Language and Reflection

An Integrated Approach to Teaching English

Anne Ruggles Gere
University of Michigan

Colleen Fairbanks
*Saginaw, Michigan, Public Schools
and the University of Michigan*

Alan Howes
University of Michigan

Laura Roop
*Oakland Intermediate School District
Waterford, Michigan*

David Schaafsma
University of Wisconsin

Macmillan Publishing Company
New York

Maxwell Macmillan Canada
Toronto

Maxwell Macmillan International
New York   Oxford · Singapore   Sydney

Senior Editor: Robert B. Miller
Production Editor: Mona M. Bunner
Art Coordinator: Ruth A. Kimpel
Cover Designer: Marsha McDevitt
Production Buyer: Patricia A. Tonneman

This book was set in New Baskerville by TCSystems, Inc. and was printed and bound by R. R. Donnelley & Sons Company. The cover was printed by New England Book Components.

Macmillan Publishing Company
866 Third Avenue
New York, New York 10022

Macmillan Publishing Company is part of the
Maxwell Communication Group of Companies.

Maxwell Macmillan Canada, Inc.
1200 Eglinton Avenue East, Suite 200
Don Mills, Ontario M3C 3N1

Library of Congress Cataloging-in-Publication Data
Language and reflection: an integrated approach to teaching English/
    Anne Ruggles Gere...[et al.].
        p.   cm.
    Includes bibliographical references and index.
    ISBN 0-02-341450-2
    1. English language—Study and teaching—United States.
    2. Language arts—United States.   I. Gere, Anne Ruggles (date).
LB1576.L2936   1992
428'.007'073—dc20   91-24608
                                                            CIP

Printing: 1 2 3 4 5 6 7 8 9   Year: 2 3 4 5

Photo credits: Bentley Historical Library, University of Michigan, p. 20; and The Bettmann Archive, pp. 21, 22.

Acknowledgments

When the five of us taught the Professional Semester, an experimental program of courses for future teachers, in the fall of 1988, we had no intention of writing a book. We simply wanted to do the best possible job with the group of prospective English teachers who had signed on at the University of Michigan for twelve credits of methods, observation in schools, advanced expository writing, and literature study. This block of courses gave us an opportunity to draw on our 100+ collective years of teaching and to think together about what it means to teach English. We and the students challenged one another, addressed complicated issues, and continually reexamined ideas throughout the semester. Without the 1988 Professional Semester, this book could not have been written. A timely visit from Robert Miller, Education Editor at Macmillan, helped us see that writing a book could enable us to share our thoughts with some of our colleagues, and that our differences in perspectives and backgrounds could enrich the book just as they had enriched the Professional Semester. We are grateful to Robert for extending our collaboration across several years.

Determined to enact our vision of collaboration in the process of writing, we worked as a group to create an overview for the whole book. During the process of drafting and revising each chapter, each of us was involved at some stage. Mallory Hiatt, secretary for the Joint Ph.D. in English and Education at the University of Michigan, made our active collaboration possible by spending many busy hours at her computer. Thank you, Mallory.

As we moved toward a final draft, a number of readers helped us refine the text. The 1989 Professional Semester (taught by Alan Howes and Tom Philion) contributed several key texts. Students in the 1990 Professional Semester (taught by Anne Gere, Ted Lardner, and John Stratman), in Cathy Fleischer's methods class at Eastern Michigan University, and in Dave Schaafsma's methods class at the University of Wisconsin all read the manuscript and offered valuable perspectives. Ted Lardner, Sarah Robbins, and John Stratman of the University of Michigan and Dawn Perkins of the University of Wisconsin provided many useful suggestions for revisions. And the reviewers—John H. Bushman, University of Kansas; John Conner, University of Iowa; Margaret Early, University of Florida; W. Geiger Ellis, University of Georgia; Ted Hipple, University of Tennessee, Knoxville; Ruie Jane Pritchard, North Carolina State University; Linda K. Shadiow, Northern Arizona University; and Richard J. Zbaracki, Iowa State University—responded to drafts in helpful ways.

Mona Bunner guided us skillfully through as accelerated production schedule, and Ursula Smith distinguished herself as an outstanding copyeditor and general coordinator during the final days of manuscript preparation. They and their colleagues at Macmillan made even the most frantic days endurable.

Introduction

What is important is anyone's coming awake and discovering a place, finding in full orbit a spinning globe one can lean over, catch, and jump on. What is important is the moment of opening a life and feeling it touch—with an electric hiss and cry—this speckled mineral sphere, our present world.

Annie Dillard
An American Childhood

In choosing to teach, you take on the role of assisting young people to come awake and to discover their places in the world, even as you are coming awake to the profession of teaching. You've chosen a complicated task, and chances are you won't know whether you will become a good teacher until you try to catch and jump on the spinning globe of classroom life. It is also true that your chances for success will be greatly enhanced through research and reflection before you step into that world. You might ask yourself: What does it mean for students to open their lives in the English classroom? How do reading and writing in the classroom allow students to discover not only their present world, but past worlds, other worlds, too?

You may be a prospective teacher taking a methods course or you may be an experienced teacher interested in further growth. In either case, this book asks you to examine your beliefs about language, the beliefs of other educators, and the implications of those beliefs for English classes, where the primary goal is to foster language development through reading, writing, listening, and speaking. We offer it is a catalyst to the ongoing process of research and reflection that is an essential part of good teaching.

The teachers and students who come to life in the brief scenarios opening several of the chapters are composites, although they have been drawn from our experiences; the students and teachers we quote in other contexts are real people. We draw upon them to show the various ways that English can be taught, emphasizing the complementary nature of all facets of language learning. We believe that the theory of language and language learning that an English teacher embraces determines how the various domains of English (reading, writing, listening, and speaking) are incorporated into classroom activities. The four perspectives on language—as artifact, as development, as expression, as social construct—are quite different from each other, although they overlap in places; some ideas and techniques are applicable to more than one perspective.

We have included examples of the way you might go about implementing each approach at different levels and in different kinds of classrooms. These suggestions are not "lesson plans" in the usual sense; instead they demonstrate the kinds of resources or strategies you might use to create your own teaching plans, suited to your particular classroom context. In addition to the four major perspectives on language and language learning, this book addresses the history of the teaching of English and the effect that history has on present-day teaching, the personal and social factors essential to understand individual students and particular classrooms, the various methods of evaluation English teachers can use, and the societal forces that impinge upon the English classroom.

Keep in mind that coming awake to a teaching life can only happen with practical experience in a classroom; still, you will be better prepared to teach if you reflect on your initial classroom observations, consider alternatives, and begin early on to articulate your beliefs about kids, language, and learning. As you read this text, you will begin to develop a philosophy to guide your initial teaching experiences. We believe that this process begins by reflecting on your own experiences as a learner and the experiences of your fellow learners, as well as those of other English teachers, some of whom you will encounter in this book. Through such reflection, you can begin to identify who you want to become as a teacher of English.

We wrote this book in much the same way we would urge you to develop a theory of teaching—by collaboration and discussion. Each chapter was orginally drafted by two of the five authors and then the entire group discussed these drafts, offering suggestions and alternatives. For final revisions we shuffled the original pairs so that two different individuals did the last version of each chapter. During this process, different perspectives emerged and individual understanding was broadened. Similarly, we believe that good teachers use many approaches, but that they jump into the teaching world as a particular place. As their experience grows, they do not remain immobilized in their location, but move consciously in and around the perimeters of that world, crossing boundaries and weaving circuitous paths. We hope that your reading of this text will help you begin to find your own place in the world of teaching at the same time that it introduces you to the many places where teachers play out their professional lives.

Contents

CHAPTER 7

Language as Social Construct   *184*

CHAPTER 8

Exploring and Evaluating the Approaches   *214*

CHAPTER 9

Evaluation   *235*

1
Why Teach English?

WHY TEACH ENGLISH? If you ask your peers or other, more experienced English teachers, their answers will probably range from "I love literature, and I want to help young people understand the contributions of great writers like Hawthorne and Shakespeare" to "Kids need to be able to read and write effectively in order to function in the world of work" to "I think students can boost their self-esteem by learning to write journals, stories, and poems."

Those personal reactions to the question point to a broader question: Why should a subject named English be part of school curricula? Responses to this question by citizens, politicians, and public figures coincide with what individual teachers tend to say during public discussions of the teaching of English. Individuals explain their reasons for teaching English in various and complicated ways, but their statements usually fit into one or more general categories. Similarly, at any given historical moment, one or two general reasons for including English in curricula dominate the public discussion, but these reasons also fit into categories.

Reasons for Teaching English

Six primary reasons, or goals, which sometimes overlap, are frequently named when Americans argue the why and hows of literacy. (Although they are not assigned sole responsibility for it, English teachers are seen as playing a major role in literacy education, so the term "literacy" is heard frequently when Americans talk about the teaching of English.) We discuss the six reasons here in their historical context.

- *To improve morality*   From the time of the Reformation, Protestant religious groups have connected literacy with piety or devotion, and Europeans who came to the North American continent in the seventeenth century were no exception. These early immigrants believed that ability to read (the Bible, specifically) was essential to their salvation, and although the religious fervor of this group dissipated as the population in the United States became more diverse and more secular, the connection between reading and improvement of self remained in the public consciousness. Much of the power ascribed to religious texts was transferred to literature, and English was seen as a discipline capable of contributing to morality.

  English teachers who espouse this view assign special value to the study of literature. They assume that students will become better human beings if they read what British poet Matthew Arnold called "the best that has been thought and said."

- *To prepare good workers*   As American society became increasingly specialized and mechanized, politicians, industrialists, and educators tried to ease the transition from rural to urban life. Schooling was viewed as the key; as future workers, students could learn to be prompt, to obey authority figures, and to follow arbitrary schedules and routines. In this view, English teachers, especially those in classes geared for the non-college-bound, could help train workers.

  In English classrooms where training workers is the aim, functional literacy is the obvious goal. Students may be asked to write for the "real world"—business letters, forms, resumes—and to read such texts as manuals and newspaper want ads. They may also be asked to perform drills designed to improve their knowledge of correct usage, drills we often call "grammar."

- *To create an elite*   While this purpose may seem somewhat inappropriate in a democratic society, it played a significant part in American public education. Concern about students' preparation for elite institutions has long dominated English curriculum planning. In 1894, the Committee of Ten was convened by the National Association of Education to examine the high school curriculum. Chaired by Harvard's Charles Eliot, the committee attempted to institutionalize a secondary English curriculum, developing a list of required readings and admissions criteria.

  Secondary school English teachers who are influenced by the "elitist" position tend to believe that students should be grouped according to ability level so that those in the college preparatory track will be exposed to advanced work. The classes taught by such teachers tend to mirror college courses in method and emphasis and frequently include lectures about literature.

- *To produce good citizens*   Obviously, this purpose is related to the previous ones. Citizens of a democracy must be literate in order to make informed decisions, the argument goes. Students should know the history of American ideas, should responsibly follow current events, and should acquire the (rather advanced) literacy skills needed for voting and becoming taxpaying wage earners.

  Many secondary English classrooms reflect this concern, focusing on dilemmas and decisions facing characters in texts by selected American writers. Frequently teachers who follow this approach impose a thematic organization on the curriculum. Certain concepts, said to be "American," are emphasized in discussions: religious tolerance, the importance of the individual, the pioneering spirit, and the work ethic.

- *To foster personal growth*   Undergirding this goal is the notion that education—English studies specifically—can lead to happiness. By studying one's place in the world, by coming to understand the perspectives of other people and other cultures, one can enhance self-esteem and understanding.

  In English classrooms, teachers who emphasize personal growth may ask students to keep journals and make connections between their lives and literary texts. These teachers are typically less concerned about preparing students for a specific goal such as attending college and more interested in helping students become productive and well-adjusted adults.

- *To offset inequity*   Although schooling has tended to sharpen economic and social disparities, its brightest promise is to promote equity. Women, minorities, and the poor have regarded public education with great hope; without education, these groups have virtually no access to economic or political power.

  English teachers trying to offset inequity lead students toward critical consciousness of power relationships and validate the literacy practices of students' particular cultures. This often means seeing the classroom walls as permeable and encouraging frequent communication between school and the larger world. Students in such classes often do projects—such as conducting interviews—that involve their own communities.

Two or more of these goals may dominate the basic rationale for English education at any point in history. For instance, in the late 1980s, E. D. Hirsch's *Cultural Literacy* greatly affected public perceptions about what schools should teach. Columnists, parents, and some educators, bemoaning students' ignorance of Western texts, beliefs, and artifacts, called for schools to teach canonical works. During that same period, however, a competing position, that schools should offset social and economic inequity by providing opportunities for so-called at-risk students, also received public attention. In addition, American businesses argued that public schools weren't equipping students with the necessary literacy skills for the workplace.

Just as more than one perspective can dominate public discussion at a given time in history, so individual English teachers frequently embrace more than one perspective as they plan their classes. The teacher who says, "I love literature, and I want to help young people understand the contributions of great writers like Hawthorne and Shakespeare," could, on the basis of this statement, be described as one whose goal is *to create an elite*. Yet this same teacher might also say, "I think students can boost their self-esteem by learning to write journals, stories, and poems," and thereby reveal himself or herself as a teacher whose goal is *to foster personal growth*.

The History of English Instruction

As you think about becoming a teacher, the history of English instruction probably seems unimportant. Your mind no doubt turns to questions about classroom management and writing lesson plans. These things are, of course, important, but understanding the history of English instruction can give you valuable perspectives on today's classrooms. Faced with an unruly group of students, you may find comfort in the fact that you are not, like your counterpart of 100 years ago, expected to cane the trouble-makers. More important, understanding the issues that have been central to English studies over the years may help you decide what to emphasize and how to proceed with a given unit of instruction.

Even as we trace the history of English instruction, we remind ourselves—and you—that the public discussions about English education have historically had remarkably limited effect on the classrooms of individual teachers. As the vintage photos on pages 20 and 21 demonstrate, the English classrooms of the nineteenth and twentieth centuries bear a number of similarities. Students still sit at desks placed in rows facing the teacher, and the teacher's desk is considerably larger and less movable than those assigned to students. Blackboards still cover the walls and serve as sources of information.

As you read this history, you will notice that we give considerably more attention to recent decades. This is deliberate. We believe that English instruction owes much of its current shape to decisions and movements that occurred within this last century.

Change in American schools has been contingent more upon demographic change than on shifts in public views or introduction of innovative methodology. During the nineteenth century, for example, the belief in public education for all began to take hold nationally, and the number of schools in the United States grew significantly. Children who would have remained unschooled, working in fields, homes, or factories, instead began attending school en masse.

Immigration, emigration, and changing notions about what literacy entails affect public discussion profoundly, though not always explicitly. Therefore, to understand English instruction at any given historical juncture, we need to ask the following questions: Who attended school? For what purposes? If we keep these questions in the foreground, the history of English education becomes comprehensible and relevant to today's debate.

Reading and writing in the English language were the province of the earliest American schools. Puritan settlers passed laws requiring the formation of reading and writing schools in communities of a certain size before 1700, chiefly *to improve morality*. Schooling was seen as a means of warding off evil. Texts used in schools and texts owned by individual households were largely of a religious nature, and reading received more emphasis than writing, although simple writing tasks were assigned. Between 1640 and 1715 about 60 percent of male New Englanders were able to sign their names to legal documents; signing rates were slightly lower for white males in other colonies. Signing rates for women and for African Americans were dramatically lower, although there is some evidence that a majority of women colonists were able to read.

Schools assumed different functions as the colonies grew and prospered. In the middle of the eighteenth century, two other reasons for attaining literacy began to compete with religious motivations. As communities grew large enough to support schools and commerce, literacy became necessary for the workers who needed to keep accounts and correspond with clients. Thus an increasingly apparent goal in the teaching of English was *to create good workers*. In addition, those who had managed to accumulate wealth and power in the new society wanted to ensure their sons' positions as well; these families looked to the schools *to create an elite*.

The English curriculum in these early American schools focused on reading, writing, and grammatical skills. Pupils were expected to learn English grammar, to read short passages aloud, to spell, and to communicate in writing. Students often memorized passages from the Bible or from classical texts, but their exposure to English literature in school was limited to the occasional poem or brief prose passage.

After the Revolutionary War, literacy acquisition became important to the new nation. First, it was necessary *to produce good citizens*. The ability to read and write seemed crucial for the citizens of an American democracy. As Thomas Jefferson said, "Were it left to me to decide whether we should have a government without a newspaper, or newspapers without a government, I should not hesitate a moment to prefer the latter. But I should mean that every man should receive these papers and be capable of reading them."

Second, the country experienced a newfound sense of self-confidence and purposefulness. Literacy was a way *to foster personal growth.* Citizens of the new nation believed that knowledge, like the continent itself, was only half discovered, and they felt that learning more constituted a form of self-improvement.

Finally, the Declaration of Independence had claimed, "All men are created equal"; by becoming a literate citizen of a democracy, one was able *to offset inequity,* even if born and raised in rural poverty. Benjamin Franklin, who had only two years of formal education, embodied this belief. Rising from his humble origins to become one of the most respected citizens in the United States, Franklin credited his success to his literacy skills.

However, until 1840, access to education remained rather limited. Boys had greater access to schools than girls, wealthy and middle classes greater access than the poor, and urban youth greater access than rural youth. African Americans and other oppressed minorities were largely denied access to education. Slave owners explicitly forbade their slaves to learn to read and write because such skills might have aided their escape. Despite these prohibitions, some slaves did gain literacy skills, and passed them on in so-called secret schools. Many of the African Americans who became literate during the slave era helped develop the Sabbath Schools that worked *to offset inequity* by educating former slaves after the Civil War.

As the notion of public schooling took hold in the midnineteenth century, schoolhouses began to dot the countryside and communities began clamoring for the services of teachers. Businessmen and industrialists saw schools as a way to transform isolated rural farm workers into disciplined factory workers. More importantly, the idea of education for all captured the imaginations of the disenfranchised and the marginalized. African Americans valued education's potential to destroy slavery and to help them achieve economic and social equity. Women saw education as a means to broaden their opportunities and to gain access to the vote. Powerful and powerless Americans alike seized upon this democratic concept, though for somewhat different reasons. Movements for public education, higher education, and self-education flourished during the last decades of the nineteenth century.

In the 1890s, as schools opened their doors to a more diverse population of learners, and as colleges expanded to admit more than a mere handful of elite pupils, the curricula of schools, high schools and colleges especially, were scrutinized and revamped. The most powerful influence on this reshaping, at least with regard to the English curriculum, was the Committee of Ten. Headed by Charles W. Eliot, the president of Harvard, the Committee of Ten was convened in 1892 by the National

Association of Education to examine curricula in each of nine subject areas.

With its final report (1894), this committee managed to unify a diverse set of studies in English into a whole that superseded other subject areas in terms of status and significance. Literature, American literature in particular, gained a foothold in secondary schools once colleges made it clear that entrance examinations would involve writing based on specific literary texts. "Uniform Lists," as they were called, were established by the National Conference on Uniform Entrance Requirements in English. These lists specified the literary texts on which students should be prepared to write entrance examinations, and works such as *Julius Caesar* and *Silas Marner* thus established themselves in the curriculum. The English classroom was once again helping *to create an elite.*

Not all teachers of English found the Committee of Ten's work helpful, however. Some secondary teachers noted that they had been virtually excluded from the process of curriculum development; others wondered whether the texts on the Uniform Lists were appropriate for their students. The effect of the Committee of Ten's report was inevitable (and remarkably long-lasting): Secondary English would be shaped by and subordinate to college English.

Within five years of the time the Committee of Ten and the Conference on Uniform Entrance Requirements submitted their reports, Uniform Lists drove the secondary curriculum. But protest was brewing. Fred Newton Scott, a University of Michigan professor active in English education, regarded the examinations, used mainly by Ivy League colleges, as "feudal." He believed that a better route toward preparing high school students for college lay in involving college professors in the accreditation of high schools. Classroom teachers in several states tried to pressure the colleges to broaden the Uniform Lists, but they met with limited success.

In 1911, organized dissent in New York state gained a national impetus, and the National Council of Teachers of English (NCTE) was formed. NCTE's first members were reformers at heart; they aimed to revise the Committee of Ten's vision of English education. In their view, the study of English should be active and engaging for all students, not just for the college-bound (*to offset inequity*). While they accepted literature as the centerpiece of the English curriculum, they supported dramatic and cooperative activities in the classroom as well. They held that the aim of education was not necessarily college admission, but *to foster personal growth* and to meet the practical demands of the workplace and democratic government—that is, *to prepare good workers* and *to produce good citizens.*

The reformers' efforts bore fruit. *Reorganization of English in Secondary Schools* (1917), a major report that countered the college preparatory emphasis of the Committee of Ten's report, broadened English education to address the needs of students from various backgrounds. Although this report stopped short of discarding uniform lists of the "classics," it took a much broader approach and touched upon all six goals in justifying the study of English.

With the onset of World War I, two reasons for studying English—*to prepare good workers* and *to produce good citizens*—received special attention. Current events, American literature, and communication skills regarded as necessary for warfare and diplomacy became the focus of study in the English classroom. The American Psychological Association's use of IQ tests to determine placement, and hence, status, in the armed forces had a powerful effect on secondary classrooms in English and other subject areas as well. Once citizens, teachers, and administrators accepted the notion that student potential and performance could be measured "objectively," it seemed logical to divide students according to ability for more "efficient" and "functional" teaching.

Thus, with the onset of war and the growth of scientific study, the discussion of English education took a new turn; instead of talking about enjoyment and enculturation through literary study, English educators began to speak about the "efficiency" and "practicality" of English study. In 1922, NCTE's Committee on the Place and Function of English in American Life sponsored a huge national study of English skills utilized by America's work force. Some of the recommendations made in the committee's final report included increased attention to verbal communication and the writing of memos. This sort of functionalism served as justification for English's place in the secondary curriculum and for tracking, but the teaching of English continued to center on literary classics.

The progressive movement in education began to make itself felt in English studies during the early decades of the twentieth century. Emphasizing the importance of developing students' social and emotional natures as well as their minds, the "progressives" urged changes in both the methods and content of English classrooms, changes intended *to foster personal growth*.

In response to the Great Depression, which began in 1929 and continued through much of the next decade, educational leaders began to describe the teaching of English in different terms. A 1935 report titled *An Experience Curriculum in English* emphasized the social value of English. In this view English teachers should foster socially useful skills, a perspective that helped justify English's place in the high school curriculum. Underlining the social value of English indirectly promoted the utility of schooling at a time when less than 50 percent of the population of the United States had graduated from high school.

This emphasis on social utility could be justified, as could the earlier emphases, by citing several of the primary reasons for teaching English. The skills students learned in English classes would *produce good citizens* in a country that wanted to avoid civil strife during the economic crisis of the

Great Depression. The kinds of skills prescribed by *An Experience Curriculum in English,* however, could also be described as useful in *creating an elite,* since the curriculum included skills such as writing invitations and thank-you notes, which reflected white midde-class and upper-class values. (As Box 1.1 shows, such skills continued to occupy a place in English classes for the next two decades.) On the other hand, teaching these skills to all students, especially students from working-class families, also offered a means *to offset the inequity* of class. Students whose homes did not provide them experiences with the social graces could, in this view, gain access to some of the cultural capital of their more privileged peers.

An Experience Curriculum in English highlighted the importance of considering student experience in curriculum development and teaching. This meant considering issues of interest to students and creating teaching units based on themes drawn from these issues. While writing and language tasks in the Experience Curriculum were concerned with social values, instruction in literature focused on relevance to student experience and interest, rather than on literary history. As the authors of the guide explained, this would mean looking at texts such as *David Copperfield* or *Two Years before the Mast* from the perspective of human development or thinking about Whitman's "I Hear America Singing" in terms of international relations. As these themes suggest, this aspect of the Experience Curriculum aimed at producing good citizens, but its major emphasis was personal growth. This was an approach to teaching English that placed the affective lives of students in the foreground. Like contemporary thematic units, the approach of the Experience Curriculum was designed to engage students emotionally as well as intellectually so as *to foster their growth* as persons.

The motivations of *producing good citizens, fostering personal growth, creating an elite,* and *offsetting inequities* continue to operate, as they always have, among English teachers, but the Experience Curriculum gave way to other concerns after World War II. School enrollments grew dramatically during the postwar years, and an ever-higher percentage of students stayed on to graduate from high school. The English curriculum responded by narrowing its scope. By the 1950s English teachers were once again more likely to adopt a chronological approach to literature, and *creating an elite*—in this case an elite that would enroll in college—played an increasingly important role in high school classrooms.

The narrowing of the English curriculum took another form as Warriner's *English Grammar and Composition* made its first appearance in the late 1940s and was enthusiastically received by English teachers. The prominent place given Warriner's, with its emphasis on correctness and parsing in language, illustrates how one dimension of the English curriculum can produce different results for different students. The dialect of English privileged by Warriner's was, not surprisingly, that of middle-class whites, so its version of grammar study served to reinforce the

---

BOX 1.1
SOCIAL ETIQUETTE

You spend a great deal of your time every day in conversation. You exchange information, opinions, and experiences with friends and acquaintances. You chat about ordinary things—school affairs, movies, sports, dances, and similar matters.

Would you like to improve your social conversational skill? With study and practice you can learn how to converse with greater satisfaction to yourself and others. A person who converses easily and pleasantly is popular, and rightly so.

MAKING SOCIAL
INTRODUCTIONS

The purpose of introducing one person to another is to make them acquainted so they may enjoy each other's company.

The etiquette of introductions is simple. No set expressions are used. You may simply mention the persons' names. However, be sure to pronounce each name distinctly. For example:

Edna, Joe Everett.

Mother, this is Neil Smith.

Miss Brown, Mr. Philips.

Or you may say something like this:

Edna, may I introduce Joe Everett?

Mother, I'd like you to meet my friend Neil Smith.

Miss Brown, I'd like to present Mr. Philips.

It is desirable to add a remark that will help start a conversation. For example:

Edna, may I introduce Joe Everett, who captained our tennis team this season?

How are you, Joe? I've seen you play many times. That was a close match with South Side High, wasn't it?

Mother, I'd like you to meet my friend Neil Smith. Neil is editor of our school yearbook.

How do you do, Neil? Editing a yearbook must take a lot of your time. Have you decided on the theme of this year's book?

Introduce a Man to a Woman. Mention the woman's name first. A man is always introduced to a woman even if he is older. The woman need not rise and she need not extend her hand unless she wishes to. For example:

Sue, this is my Dad.

Sis, I'd like you to meet Charlie Hyams. Charlie, this is my sister Kate.

Miss Teen, may I present Mr. Well-Known.

Miss Middle-Age, this is my classmate Ed Thomas.

Introduce a Young Person to an Older Person of the Same Sex. When introducing one man to another, it does not matter which name is mentioned first unless there is a great difference in their ages. In such a case, introduce the younger man to the older. The young person should not call the older man by his first name unless invited to do so. For example:

Dad, this is Ed Burke.

Mr. Ancient, Mr. Youngman.

Mr. Principal, this is my brother Bob.

Bill, this is my son Jack. Jack, this is Mr. Butler.

Similarly, a young woman is introduced to an older woman. Mention the older woman's name first. (Marriage makes no difference in introduction. A young married woman is presented to an older single woman.) For example:

Mother, I'd like you to meet Susie Blair.

Miss Grayhair, this is Mrs. Honeymooner.

Miss Elder, may I present Miss Young.

At social gatherings young people generally use first names and disregard the titles Mr., Miss, and Mrs. For example:

Dorothy Keaton, Tom Fielding.

Marion, this is Katherine Hayden.

Esther, I'd like you to meet Joe and Estelle Metz.

When introducing groups of persons, the simplest procedure is to mention the names of those in one group and then the names of those in the other. For example:

Ella and Sue, Grace and Loretta.

Eileen, Kate, and Sally, may I introduce Joe Smith and Tom Fitzpatrick.

ACKNOWLEDGING AN INTRODUCTION

Respond to an Introduction Courteously and Properly. Respond to an introduction in such a way that the new acquaintance feels you are really pleased to know him.

In formal situations the usual reply is, "How do you do?" Add the person's name to fix it in your mind.

In informal situations there is no fixed reply. Any sincere and pleasant acknowledgment will do. If you can think of nothing better, "How are you, Mr. Jones?" or "Good afternoon, Mr. Jones" may be used. Avoid shopworn expressions like "Pleased to meet you" and "Glad to know you."

Exercise 1. In groups of two or three, one person acting as host and the other two as the persons indicated below, demonstrate good form in the following introduction situations.

1. A teen-age boy and a teen-age girl.

2. A teen-age boy and a city official.

3. A young girl and an older woman.

4. Two older men.

5. Two young men.

6. A young married woman and an older married woman.

7. A young married woman and an older single woman.

8. A young woman (seated) and a young man (standing).

9. A young woman (seated) and an older man (standing).

10. An older woman (seated) and a young woman (standing).

11. A young man (seated) and an older man (standing).

12. Two young girls.

Exercise 2. With one person acting as host and others as members of the following groups, perform these introductions.

1. Two boys to a group of three girls.

2. Two girls to a group of three girls.

3. One of your friends to your father and mother.

4. Your father and mother to your teacher.

—Excerpts from *English Grammar and Composition*, Grade 10, by John E. Warriner and Francis Griffith, copyright © 1963 by Harcourt Brace Jovanovich, Inc., reprinted by permission of the publisher.

linguistic patterns of white middle-class students. (See Box 1.2.) Rather than learning rules, these students could often "trust their ears" to tell them the correct answer to questions about usage. This kind of reinforcement often gave these students a feeling of self-justification and confidence that aided their movement into the elite of the college-educated. For students from other backgrounds, the kind of language study fostered by Warriner's was largely a negative experience because it conveyed the message that their dialects (and perhaps they themselves) were inadequate. Students who could not trust that their own ears—their internal language sense—would help them answer usage questions were not likely to be as confident about their capacity to join the elite group entering college.

Indirectly, then, this kind of language study helped *to prepare good workers* because it fostered feelings of inferiority among certain students at the same time that it familiarized them with the language commonly used in business. For a few rare students the opportunity to learn the dialect of power provided a means to become upwardly mobile and thus *to offset inequity,* particularly during the 1960s as the U.S. economy expanded. Students who learned, as a kind of second dialect, the conventions fostered by Warriner's were sometimes able to improve their socioeconomic status.

When the USSR launched Sputnik in 1957, the United States responded with considerable public concern about the education of its youth, and perspectives on the teaching of English shifted again. Federal funds poured into education, and English teachers, like teachers in all disciplines, began to see their mission as tied to national interests. They were *to produce good citizens,* who, by definition, would be able to compete intellectually in the global sphere. College education became less a matter of enabling individuals to transcend their origins and more an issue of national interest. By doing better in school, individuals would contribute to the nation's intellectual capacity to compete with the Soviet Union.

BOX 1.2
CORRECT USAGE

The words and expressions listed below are common errors in English. Ask yourself whether you ever use any of them. If you do, now is the time to eliminate them from your speech and writing.

aint. Don't say it!

all the farther, all the faster. Poor English when used to mean as far as, as fast as.

> *Wrong:* This is all the farther you can go.
>
> *Right:* This is *as far as* you can go.

and etc. Since *etc.* is an abbreviation of the Latin *et cetera*, which means *and other things*, you are using *and* twice when you write "and etc." The *etc.* is sufficient.

anywheres, everywheres, nowheres. Use these words and others like them without the *s*.

> *Right:* *Everywhere* I looked, I saw mountains.

at. Don't use *at* after *where*.

> *Wrong:* Where were you at?
>
> *Right:* Where were you?

being as, being that. Poor English. Use *since* or *because*.

> *Wrong:* Being that there was no snow, we postponed our sleigh ride.
>
> *Right:* *Since* there was no snow, we postponed our sleigh ride.
>
> *Wrong:* Being as he's the boss, we do what he says.

> *Right:* *Because* he's the boss, we do what he says.

bust, busted. Use *broke* or *burst* instead.

> *Wrong:* While skiing, he busted his ankle.
>
> *Right:* While skiing, he *broke* his ankle.
>
> *Wrong:* The frozen pipes busted.
>
> *Right:* The frozen pipes *burst*.

bursted. Incorrect past form of *burst*. The principal parts of *burst* are *burst*, *burst*, *(has) burst*.

> *Wrong:* The gasoline tanks bursted into flame.
>
> *Right:* The gasoline tanks *burst* into flame.

Exercise. The following sentences contain the errors just listed. Rewrite each sentence correctly. Practice saying *aloud* the correct sentences.

1. Being as we were tired of rising early, gulping our breakfast, catching the bus, and etc., we were glad to move nearer to school.

2. When I sat on the trunk, it busted wide open, and the contents flew everywheres.

3. Is this all the faster your car will go?

4. In Chicago where did you stay at?

5. A mob of children bursted through the doors.

6. I saw your sister somewheres downtown.

7. Being that the fog was heavy, we didn't know where we were at.

8. The bumper was busted and one of the tires had bursted.

9. Boards, bricks, window frames, and etc., were everywheres around the new house.

10. This is all the farther the road goes.

11. Terry busted his leash and we couldn't find him anywheres.

12. Being that the boiler has a safety valve somewheres on the top, it won't bust.

—Excerpts from *English Grammar and Composition*, Grade 10, by John E. Warriner and Francis Griffith, © 1963 by Harcourt Brace Jovanovich, Inc., reprinted by permission of the publisher.

Language study now emphasized a more scientific approach to language. Thanks to the influence of the Commission on English created by the College Entrance Examination Board in 1959, the English curriculum comprised the trinity of language, literature, and composition. This "Tripod," as described in *Freedom and Discipline in English*, the commission's report, emphasized the intellectual, or academic, dimension of English (*to create an elite*) at the expense of other aspects, and the summer institutes sponsored by the Commission on English generated curriculum guides designed to foster that dimension. (Box 1.3 gives an excerpt from a passage from the report.) Issues such as personal growth and offsetting inequities receded into the background as intellectual dimensions seized the foreground in the teaching of English.

This intellectual emphasis diminished with the onset of the social upheavals of the latter half of the 1960s. English teachers, along with other groups in society, began to question tradition and challenge authority, and the Tripod approach came under scrutiny. The 1966 Dartmouth Conference, a meeting of British and American English educators, galvanized English teachers in this country into shifting away from the Tripod toward a program that gave greater attention *to fostering personal growth*. (The Tripod did not, of course, disappear entirely, and you can find evidence of the language/literature/composition approach in many of today's classrooms.)

Americans, impressed by the "infant schools" in Britain, moved toward a more student-centered curriculum. In addition, English at the college level moved toward giving students considerably more choice than they had enjoyed previously, and this move away from a prescribed program of study also led to changes in English study in high schools. As alternatives to American and British Lit classes, elective courses, frequently organized around thematic topics such as death, romance, and growing up, emerged. Students were encouraged to write about their feelings as well as about literary figures.

The civil rights movement of the 1960s led to greater inclusion of literature by women and minorities in textbooks, thereby providing an-

---

BOX 1.3
ENGLISH REDEFINED

What is the school and college subject called "English"? This question the Commission took as its starting point. The report that follows provides an answer arrived at largely by discussion among its members and with hundreds of teachers. The answer rests on the unstartling assumption that language, primarily the English language, constitutes the core of the subject, and on the further and equally unstartling assumption that the study and use of the English language is the proper content of the English curriculum.

So simple and obvious an answer may seem too slight to justify elaboration into a formal report, but the perusal of scores of school curriculums has convinced the Commission that a simple answer is needed at the present time. The need can best be illustrated by a comparison. When the work of this Commission began, that of the College Board's Commission on Mathematics was coming to a close. What the mathematicians found in the school curriculum was a disciplined but largely anachronistic program of study, rigidified in its sequence and unresponsive to important developments in mathematical theory. They recommended drastic revisions in content, methods of instruction, and the ordering of elements. Their recommendations, in conjunction with those of other groups working on the same problem at the same time, and in conjunction with groups independently studying school curriculums in the sciences, have produced dramatic changes in less than 10 years. Where these recommendations have stimulated the development of new

programs, it may reasonably be claimed that curriculums in mathematics and the sciences are "up to date."

For English the situation is quite different. "English must be kept up," wrote Keats; but keeping it up is not primarily a matter of keeping it up to date. To a large degree, the study of English or of any of those subjects loosely classified as "the humanities" is not a matter of making new, but of constant renewal, constant rediscovery, constant restoration. The sciences and mathematics lose their relevance if they fail to keep close to the working front of their disciplines. The humanities most often suffer from having their essence diluted or obscured by what appears to be new. This is not to say that current knowledge has no meaning for the humanities, but only to insist that the accumulation of the past is for them far richer than for the sciences. Yet, precisely because the humanities, the study of one's native language and literature among them, are so thoroughly implicated in everyday human activity, they are highly susceptible to immediate and ephemeral influences. The fashion of a time often so overlays them, particularly in their popular forms, that their real nature is all but lost sight of. The English curriculum in the average secondary school today is an unhappy combination of old matter unrenewed and new matter that rarely rises above the level of passing concerns. *Macbeth* vies with the writing of thank-you notes for time in the curriculum, and lessons on telephoning with instruction in the processes of argument.

The first job, then, of the Commission

on English was to distinguish between the passing and the permanent, to affirm and describe the nature of English as a subject. In making its description, the Commission was well aware that a curriculum should in every case derive from a particular situation. It therefore quite deliberately chose to concentrate its attention on the program for secondary school students who are preparing for college. The Commission believes that the sooner the program in English for college preparatory students can be given sound underpinnings, the sooner corollary programs for other students can be thoughtfully designed. Even for college preparatory students, emphasis and curriculum materials will and should vary from program to program, but the main concerns remain the same, and it is to them that the Commission has directed its attention. In choosing to describe only the English program for the college-bound student, it has simply adopted the principle of beginning work where resources are at present largest and where a solution may most readily be found.

—From the Commission on English, *Freedom and Discipline in English* (New York: College Entrance Examination Board, 1965), pp. 2–4.

other way for English teachers *to offset inequity* in society. At the same time, English teachers began to give more attention to compensatory and remedial education. The term "relevance" became important in discussion of the English curriculum (see Box 1.4), and elective courses provided educational experiences that seemed more directly connected with students' lives. Rather than portraying literature as written mostly by dead white men, textbooks began to offer a broader perspective, one that encouraged females and students from so-called minority populations to consider their own places in the literary tradition.

In reaction to the educational expansion of the 1960s and early 1970s, a "back-to-basics" movement flourished through the late 1970s and into the 1980s. Public discussion of schools, and of English in particular, focused on the underpreparation of students, particularly in the area of writing, and frequently cited electives and other "relevant" features of the curriculum as responsible for this underpreparation. A 1975 issue of *Newsweek* focused on "Why Johnny Can't Write" (see Box 1.5), and several subsequent reports on high schools in the United States called students' literacy skills into question. Many English educators responded by renewing emphasis on grammar drills and other exercises designed to improve students' writing skills. This occurred despite the fact that research conducted during the previous decade had demonstrated that there is no correlation between study of isolated grammar skills and improvement in writing.

This research in writing brought terms like "composing process" into the language of English teaching, and writing instruction began to play a more prominent role in the English classroom. Rather than simply giving

---

BOX 1.4
SOCIAL RELEVANCE

NOTES FOR A
MOVIE SCRIPT
by Carl Holman

Fade in the sound of summer music,
Picture a hand plunging through her
  hair,
Next his socked feet and her scuffed
  dance slippers
Close, as they kiss on the rug-stripped
  stair.

Catch now the taxi from the station,
Capture her shoulders' sudden sag;
Switch to him silent in the barracks
While the room roars at the corporal's
  gag.

Let the drums dwindle in the distance,
Pile the green sea above the land
While she prepares a single breakfast,
Reading the V-Mail in her hand.

Ride a cold moonbeam to the pillbox,
Sidle the camera to his feet
Sprawled just outside in the gummy
  grasses,
Swollen like nightmare and not neat.

Now doorbell nudges the lazy morning:
She stills the sweeper for a while,
Twitches her dress, swings the screen-
  door open,
Cut—with no music—on her smile.

"Notes for a Movie Script" by Carl
Holman. Copyright 1945 by M. Carl
Holman. Reprinted by permission of
Mariella A. Holman.

Talking It Over

1. How does the title fit the poem?

2. The poet has given several pictures,
   or images, to suggest a story. What
   scenes indicate how the man and
   woman feel about each other?

3. a. Each brief picture, or image
      creates a mood. What is the mood
      of the first stanza? What do the
      directions for music add to the
      image?

   b. What is the mood of each of the
      other four stanzas? There is a sec-
      ond direction for music in the last
      stanza. How does the feeling cre-
      ated here differ from that in the
      first stanza?

   c. What are the two references to the
      young man's feet? How do they
      create very different moods?

4. a. What has happened to the young
      man? How is this to be shown in
      the movie?

   b. How would the woman's expres-
      sion change from the time she
      opens the door to the time she re-
      alizes what the message is?

5. Is this sketchy telling of a story as effective as a more complete version
   would be? Why or why not?

Of this poem Carl Holman says:

I suppose it grew out of my then very
personal feelings about the split worlds of
the soldier and the civilian—involving
also reactions to . . . the movies we were
seeing, the headlines we were reading and
the letters and numbers (including casu-
alty lists) behind which it was sometimes
hard to realize separate and unique human beings.

> Holman has written poetry, fiction, and reviews. His work has appeared in various magazines and in anthologies, *Soon One Morning* and *Poetry of the Negro.* He has received many awards and fellowships for his writing.

—From Robert C. Pooley, Alfred Grommon, Virginia Lowers, Elsie Katterjohn, and Olive Niles, eds., *Accent: U.S.A.* (Glenview, Ill.: Scott, Foresman, 1965), p. 370.

a writing assignment on Monday and collecting it on Friday, English teachers began to show students *how* to write. As they intervened in the composing process, English teachers often introduced new activities in their classes. Students were sometimes encouraged to work in small groups, to share ideas about writing, and to respond to one another's drafts.

The appearance of the personal computer in the marketplace contributed to another kind of change in English classrooms. Computers began to appear in some classrooms, sometimes for grammar drills and sometimes for word processing. Usually the justification for providing computers was *to prepare good workers* by introducing them to an important technology. In other cases, computers were presented as a means *to offset inequity,* since they could be used for the routine tasks and free teachers for more significant work with individual students. When they are available for students in composition classes, computers reinforce the composing process, since word processing makes it so easy for students to revise and edit their work. But problems of access and incompatible systems still stymie many English teachers who wish to incorporate computer-assisted instruction in their classrooms.

Another dimension of research on writing emphasized its capacity to aid learning. As they recognized the value of "writing to learn," some high schools adopted writing-across-the-curriculum programs. These programs conceive of writing as a means of learning in all subjects and encourage teachers to use informal writing to foster learning. English teachers have, not surprisingly, taken the lead in helping their colleagues in other disciplines develop strategies for using journal writing and other kinds of informal writing in science, math, and social studies classes.

Reflecting on the History

Recounting the history of English teaching in this country can create the impression that the curriculum moved smoothly from one emphasis to another, that terms like the Progressive Era or the Tripod describe sweeping changes that transformed English classes in every decade. The reality of English teaching then, as now, is a good deal more complicated.

BOX 1.5
QUESTIONING LITERACY SKILLS

If your children are attending college, the chances are that when they graduate they will be unable to write ordinary, expository English with any real degree of structure and lucidity. If they are in high school and planning to attend college, the chances are less than even that they will be able to write English at the minimal college level when they get there. If they are not planning to attend college, their skills in writing English may not even qualify them for secretarial or clerical work. . . . The 1960's . . . brought a subtle shift of educational philosophy away from the teaching of expository writing. Many teachers began to emphasize "creativity" in the English classrooms and expanded their curriculums to allow students to work with contemporary media of communication such as film, videotape and photography. In the process, charges Dorothy Matthews, director of undergraduate English at Illinois, they often shortchanged instruction in the written language. "Things have never been good, but the situation is getting a lot worse," she complains. "What really disturbs us is the students' inability to organize their thoughts clearly." An essay by one of Matthews's Illinois freshmen stands as guileless testimony to the problem: "It's obvious in our modern world of today theirs a lot of impreciseness in expressing thoughts we have."

—From "Why Johnny Can't Write," *Newsweek,* December 8, 1975, p. 58. Copyright © 1975 Newsweek, Inc. All rights reserved. Reprinted by permission.

In his *How Teachers Taught: Constancy and Change in American Classrooms 1890–1980,* educational historian Larry Cuban has described education as a vast ocean where various approaches and theories crash against one another like waves on the surface. Meanwhile individual teachers in their classrooms on the ocean floor continue doing what they have always done. While this metaphor overstates the case, it does make an important point about the continuity of English education. For the most part, today's classrooms don't look much different from those of 100 years ago as the nineteenth-century photograph of Coldwater High School on page 20 demonstrates. The teacher stands at the front of the room, and students sit in neat rows facing the front. Superficial differences (in students' clothing or style of flag salute—as in the photograph on page 21) can obscure the similarities of classrooms across time. In many of today's English classes, as was true a century ago, the teacher does most of the talking, and media play a relatively small part in daily class work. Literature often serves as a stimulus for writing, and language study usually includes grammar drills. Most students read a comedy and a

tragedy by Shakespeare during high school, and their spelling errors are still circled in red.

Despite all that remains constant in English instruction, we can point to a number of areas where changes seem to have filtered into the classroom. Literature anthologies of the 1990s include more works by women and minorities than did their counterparts forty years ago. Standardized tests and district/state writing assessments play a larger role in English classes than they did a generation ago. Terms such as "composing process" and "revising" are used in many classrooms. Many students write on word processors, either at home or at school. Some teachers in disciplines other than English ask students to write as a way of learning subject matter. Student desks may still be in rows, but they are no longer bolted to the floor, and some classrooms, like the one pictured on page 22, encourage students to work in small groups.

Some English teachers have embraced a new professionalism. They see themselves as producers as well as consumers of research in English education, and this research enlivens and informs their teaching. A number of sources can be cited for this new professionalism, but the National Writing Project (NWP) stands among the most prominent. Founded in Berkeley, California, as an in-service training program for teachers of writing, the NWP assumed that teachers' experiences in classrooms gave them an expertise worth sharing with other teachers. It also assumed that those who teach writing should themselves write. NWP sites are located in nearly every state and in several foreign countries, but the procedure is essentially the same in all locations. Experienced teachers are selected to participate in an intensive three- to five-week workshop in which they write and learn from one another's classroom experiences. When these teachers return to their own classrooms, they are more likely to employ

workshop techniques, to give more diverse writing assignments, and to invite students to decide what they will write about.

Just as we can point to innovations in English instruction, so too can we see that today's English teachers face questions that did not exist for their predecessors. Many of these questions center around two issues: changing demographics in our society and shifting definitions of literacy. Recent population statistics suggest demographic shifts that have implications for English teachers. In 1955, 60 percent of the nation's households conformed to the traditional notion of a two-parent family, with the father serving as the wage earner, the mother performing household tasks, and two or more children in school. In the 1970s women entered the work force in record numbers so that by 1986 only 4 percent of American households conformed to this image.

In the fall of 1986, 3.6 million children began their formal schooling One-fourth of them were from families who lived in poverty. Fourteen percent of them were the children of teenage mothers. Forty percent of today's school children will live in a single-parent home before they are

18. The population has changed in other ways as well. The nonwhite school population has increased from 24 percent in 1976 to between 30 and 40 percent in the 1990s. As many as 15 percent of students in schools in 1990 are immigrants whose first language is not English. Many of these immigrants join a growing "underclass" in this country that includes African Americans, Appalachian whites, Hispanics, American Indians, and Southeast Asians. In some states, and in many metropolitan areas, whites have become the minority population in schools. We are said to be a nation composed of a "majority of minorities."

These demographic changes in the United States suggest that English teachers will face an increasing number of students who do not fit white middle-class norms. Their family backgrounds, medical histories, and linguistic heritages will raise certain questions: What roles, once played by parents, should English teachers assume? How do English teachers establish relationships with the community from which their students come? How does an English teacher work effectively with students suffering from drug- or alcohol-centered disabilities, neglect, stress, abuse, poverty, or other conditions that interfere with learning? What adjustments should an English teacher make in working with students for whom English is a second language?

Not surprisingly, changing demographics in the United States are paralleled by changes in literacy rates in this country. Twenty-five percent of all students who enter school today drop out before they complete high school, and most of those who drop out are from the increasingly "majority minority" population. In many urban districts, the dropout rate approaches 50 percent. As Jonathan Kozol pointed out in his 1985 book *Illiterate America,* there were 60 million Americans that year, by his estimate, who could not read his book.

Simultaneously, this nation's definition of literacy is changing, as it has changed since Europeans first arrived on the North American continent. During the colonial period literacy meant the ability to sign one's name and read familiar biblical texts. Today literacy implies the ability to operate effectively in our complex society. Computer literacy is one of the many types of "new literacy" that raise special questions for English teachers: What will be the place of computers in English classes? How will inequities between students who own computers and those who do not be addressed? How can English teachers address the gender gap between boys who feel at ease with computers and girls who frequently do not? What will be the relationship between the teacher and the computer? What role will computer networks play in writing instruction?

The expanded definition of literacy prompts other questions. What kinds of texts should be used in English classes? What genres of writing should receive attention? If literacy means the ability to operate effectively in society, how can English teachers help students make connections between the classroom and the larger society? How should English teachers negotiate the conflicting claims of emphasis on critical thinking and what has been called "cultural literacy"? What is the place of media in English classes? What does it mean to include media in the definition of literacy?

As literacy has been redefined, teachers and researchers alike have explored new ways to teach. Collaboration and writing across the curriculum have emerged in English classrooms. The popularity of "cooperative learning," the use of workshop techniques with drafts of student writing, and new approaches to evaluation all testify to the emergence of collaboration in English classrooms. And collaboration prompts even more questions: How does the English teacher's role change in collaborative learning situations? How can old systems of evaluation be modified to fit collaborative learning environments? What does collaboration imply about relationships among teachers? What effect does collaboration have on student motivation?

The emergence of writing-across-the-curriculum (WAC) programs also raises questions for English teachers: How does WAC change the definition of writing and the meaning of terms such as "writing process"? What role should English teachers play in developing WAC programs? How does the role of English teachers change when teachers in many disciplines use writing as a tool in their classes?

This book does not contain definitive answers to the questions spawned by changing demographics and shifting definitions of literacy, but it does provide considerable information for thinking about the questions. As you consider them you may find it helpful to keep in mind the various goals inevitably cited in public discussion of the teaching of English:

- To improve morality
- To prepare good workers
- To create an elite
- To produce good citizens
- To foster personal growth
- To offset inequity

As the history of English teaching in this country demonstrates, the various goals recur across time, though their relative prominence is constantly shifting. Thinking about the meaning and importance of each of these reasons to teach English will help you as you begin to look closely at English classrooms. Each of the approaches you'll encounter in this text emphasizes some goals more than others. Similarly, the teachers you observe will privilege some goals over others. Through these encounters with the many ways of teaching English, you can decide for yourself the relative prominence you'll give each goal in your own classroom.

Suggested Reading

APPLEBEE, ARTHUR, N. *Tradition and Reform in the Teaching of English.* Urbana, Ill.: NCTE, 1974.

This book describes three traditions—the ethical, the classical, and the non-academic—that have contributed to the teaching of English.

CLAPP, JOHN M. "Report of the Committee on Place and Function of English in American Life." *English Journal* 15 (February 1926):110–34.

Based on a 1920s study of how English was being used outside of school, this report led English teachers to give attention to telephone conversations, written reports, letters, and informal notes.

DIXON, JOHN. *Growth Through English.* Reading, Eng.: National Association for the Teaching of English, 1967.

This book offers a British perspective on the Dartmouth Conference, a 1967 meeting of British and American English educators, which led to more emphasis on language learning in American classes.

Freedom and Discipline in English: Report of the Commission on English. New York: College Entrance Examination Board, 1965.

The text outlines the intellectual premises underlying the Tripod approach. The commission, which included a number of college English professors, emphasized the high school's role in preparing college students.

HATFIELD, W. WILBUR. *An Experience Curriculum in English.* New York: D. Appleton-Century, 1935.

This text documents the work of a commission created by NCTE with representatives from NEA and North Central Association and charged with developing a pattern for a curriculum in English to serve as a reference for schools and teachers. The resulting curriculum advocates both personal growth and socially useful skills.

NATIONAL EDUCATION ASSOCIATION. *Report of the Committee of Ten on Secondary School Studies.* New York: American Book Company, 1894.

Written by a committee organized to address the issue of a uniform curriculum for the nation's schools, this report influenced the secondary school English curriculum greatly.

2

Reading Kids
and Classrooms

Fumbling handouts, seating charts, literature textbooks. Checking your teeth for any leftover danish, checking the floor for stray electrical cords. You don't want to embarrass yourself on the very first day. Blank-faced teenagers merely glance in your direction, then swivel toward their neighbors and launch into animated conversations. You study, once again, the lesson plan on Huck Finn *you so painstakingly prepared, praying it will consume an entire class period. The bell rings and—gulp!—you're on.*

THE FIRST FEW DAYS, even weeks, of teaching may be nerve-wracking for you, the new teacher, no matter how well prepared you are. It's also natural to be self-conscious about your classroom persona. You feel like you are on center stage, learning a new, more responsible role, and you may not feel ready to accept this responsibility. So why are you here, standing in front of this English classroom? In Chapter 1 we read about the reasons given over time for the teaching of English. That historical focus brings us to the present, and to your own place in the classroom. Why do you feel it is important to teach English? Most of us would answer this question by incorporating one or more of the reasons discussed in Chapter 1, but we might also include in our answers a commitment to sharing our love of reading and discussing literary texts. As English majors, we have likely been well prepared to read and interpret texts, especially literary ones, and we can imagine ourselves sharing our enjoyment in these texts in classrooms with our students. After all, we have been doing this for years, in our experience as students, from early grades through university course work.

Important as the skill of reading texts is for our preparation as English teachers, it is perhaps of even greater importance to be careful "readers" of students and classrooms. In fact, of all the many aspects of becoming a teacher—preparation in subject matter, familiarity with learning taxonomies, lesson plans, disciplinary methods—nothing may be more important than a teacher's commitment to knowing students as learners. The ability to "read" individual students and use those observations to create meaningful learning experiences is what separates the good teacher from the mediocre. Good teachers study each student's particular configuration of abilities and interests, not out of mere curiosity, but out of need: Successful teaching demands such knowledge.

As you observe different classrooms, it's easy to be distracted by the "performance" of the teacher—the rituals, the motivational antics, the little lectures. You may learn some handy tricks of the trade, but spending valuable observation time on the superficial will not help you much in becoming a responsive teacher. Instead, you might begin by watching how the teacher interacts with individual students. How does the teacher talk with students before, during, and after class? To what extent does this teacher seem to know the students as human beings? We emphasize here the importance of seeing teaching as developing a relationship with students—a relationship with whole classrooms and with individual students.

The excellent teacher knows his or her students very well, and knows them through paying close attention to them as individual learners. By systematically observing individual students' learning patterns and making inferences from your observations, you can practice the kind of reflection that epitomizes the excellent teacher.

Good teachers of English are constantly assessing their students' reactions and performance. They wonder what each student's attitude is toward each reading, writing, or speaking activity. They watch for sparks of interest, points of struggle, and signs of growth. They are curious about students' literate lives beyond their particular classrooms: Do these students read and write for pleasure or for other self-initiated purposes outside school? Good teachers are constantly seeking ways to reach (and teach) every student in the class.

Educator Herbert Kohl suggests (see Box 2.1) that the heart of the process of becoming a teacher must be "loving students as learners." Vito Perrone, in *A Letter to Teachers* (San Francisco: Jossey-Bass, 1991), suggests that the "larger purposes" of education—such as we discussed in

BOX 2.1
LOVING STUDENTS AS LEARNERS

Faith in the learner leads some teachers to find strengths where others see nothing but weakness and failure. Such faith, which is a component of teaching sensibility, is a form of what I call the love of students as learners. It is important to pause over the idea of loving students as learners, which is not the same as simply loving students. Each of us has only so much love we can offer, for love is not cheaply won or given. I care about all of my students, and respect them, but love grows slowly and requires attention and effort that cannot be spread around to twenty or thirty people simultaneously. . . . I don't trust teachers who say they love all their students, because it isn't possible to love so many people you know so little about and will separate from in six months.

Yet a certain kind of love is essential to good teaching, and that is what I choose to call loving students as learners. I once worked with a fourteen-year-old boy who could not read at all. He was very big and often defied his teachers. Occasionally he would explode with an uncontrolled and undirected violence that made people afraid to go near him. His parents came to me in despair. I promised to work with him two days a week after school. I was afraid of him too, though I considered being alone with him one of the risks and challenges of teaching. Since he had little sense of humor and seemingly no affection, I didn't particularly like him. Still, I responded

to the teaching challenge, and as we worked together, loved the way he came to master first his energy, then the alphabet, and then later books and writing. . . .

. . . [W]e talked about what was in different books. I read sections from books that dealt with subjects he was interested in, such as sea adventures and animal life. . . . Anyway, his whole attitude toward reading began to change. I felt that my love of learning and my pride in teaching him gave him a very different perception of himself as a learner. I loved to see him learning and, of course, to feel that I was some part of that process. . . . I took great pleasure in seeing him focus his previously undisciplined energy and learn to read. I loved him as a learner: it was a job-related affection. That affection led me to study him carefully and build on the strengths and personal interests I could tease out of him. It required that my personal feelings about him be subordinated to my feelings about him as a learner.

Teachers have preferences and can't be expected to like every student equally. And though teachers want to be liked by all their students, they shouldn't expect that to happen, either. Nevertheless, a teacher has an obligation to care about every student as a learner, just as every student should respect a decent caring teacher whether or not he or she likes that teacher.

—Excerpt from **BECOMING MINDS: On Becoming a Teacher** by Herbert Kohl. Copyright © 1984 by Herbert Kohl. Reprinted by permission of HarperCollins Publishers.

Chapter 1—must inform everything we do in the classroom. As he says, "Teaching is first and foremost a moral and intellectual endeavor, always beginning with children and young people and their intentions and needs." "Loving students as learners" is at the heart of these larger purposes; it also drives the very process of reading kids. Getting to know and care about your students as learners will lead you to pay close attention to the different ways that they learn to read and write. While it is important to observe closely the students you have the privilege to teach and learn with, it is also important to keep these larger purposes in mind as you observe classrooms and kids: What is it you really want students to come to understand as a result of their schooling? What kinds of values and commitments do you as a teacher represent? The focus in Chapters 3 through 8 is on developing a view of language—what Nancie Atwell calls "an awareness of language processes" (see Suggested Reading at the end of this chapter)—that will in part form the basis for your teaching. What is the nature of language and learning? How do students, in general, best learn? How can we best "love students as learners"? To keep these larger purposes before us is to commit to growth and development as teachers, to commit to learn with our students about teaching and learning.

Reading Individual Kids as Learners

In the following case studies, you have the opportunity to practice "reading" students of English. As you examine each case, it may be helpful to make some notes:

- What are this student's apparent strengths and weaknesses in language learning?
- What strategies does this student need to learn?
- What could a teacher do to tap into this student's abilities and interests?

When you finish reading each case, you can compare your analysis with that of the student's teacher. You might also note the extent to which each teacher seems to follow Kohl's and Perrone's advice about attending to students' needs as learners. As you see it, how does each teacher demonstrate, or in some way fail to demonstrate, this principle? Is there a different approach you might have taken?

Yolanda

Yolanda attends high school in a midsized, rust-belt town. The district is poor, but most students remain hopeful about school and their futures.

Like the majority of students at her school, Yolanda is African American. She lives in an all-black neighborhood that suffers from the problems plaguing most poor, urban communities: discrimination, drugs, and violence. Still, she doesn't dwell on the misery. Yolanda has taken up drums, playing in the highly regarded high school jazz band. She wants to go to college to study music.

From the very first day of school, it is clear that Yolanda wants to be a good student. Alert, poised, and smiling, she takes interest in her tenth-grade English class, volunteering comments and asking questions. On a survey given at the beginning of the semester, she says that she doesn't consider herself a reader or a writer, but that she likes both activities. She says that spelling and grammar pose the greatest writing problems for her. In reading activities, Yolanda feels that keeping up with the assignments presents the most difficulty.

Her first journal entries, written as letters in response to stories from a student-authored collection, introduce her as a writer:

Dear Tomika

The story "My Two Friends" (p 59) it was about two friends. And it was kind of different to me. One character was unfair to another. And the other character is really being a friend I would say so. But I think that this really happens in persons lives but I have been through it to. So by me reading this maid me understand how certain people be. But it is a alright stories you should read it. But things like that won't happen to me any more.

Sincerely,
Yolanda

Surface errors aside (for the moment), Yolanda's entry gives the reader a sense that she has understood the theme of the story and connected it to her personal experiences. She seems to make references to events that a reader other than Tomika might have trouble understanding. (Tomika is one of Yolanda's friends in the class.) The surface errors, while troublesome, follow specific patterns: difficulties in using conjunctions ("and" and "but"), missing punctuation or inappropriate authorial commentaries ("I would say so"), and the use of dialectal "be" ("how certain people be").

When Yolanda writes longer pieces, the problems in her writing become more evident. In response to a journal entry about threats to friendships, she writes:

My close Friend now almost because my enemy.

Well I had friend name Lanette. She is 15 teen years old we grew up together. From 1st grade to now. We went to church, school, parties, name it we did it together. But when we started to grow up about 13 teen I was in the 7th and she didn't pass she was in the 6th. But she thought I was going to change but I didn't. So we used to go places and most would try to talk to me. So she loves boys she had a baby in the 6th grade and he didn't even claim it. So I used to babysit and I still was her homie. But this boy she went with in the 12th grade and she was in the 8th I was in the 9th. She always wanted me to go over her house with her. But when he tried to talk to me I just wouldn't so he told her I tried to talk to him but I really didn't I swear. So she asked me and I said no but she started calling me all kind of names Bitches, Hoes, and everything you name it. So I said stop I swear I didn't. And she ran in the house crying I was going in the house after her but she grab her mother big knife and stabbed me in my leg and then I start to fight her back. But he really didn't like her and she didn't know it. But I had 16 stitches. And she came out there to see me and I didn't won't to see her. So the next day she came to my house I said come in she told me she was sorry and I said why did you go off like that she said because she was pregnant again but I said what did I have to do with it she said she wanted him to stay with her not leave her but they still broke up and we stayed friends.

Yolanda's story is startling, but its themes are not unusual in her community. The story is also troubling for its problems with coherence and sequencing. The disjointed narrative with all of its grammatical and structural problems stands in stark contrast to Yolanda's spoken performances in class. During discussions, she is vocal and demonstrates few of the problems that appear in her writing.

As we said, Yolanda has some trouble completing reading assignments. This is true even when she is given ample time to read in class. She has never finished a novel in school, though she has read some books on her own that she occasionally carries with her in school. She says she likes to read when the material interests her. She has an open attitude toward reading and writing, readily sharing the difficulties she encounters. She is also a willing learner in conferences with her teacher about her reading and writing, listening carefully to suggestions.

Yolanda's Teacher on Yolanda

While her work presents many challenges to a teacher, Yolanda also possesses many strengths. Her openness to learning, eager attitude, and genuine interest bode well for her potential in school. As her teacher, I have found that patience and quiet assistance have helped her the most. Despite the many skills she needs to learn, I want to encourage her, not defeat her by overwhelming criticisms or suggestions. After observing her classroom performance, I'm convinced that Yolanda learns best by hearing others; both her musical talent and her greater skill at discussions bear out this conclusion. As a result, I try to conference with Yolanda as she's writing, reading her work aloud to her and asking her to listen to how it sounds. It helps having her work with other students, too.

I see her written texts as almost an interior dialogue, not sufficiently attuned to an external audience. She seems, in other words, to be writing to herself, not to others (her teacher, her classmates, etc.). Moreover, Yolanda's text tries to do too much at once—in her friendship story she tries to tell everyone's perspective at once, mixing them up in any given sentence. In conferences we've worked together, sorting out who's doing what and in what order. We've also discussed the need to explain background knowledge to the reader; she must watch carefully for assumptions about relationships or events that the reader doesn't share. Sometimes we even take an individual sentence, dividing it into the separate ideas that she tends to conflate.

Yolanda also brings many strengths to her writing. Her work exhibits much implicit knowledge about writing, especially about punctuation, spelling, and fluency. She gives the reader many details about events, providing nuances that bring life to her characters, even though her telling of the details sometimes interferes with the narrative progression. She is also concerned about improving her writing skills. Once, after she had worked through several drafts of an essay, I asked her to go back and read her first draft. Horrified, she exclaimed, "Oh, no! It was too awful! It's so much better now, I don't even want to look at what I wrote before."

It will take Yolanda some time to write more proficiently. Indeed, in another district, Yolanda might have been labeled learning-disabled because of the disparity between her spoken and written proficiencies. Her plight is not hopeless, though. She willingly takes initiative, writing many more drafts of a text than other students. She can also benefit from specific exercises, such as copychange (an exercise where students take a piece of text and substitute words to create a text of their own), as long as the utility of such exercises bears directly on her own writing. Yolanda has clear positions about the events going on around her. These events can help her learn argumentation, as well as help her develop a voice that can persuade readers. I try to help her build on her interest in music for writing topics as much as possible. I also try to help her appreciate the musical quality evident in her own language use.

Yolanda needs some help with her reading, too, and I give this to her when I can. Though I think it is important to challenge all students, I give my students the opportunity to read books that they will enjoy in terms of their own interests as much as possible, and I encourage them to respond to literature in ways in which they will feel comfortable. Yolanda seems to appreciate this approach, and she does read, with encouragement and some help from me and her peers. Recently, for instance, she read most of a biography of Aaron Copland, and an article about the history of jazz music. We regularly have small-group discussions about our reading, and her classmates help her there, of course.

Yolanda can continue to grow as a reader and writer with lots of practice and positive feedback, writing and reading things that she enjoys as much as possible. I encourage and expect her to read and write much, both in and out of class, with as much response from me and others as she can get. She is a pleasant, likable person, and likes to talk; I try to build on that ability as much as possible by having her talk in class and in small groups about her reading and writing. We try as often as we can to examine the relationship between talk and writing. Yolanda is a hard worker and really wants to learn. You can't give up on students like her.

Pete

Pete looks like a scholar—tall, curly-haired, quiet with wire-rimmed glasses—but his performance in eleventh-grade honors American Literature class seems to tell a different story. "I dunno," he answers to almost every directed question. In class discussions of assigned texts, he seems lost. When writing in class, he works very slowly, and the theses he formulates are usually pedestrian and poorly supported. For instance, when asked to compare the written works of William Byrd and Captain John Smith, he stares out the window for twenty minutes, then makes a brief list of facts about Smith's life. He begins the first draft of his essay, "Captain John Smith wrote much of his adventures. Smith tried to express in his writings that the new land was adventuresome." He rewrites these sentences, with a few minor changes, several times before settling on a different approach. Pete's final draft, after three days of in-class writing, is less than a page in length.

Contrast Byrd and Smith

The styles of writing of William Byrd II and Captain John Smith are vastly different.

The purpose and audience of the two authors were the same, basically, but that is where the similarities terminate.

As few people there were in Jamestown, Virginia, Smith needed more to help the colony get along. He wrote of the new land as adventuresome as could have been and more some. Smith also told of stories that could have hardly been believed to catch people's eyes and attention hoping they

would come over. Smith tells of "Having feasted him after
their *best* barbarian manner they could . . . then as many
could laid hands on him, dragged him to them, and thereon
laid his head, and being ready with their clubs to beat his
brains out. Pocahantas, the king's dearest daughter, got his
head in her arms and laid her own upon his to save him from
death . . ." (p. 6) This is one of the examples of the far-fetched
tales Smith tells about. No king would treat a guest with the
best of manners and then try to have him clubbed to death
only to have the king's dearest daughter ready to throw her
life away for him.

Pete's written texts occasionally showcase a fairly good vocabulary
and some knowledge of prose patterns, but the ideas expressed seem
undeveloped, even confused, as in the following excerpt from the beginning of a paper on *Huckleberry Finn*. (In history class Pete had seen a
program on paradigms, but he later admitted that he hadn't read Twain's
novel.)

Paradigms exist throughout history; paradigms of
restricting rules and regulations and paradigms of just plain
patterns, repeating themselves throughtout different epochs.
In Mark Twain's *Huckleberry Finn*, Jim's hunger for freedom is
unparalleled, to a certain degree, by what is happening in
today's society in Eastern Europe and also for that matter,
what happened just a little bit ago with China.
    Superstition is not a paradigm, but has existed throughout
history; just as the idea of having one's own freedom has.
Mark Twain expresses the usage of superstition throughout
Huckleberry Finn (as well as its . . .)
    The paradigms of freedom and the use of Superstition,
from Mark Twain's *Huckleberry Finn*, in relevance to today's
society (as a general whole) will be discussed in this paper.

Pete is tense and quiet during one-on-one conferences. Although he
is not antisocial during small-group activities, he doesn't really have any
close friends in this class. In the hallway, however, he often speaks quite
animatedly with a group of five or six students, an eccentric lot who
operate on the fringes of the "popular" crowd.
    In a survey given at the beginning of the semester, Pete reports that
he is good at math, science, and art, and his grades in these other classes
seem to reflect this assertion. But English is his problem: specifically,
composing texts and reading novels. He believes he needs work on vocabulary, because "the right words just don't come." He prefers to compose
on the word processor because "it's less messy—no crossed-out words, no

chicken scratching." Outside of the classroom, Pete enjoys reading informative texts such as factual and self-help books, although he believes he reads too slowly. He finds it difficult to study at home and in class because of interruptions and distractions.

Pete's Teacher on Pete

Pete is a classic underachiever, a bright, quirky thinker who purposefully remains anonymous. Bored and frustrated with school tasks, he resists so quietly that he is often misjudged by his teachers, who sometimes mistake his reticence for a lack of intelligence. Even Pete's parents were wondering whether he was learning-disabled. I met with Pete after school one day to discuss his work.

As we talked, I noticed that Pete seemed to have a lot of underlying anger toward typical English activities and texts. "I hate third-person narrators," he said. "I can't stand it when writers play God." He often wouldn't read such texts, relying instead on tidbits picked up during class discussions or lectures. Thus his written texts were based on flimsy clues, not on thorough reading. Pete also thought he should read texts word for word in order to get "the full meaning." Apparently, a middle school teacher had told him that was the proper way to read. Reading at such a painstaking pace caused him to lose track of meaning. When I explained to him that readers needed to vary their rates depending upon the text and the situation, and that a faster rate sometimes made the text more comprehensible, Pete was livid: "Why do teachers teach the wrong things like they're the truth?"

School writing assignments seemed silly and formulaic to Pete. Generally his teachers assigned topics and required him to outline, brainstorm, and write several drafts. Like Bartleby the Scrivener, Pete "preferred not to." He procrastinated. Thus those rather pedestrian papers, outlines and all, had been written during lunch or a half-hour break. Because his English grades were so poor, his college opportunities were narrowing.

At the same time, Pete was setting his own learning agenda during his free time. He had started a journal and was reading *Past Life Regression,* in part because his mother had been talking with him about reincarnation.

Although it may be hard to believe after you've seen some of his papers, Pete was also a perfectionist with his own writing. He really seemed to fold up under the pressure he put on himself to be a good expository writer. He had very high standards for himself as a thinker. But in the end he just generally stopped trying, again partly out of his resistance to the task itself.

In our conferences, we explored the similarities and differences between novels and informative writing; we talked of setting goals and of tailoring school tasks to fit Pete's personal interests. He began to examine the consequences of his resistance. "By not trying, I'm never put on the line," he admitted. "I'll never know if I really can do it." We talked about his responsibility as a student to make English meaningful to himself. I suggested that Pete create his own assignments and negotiate with me to substitute his writing tasks for mine.

I think this might have been the key for him, though it may be too early to tell. His writing is starting to be less stiff, reflecting more of his own style and voice. I encourage him to write about more personal topics, things he cares about. I'm trying to get him to loosen up, to have more fun with his prose, to build on his appreciation of different kinds of writing.

Jerrod

Jerrod races to the room just as the bell rings for fifth hour. "Pimp walking" across the room to his desk, he brushes against the hair of two or three girls on his way. The girls immediately take offense, hollering at him as he moves away. It is a typical entrance; Jerrod does not seem to be able to interact simply, verbally, with other students. There is always some kind of physical contact, usually irritating. He laughs at the girls, makes it to his seat, and elbows Wallace, his best friend in class. Then he remembers he hasn't taken his journal with him—it's still in the plastic crate at the front of the room. Up again, he manages to get his journal with only minimal disruption.

A tall, thin boy, Jerrod does enjoy his English class. He often contributes important ideas to discussion, but too often ends them with a silly comment, trying to get a rise out of the other students. He usually takes a more serious posture in his journal writing. Writing about a close relationship he's had, Jerrod chooses his uncle:

A Close Relationship

I have a close relationship with someone. He is my uncle, but he's more like a friend to me. His name is Charles Scott Grant. Charles used to let me hang out with him. He taught me Tae Kwon Do. In fact, he taught me everything I know from basketball to girls to fighting. He wouldn't let anyone mess with me. He didn't just take time with me, he also took time with my brother.

When Charles graduated from high school, he moved to Los Angeles with his girl friend, but he comes back every year to visit the family. When he gets here, he always tells me what's going on in LA, and I tell him what's been going on here.

He's named after his father, or my grandfather, and he named his son Charles Scott, too. I really miss him.

Jerrod is also a good, generally enthusiastic reader. He enjoys the class reading of *Catcher in the Rye,* finding Holden Caulfield a strange character, but someone to whom he can relate. He even says that he and Holden are a lot alike. During class discussion, many students argue that Holden is immature and a troublemaker, but Jerrod defends him. "He's mixed up, but at least he doesn't fight with people. Besides, what he says about people is mostly true. Lots of people are phonies. We just don't want to hear it from a kid." His comments help his classmates reconsider their interpretations of the character. Later in the hour, however, when students read silently, Jerrod giggles and squirms, disrupting his neighbors' reading. Finally he is asked to move, so the other students can finish the reading assignment in peace.

Group projects are without a doubt Jerrod's favorite activities. He brings an enthusiasm to them that infects the rest of his group. Always humorous, he teases and cajoles his group into creative ideas that in their worst moments border on the ridiculous. He likes being in groups with his friend Wallace but doesn't object strenuously when the groups change. Being able to move around, reorganize the room, and talk to others seems to keep his active imagination focused on the learning task.

Jerrod's Teacher on Jerrod

Jerrod can be my greatest joy or my worst nightmare. His high-energy personality can spark lively debate that involves all members of the class. At other times, his inability to stay focused on an activity can disrupt the most carefully planned lesson. I confess he sometimes baffles me because he is so unpredictable. Yet he is a member of my class, and I have to keep trying to find creative ways of harnessing his restlessness. Most often, giving Jerrod some latitude—allowing him to move or to work with a partner—has the best results. There are, however, times when he must learn to work independently and silently. In these instances, he usually sits away from the group, either voluntarily or at my insistence, because the other students provide too great a distraction for him.

As a reader and writer, Jerrod shows above-average abilities. He reads insightfully. Few of my students grasp the subtleties of novels the way Jerrod can. That is, of course, provided he has bothered to read them. His writing displays his wit, but like his reading habits, it can be carelessly executed or left entirely undone. Capturing his attention for a sustained period of time is the key to his better performances. For example, when our class explored the history of African Americans in the community during Black History Month, Jerrod spent hours researching his family's migration from the South. It was a topic that he found personally stimulating, worthy of his attention.

Part of Jerrod's behavior has to do with maturation—as he matures, he will most likely settle down. Another part is simply his personality. The best I can offer him now is a place where there are flexible limits. He can't aggravate other students, but I can allow him to work more often in groups. I can also provide the opportunities for other students, bothered by his behavior, to express their displeasure—not by hollering at him, but by telling him what they don't like. After hearing other teachers complain about him, I suspect that he visits the principal's office regularly. I'm not convinced that punishment will speed up his emotional growth, nor that it will change his personality. Sometimes I have to make it clear that there are limits to his disruptive behavior, but of course my main goal is to help him find acceptable avenues for participation in my class.

Janet

Having recently moved from a rural setting to an upper-middle-class suburb, Janet has a certain clarity beyond mere innocence that most of her peers lack. Alert and often smiling, she projects intelligence, arguing with gusto during class discussions. She is an avid reader, bringing to class novels and poetry that she reads in spare moments. She reads well, choosing texts ranging from T. S. Eliot's *Four Quartets* to Anne Tyler's *The Accidental Tourist*.

Janet loves to write poems and stories, and she regularly keeps a journal. She revises eagerly in response to suggestions from her peers and her teacher. Despite Janet's love of reading and writing, she is not doing very well in English, mainly because she has trouble with the formal analytical papers that make up the bulk of her English teacher's assignments. One teacher claims her work is "too creative," too full of description and metaphor. Often she will not bother to hand in expository assignments at all, though when she does they are often more than competent, as in the draft of an essay about her grandmother.

Blind Faith

When my Grandma was sixteen years old she contracted tuberculosis. Back then it was almost virtual death, people didn't survive from TB. I can't imagine having something like that thrust upon me. My Grandma says it has nothing to do with your maturity level. She says that it was God that saved her. She has quite a great faith in the power of Healing.

About a week ago I was sitting at my kitchen table with my grandmother. She was telling me that if anyone came into this house they would have no idea that we were Catholic, that the only way a person would know was to look in my room. Well, she is right. Nowhere in our house do we have any type of religious painting or statue except in my room. I have a small, wooden crucifix, a heavy clear glass statue of the blessed Mary and a small drawing of my patron saint. Saint Catherine of Sienna. But I honestly think that I'm in the minority. I don't think that too many high-school or college students have religious works in their rooms. I think that a lot of people, not just students, don't have any portraits of religious figures. But, I'm not saying that I'm super faithful, or God fearing. By all means, I sin my fair share of times. I really don't have a Great Faith.

Sometimes I wish I did. I think that my Grandma does. She has this blind faith. She was never exposed to half of the stuff I am. She went to a small Catholic school, she was never taught Darwinism or about the Big Bang theory. I wish I would believe like she does.

For example, when she was at one of her worst points of tuberculosis, hemmoriging and weighed in at eighty pounds (she's about 5′6″) she decided to get up out of her bed and go see Father Scienus. This first of all, I would have never done. I would have stayed right where I was. It was All Hallows Eve and she had to walk through the cemetary to get to the chruch. It was dark and there were glowing candles on all of the graves. Being on the verge of death this was not a pleasant experience for her. She got to the good prists door and he came outside with her. He said to my Grandmother while pointing to the cemetary. "Kit, over there, that's Gods and you're still here on this side of the road. Get to communion every day, regardless of how you feel." Miraculously, my Grandma did it and, thank God, she's still going to communion everyday. I just pray that someday I'll have that kind of faith.

My Grandmother did not marry a Catholic. My Grandpa Ned was a Protestant, actually being more agnostic. It all worked out in the long run my Grandfather converted and actually became quite a strict Catholic before his untimely death.

My Grandfather used to come and visit at my Grandma's house quite often. On one occasion my Grandma's dad and my Grandfather began talking about faith and my Grandpa termed the faith of my great-grandparents as blind faith. Quickly therafter he was kicked out of the house. After my Grandpa had converted to Catholism, he was much the same way as my Grandma's dad, possibily even more intolerant. He told my Grandma that her faith inspired him, that if she believed in God so strongly ther must be something tight.

I can sit down with my Grandma for hours and talk about faith, and so many times I find what she says is true. I try and say the rosary every night, which she recommended. It didn't drastically change my life, but I notice the intercession on the Blessed Mary every so often.

My Grandma inspires me. If five eights of the worlds population had half of her love and faith, this would certainly be a much better place to live. It's not bad now, we still have her. It scares me to think of my life without her, I can't imagine it. She's taught me faith better than anyone could do, and hopefully when she's gone I'll be able to carry on where she left off. She never fed the hungry in India or made the cripple walk, but she changed my life and that's enough to make her saint in my book.

Janet's creative writing teacher responded to this draft positively in her written comments and in conference, noting some of the essay's strengths, but also commenting on and questioning several issues she had noted earlier in Janet's work. (This paper was written late in the year, after her teacher had established a comfortable relationship with Janet.) An accomplished poet, the teacher encouraged the poetic impulses in Janet's prose. As she said, "I was trying to show Janet the connections between poetry and prose by concentrating on flow, on sound. In conference with her, we kept reading passages out loud, and I kept encouraging her to *listen* the way she always did when she worked on poems." The following series of drafts of a poem show the effects of the teacher's work with Janet:

Inside/Outside
(first draft)

I am coffee perkelating
waking you up
I am old-fashioned and comfort
Country homes and laughing children
A field of golden wheat
Bending and breaking

I am a warm kitchen
on a snowy winter morn
I am a sunrise, dawn
A crowd of roaring fans and old friends
toasting Christmas
A lone child on a beach
A noontime play ground.

At this point, Janet's teacher commented only on the apparently incongruous leap from the country to the beach, encouraging her to focus on the ways she might be like the country home. The second draft reflected the teacher's comments:

Inside/Outside
(second draft)

I am coffee perkalating
waking you up
I am old fashioned and comfort
Country homes and laughing children
A field of golden wheat
Bending and unbreaking

I am a warm kitchen
on a snowy winter morn
I am a sunrise, dawn
Baking cookies and tea kettles whistling
Handknit afghans
and quilts
A crackling fire
On a crisp fall day

Janet's teacher placed question marks after images or words she wanted Janet to reconsider, and she "starred" images she particularl liked. After this, Janet "went back to the drawing board," listing phrase in her journal:

sugar and cinnamon

cooked to syrup

melted and warm

sweet, mushy, and hot

burning your tongue

reminds me of *gramma*

The next day she wrote some more notes, still at the drawing board:

coffee perkalating, bacon eggs and

bread from the French Bakery-

homemade raspberry jam from raspberries

she picked herself

Snowy winter mornings

warm, comfortable, safe

Evenings: lamp hissing, crackers and cheese on the back
    porch

> fall baking: cookies, fudge
>
> tea kettle whistling
>
> The fire is crakiling (crisp and safe)
>
> Spending the days and nights with grandma, coffee
>   perkalating
>
> in the morning waking me up, I feel old-fashioned, and
>
> comfortable. Gas lamps hissing—not here—but I hear
>   them in
>
> my imagination. Her kitchen is always warm, I can see the
>
> snow falling

Some words were crossed out, some were indecipherable, and daydreaming doodles accompanied the notes.

A week later Janet handed in her final draft:

Spending My Days and Nights with Grandma

On winter mornings, the coffee percolating
and the sizzling of bacon and eggs
would wake me up.
We ate fresh bread from the French bakery
with homemade jam made from raspberries she picked.
Together, we were warm, safe and comfortable
on these bright snowy dawns.

Our fall afternoons were old fashioned and cozy
I sat and rocked with an afghan on my lap
reading by the stone fireplace.
She always made baked apples with sugar and cinnamon
sweet and mushy, burning my tongue.
Just the two of us there was no other world
but ours.

During our summer evenings we sat on the back porch
and ate crackers and cheese with the fresh lettuce
we grew together in our garden.
Our conversations were soft and simple
dwindling down to nothing.
As the night grew late, we slept to a summer lullaby
The sprinklers ticking and the gaslamps hissing.

Janet's year-end poetry collection includes this poem, but it also includes some poems dealing with such serious personal crises as her once being raped. Her introduction to the collection demonstrates an awareness of her growth as a writer and person over the course of the year in creative writing class:

> My poems over the course of this year have changed and I'm not sure if they are better or worse because of it . . . I now realize that poetry can be more of an outlet than I thought, not only for creative purposes but for personal purposes, too. I also learned there's a certain amount of putting yourself on the line in poetry, too.
>
> I like to think of poetry as a personal sort of therapy. I don't know if all poets feel this way, but the gratification of seeing an idea transform into a poem brings a certain peace of mind. It also helps to write things and see them written. It can always be spoken but to have it written down takes pieces of maybe painful or sometimes joyful memories out.
>
> I also like getting response to my poems. The response, good or bad, makes me want to go and write to make it better than before. I'm looking forward to continuing my writing career and I hope my work will continue to improve and that people derive some pleasure from reading it.

Grades do not seem to motivate Janet. She is fully aware that with her sporadic attempts at analytic writing she may never receive a grade above a C. Even brief conferences focusing on these assignments don't really prompt her to make an effort.

Janet's Teacher on Janet

Janet is in the process of becoming the wonderful, self-motivated learner we hope all our students will become. She reads and writes very well for her own purposes; in fact, she hopes to write professionally. Paradoxically, because Janet is so independent, she no longer "fits" very well in many English classrooms, especially those that require compliance. In addition, the (over)emphasis on analysis and exposition turns her off. Janet had, unfortunately, learned the false dichotomy taught by so many teachers—that "creativity" (descriptive, metaphoric, narrative text features) cannot coexist with "practicality" (expository, persuasive, analytical text features).

My job was to unteach and reteach, using the texts and ways of writing I knew she loved. I asked her to gather several poems she wanted to discuss in depth with me; as we talked, I recorded her astute analysis point by point. I helped her see that she knew how to analyze. We read a number of essays by poets and fiction writers she admired. "See," I said, "*they* sometimes find reasons to write exposition." We examined those texts for "creative" features and found plenty. We looked at the similarities in the processes of creating poems, short stories, and even essays.

After this rather intensive campaign on my part, Janet began to draft and revise essays, though never with the same fervor that the other writing inspired. I imagine she has found a way to talk herself into "doing school," and I'm hopeful that she may learn to love writing essays in the future. In the meantime, Janet makes great progress with her poetry, and though she is no longer in my class, she continues to share draft after draft of her poetry with me.

As portrayed, each of these students seems unique, and they are, just as each of the students in your classes will be a unique blend of traits, habits, experiences, skills. Yet none of them is wildly eccentric. Teaching each of them means observing what strengths and weaknesses they possess and interacting with them in ways that will help them learn to be more proficient language arts students. Janet, although very talented, cannot rest on the talent she brings with her. Her teachers need to provide challenges that will draw upon her talent in the context of assignments that don't always "inspire" her. For Yolanda, the challenge of almost any writing assignment is enough. The teacher must respond with creative learning "supports," helping her organize her thoughts so she can express them clearly. Each of these students can flourish in classrooms, with the informed and deliberate attention of teachers sensitive to their different needs.

We asked you earlier to consider Yolanda's, Pete's, Jerrod's, and Janet's apparent strengths and weaknesses in language learning as you read their case studies—and to consider too the strategies you felt each of these students needed to learn and the ways a teacher could tap into their abilities and interests. In Box 2.2 we ask you to imagine that you *are* that teacher for a few moments.

Responding to the individual needs of students may seem a daunting task at first. You may even be asking yourself now: How can I know students well enough to respond individually to each one? How can I possibly teach with such student variation in a classroom? While each teacher finds his or her own way of getting to know students, deciding that it is, in fact, important to explore their personalities, talents, and proficiencies does change the way you view your classroom. As individuals emerge from the mass of adolescent faces, it becomes possible to talk to individual students differently, using your knowledge of them to assist their reading and writing.

One important consideration in reading students as learners is what Howard Gardner calls "multiple intelligences." In his book *Frames of Mind: The Theory of Multiple Intelligences* (New York: Basic Books, 1985), Gardner outlines seven different intelligences that humans possess: musical, bodily kinesthetic, logical-mathematical, linguistic, spatial, personal,

---

BOX 2.2
TEACHING AND LEARNING WITH YOLANDA, PETE, JERROD, AND JANET

Imagine this: As an English teacher in your own classroom, you have the responsibility of teaching five classes of twenty-five very different young people for fifty minutes every day. You have your own experience as a student in a classroom to call on, and you may even have some experience working with younger people.

Imagine now that you have Yolanda, Pete, Jerrod, and Janet in your classroom—in the same classroom, as a matter of fact, since there is no tracking in your school. How might your classroom accommodate their individual strengths and weaknesses? Do you see their special needs as obstacles to your plans or as opportunities?

Take a few moments to answer for yourself the following questions.

GENERAL CLASSROOM CONSIDERATIONS

1. How will your classroom be structured? For instance, how will the desks be arranged?

2. What kind of relationship will you develop with each of these students?

3. What kind of approach to learning will you take? Give some examples of the kinds of activities you hope to do in your classroom. Why do you think it is best to take this kind of approach?

4. How does your general approach accommodate individual student needs?

QUESTIONS ABOUT INDIVIDUAL STUDENTS

1. What are your perceptions of Yolanda, Pete, Jerrod, and Janet? Do you agree with each teacher's assessment of their strengths and weaknesses? If your assessment is different, what does that mean in terms of your response to their needs?

2. How would you work with them in order to accommodate their particular interests and abilities?

3. As an English major, you are probably more like Janet than the other three students. What difference would it make to you to work with students who are not necessarily inclined to read and write as Janet generally does, and who may seem to you to be less capable learners?

---

and interpersonal. English teachers evaluate students primarily in terms of their linguistic intelligence, and most standardized tests appear to measure intelligence primarily in terms of linguistic and logical-mathematical intelligences. But Gardner argues that most adult roles require a combination of intelligences rather than a specific one, that people have varying aptitudes for any one form of intelligence, and that the combination of intelligences works in a "sum is greater than the parts" way. In making room for the individual differences of our students, it would be wise to keep Gardner's formulation in mind and, if possible, to make adjustments in our approaches to classroom content that will be sensitive to each student's needs.

Reading Individual Kids as Kids

We have underscored thus far the importance of "reading" individual students as learners. Your primary obligation as a teacher is to coach the student's performance, nurturing self-confidence and literacy skills. Closely examining students' different ways of learning will help you accomplish these goals. But in addition to observing individual learning styles, it is also important to know about and take an interest in your students as persons. You and your students will both be enriched by this very human aspect of teaching, of course. Students can be wonderful people to know and learn from! Be aware of their lives outside your classroom: What do your students like to do in their spare time? What kinds of television shows and movies do they like to watch? What kind of music do they listen to? Where do they hang out on the weekends? What school activities are they involved in? How are they doing in other classes?

By finding out about your students, their habits, their personalities, the communities they come from, and the communities they create, you can begin to address many of your own questions: what to teach, how to teach, and how to motivate your students. In his book, *The Tone of Teaching* (Portsmouth, N.H.: Heinemann, 1986), Max VanManen says, "A teacher is a child watcher . . . a child watcher keeps in view the total existence of the developing child." Reading individual kids as kids, young persons who live lives outside of your classroom, provides the broader framework for understanding them as individual learners and for adapting your classroom to their differences.

But what does it mean to "read" individual students? What Yetta Goodman calls "kidwatching," observing the details of students' academic and affective behavior, provides teachers with the information they need to make good instructional choices. (Goodman's essay is found in *Observing the Language Learner*; see Jaggar and Smith-Burke in Suggested Reading at the end of this chapter.) For instance, if you know that eight of your fourth-hour composition students rehearsed until 11:00 P.M. for the school's production of *West Side Story*, you may choose to adjust your lesson plan. It would not be, for most teachers, the day to take a principled stand against sleeping in class. When James, usually an active member of the class, sits cross-armed, sullenly refusing to take his essay test on *Catcher in the Rye*, muttering that he hates the book, you may want to investigate. What could have happened to provoke this change? Did he have a fight with Vernel, his best friend? A problem in his algebra class? Lose his after-school job? Answers to any of these questions might explain James's current state of mind. They might also help you help him get back on track.

In *Being with Children*, Phillip Lopate discusses the importance of "hanging out" in getting a feel for the life of the school. (See Box 2.3.) "Noodling around" with kids, hanging out with them and seeing how they think and feel, is an important part of the process of kidwatching. Getting to know your students as persons is part of the process of developing a view of the classroom sensitive to the students' perspective. When faced with impersonal routines class after class, students lose their enthusiasm for learning, and apathetic students make teaching arduous at best.

In contrast, *responsive teaching*, teaching that takes into consideration the full range of students' lives—their personalities, cultural and ethnic heritages, their various abilities in English and other subjects, the nuances of their daily lives—makes it possible for students to view the English classroom as relevant and meaningful. Responsive teaching also enables teachers to form productive relationships with students, so that kidwatching becomes a joyous activity. Watching students overcome personal or academic obstacles, take on new challenges, and mature into adulthood is the most rewarding part of teaching. Learning how to "read" kids may be one of the trickiest aspects of becoming a teacher, but it is an art and a science well worth studying.

Experienced teachers begin observing students from the moment they enter the building. Their observations are not limited to their classrooms; as Lopate seems to suggest, hallways, cafeterias, auditoriums, and student hangouts provide other contexts in which to learn about students. Most often, though, teachers have their first opportunity for kidwatching as students make the trek from the classroom doorway to their desks. Good teachers ask themselves certain questions while they watch their students' opening "performances."

- *How do the students enter the classroom?* The way that students enter the classroom tells teachers a great deal about them. Students who make grand entrances, with intentional rule breaking or theatrical displays, may be signaling that they want special attention from the teacher or from fellow students. Conversely, students seem to discourage interaction with others by going quietly to the back of the room and busying themselves at their desks. Other kids make a point of talking with the teacher or other students. All of this may provide clues as to how students want to be treated by their teachers, and how they intend to act in the classroom. It may provide clues to their learning styles, too. Change in an entry pattern is noteworthy, and an observant teacher will set aside time to talk with a student who begins to exhibit uncharacteristic behavior.

BOX 2.3
GENE

The easiest way for me to get to know the kids was to talk to them when I had nothing up my sleeve, when I wasn't demanding any work from them.

There was one boy, Gene, who had been singled out by Denise as someone who needed extra help. He was bright, she said, but he hated to work at anything for more than two minutes, and he loathed writing, and he had no friends in the class. He was short, blond-haired, with a dirt-streaked face and a dirty football jersey which he wore every day. Through trial and error I got the impression he did not like to be looked in the eye. Sometimes you meet a child whom you have to approach obliquely, like a deer, and stand quietly until he gets a chance to look you over and become used to your presence.

I sat next to him, looking at my hands for about a minute without opening my mouth. Then I said, still not looking at him, like two old-timers whittling on a porch: "What yer doin'?" "Makin' a drawing." "Let me see it?" It was something ghastly: a man's head being decapitated. "Nice. Looks like a horror movie," I said. "That's where I got the idea." "You like horror movies, eh?" "Yeah!" And now he began talking like a blue streak about monsters, and mealworms, and his dog, whom he loved passionately. He talked with a feverish haste, one word falling on the next. We were still conversing through sidelong glances, which would have made an odd impression to a third party; but by the end of ten minutes I had slowly worked around to gazing directly at him, and he at me. It was a start.

The key for me was having enough open, unscheduled time and making myself accessible to children to fill it. I wanted to be available for their everyday inspirations and small talk. I tried not to let my schedule get so tight that I couldn't noodle around with kids.

—From Phillip Lopate, *Being with Children* (New York: Simon & Schuster, 1975), p. 30. Copyright 1975 by Phillip Lopate. Reprinted by permission of the Wendy Weil Agency, Inc.

- *Where do students choose to sit?* Obviously, a permanent seating chart eliminates this question as a kidwatching tool, but in classrooms where seating is optional, teachers can find out about friendships, antipathies, and attitudes toward school. Some kids may sit in the front of the room because they can't see the blackboard or because they want to participate to the fullest. Sitting in the back of the room may be a way of becoming invisible. Struggling, bored, or unprepared students try to hide from the teacher's view. Occasionally, resistant students find the desks in the rear a fine platform for protest. Given the choice, some students may choose seats near friends more interested in social matters than subject matter. Knowing these social relationships can help you find ways to work with particular students.

Teachers sensitive to seating patterns will make a point of getting as many students as possible involved in discussions, regardless of where they sit. They may also, if necessary, move students to different seats. Still, students' choices about where to sit can be an important indicator of their personalities and learning styles.

• *How do they sit?* Do the students slouch in their chairs? Are they alert? Are their backs turned to you? Do they prop their heads up with their elbows? Lay them on the desktop? Do they bury their heads in their arms as soon as they come into the classroom? Answers to these questions can help observant teachers assess the readiness of students to learn and alert them to students' changing psychological and social situations.

• *What is the disposition of the class today?* When the response to the call to begin the class is met with a sigh from Marianne and a groan from Hugh, the teacher may see that these students are joking, but it is also possible that they will need help getting started. The disposition of any individual student on any given day helps the teacher understand the range of moods peculiar to that student. Some students remain cheerful and gregarious most of the time; others tend to be moody or volatile.

Teachers learn to engage students to some extent in terms of their individual personalities. Taking early notice of a sudden change in a student's demeanor helps the teacher anticipate likely reactions and plan interventions. For instance, if Jack comes in, slams his books on the desk, and scowls at fellow students, a responsive teacher will keep an eye on his side of the room—an insensitive remark by another student could lead to a blowup. That teacher could perhaps take Jack aside and talk with him immediately or perhaps offer to talk with him during small-group discussion time or after class. This might be a day when Jack is permitted to be less involved in classroom activities.

• *Are the students prepared for class?* Students need to learn to be responsible for their school supplies. As a rule, teachers spend a good deal of time reminding students to bring their books, journals, and pencils to class. Some students, however, make a career of running to their lockers after class has begun. Early in the fall, teachers can note which students are particularly forgetful. Before class begins, teachers can send unprepared students back to their lockers for materials. Some teachers have on hand extra pencils, an ample supply of paper, and extra textbooks.

Middle school and high school students generally don't do homework as diligently as most college students. Teachers have to l prepared for the fact that several students may not have read the assigned pages in *The Color Purple* and that Michael and Thomas may not have completed drafts on their arguments about lowering the drinking age.

- *Is there anything unusual about their physical appearance?* Physical appearance often gives teachers information about students' physical or emotional health. Dorothy wears the same stained outfit to school for three days. Her hair hasn't been washed, she's pale, and she's been nodding off during the discussion of Sylvia Plath's "Daddy," her favorite poem. After some discreet questioning, her teacher discovers that she has run away from home and is sleeping on the streets. In this circumstance, a beginning teacher should seek the advice of the school counselor and the department chair. The important point here is that the teacher notices the dramatic difference in Dorothy's appearance, making it possible to alert counselors so that she can get the help she needs.

Common illnesses and injuries—colds, flus, sprained ankles, and the like—may affect students' academic lives. Students who enter your classroom on crutches or with a box of tissues may not necessarily alter your lesson plan, but certain accommodations may have to be made. You may also encounter students with chronic illnesses such as asthma, diabetes, sickle cell anemia, cystic fibrosis, or epilepsy. As the responsible adult in the room, you need to identify the subtle signs of disease, recognize its effects on a student's daily performance, and know whom to contact in a medical emergency.

Emotional extremes, poor concentration, paranoia, hilarity, belligerence, or lethargy, combined with physical signs such as glassy, red-rimmed eyes or runny noses, should alert the teacher to possible drug abuse. A whiff of alcohol on the breath, a sweet smoky aroma, or the sudden appearance of marijuana leaf drawings on notebooks or clothing may feed a teacher's initial suspicions. Again, teachers should always seek out other school professionals for guidance in these situations. Though teachers cannot control the drug abuse that prevents students from performing to their capabilities, they can be aware of the problem, they can document unusual behavior, and they can work with the school counselor and other professionals to get help for these students.

As in the above case of Dorothy, sudden changes in dress may indicate personal upheaval. But students may purposely dress for effect—to startle, to shock, to provoke a response. Marissa, a ninth grader, begins the year dressing like her peers: oversized T-shirts and blue jeans. Suddenly, her style of dress changes dramatically. She appears at school heavily made up, in skin-tight miniskirts, low-cut stretch tops, and high heels. A number of Marissa's teachers, deeply concerned by the change in her appearance, share their observations at lunch, brainstorming what they might collectively do. They decide to call Marissa's parents and to talk informally with Marissa.

These observations, while somewhat superficial, can provide important first clues for understanding students. They also hint at potential obstacles to learning. For teachers, reading students as individuals lies at the heart of kidwatching and contributes to an understanding of students as learners in the classroom.

Reading Classrooms

Reading students as individual learners is important, but it is also true that these individual students come together in groups of twenty-five to thirty every hour. Being able to read whole classrooms is another important skill that a teacher must acquire in teaching. Individual classroom character is determined by many different factors, both on a daily basis and over time. Particular social relationships that exist within any given hour may contribute to vary class performance or behavior dramatically from hour to hour, even when those classes are studying the same materials. Particular classes seem to have their own personality. Ms. Hall's sixth-hour Creative Writing class likes to initiate classroom activities. For example, in late November Jenny, Gary, and Melissa begged to "experience" the first snowfall. "We'll write about it," they promised, cheered on by the rest of the class. Ms. Hall chose to abandon her prepared lesson plan, a fairly common occurrence with this group. In contrast, her first-hour Creative Writing class prefers more teacher-directed, text-oriented activities.

What are the factors that influence development of such classroom character? (Some of them will have become apparent in the discussion of our case studies above.) As you have seen, while teachers are certainly powerful forces in the classroom, they are not by any means the only force. By establishing a tone and manner for interaction through example and classroom rules, a teacher can affect the general classroom climate. However, various contextual features and group dynamics exert a more significant influence over classroom character.

Contextual Features
of the Classroom

As we will discuss in greater depth in later chapters, the nature of th community and the school help shape individual classrooms in a broa sense. The community's goals, values, and behavioral norms establish purpose for the school, providing general guidelines for classroom inte action. The school board sets rules of conduct that apply to all schools the district, and in certain school districts curricula must adhere to distr guidelines. Other constraints such as a community's concern about t scores on national, state, and local tests may affect the nature of particular classrooms. Though individual schools develop their own distinctive "personalities," as do individual classrooms within those schools, each school and classroom is affected by these external conditions.

Other factors contribute to individual classroom character. Physical arrangements, from the arrangement of desks or tables—in straight lines or in a circle—to the architecture of the room, can determine interactional patterns between students and the teacher. Varying the straight-row, face-the-teacher arrangement of desks—moving them into a circle or semicircle so that all students can see each other's faces—is one way teachers have of creating a different atmosphere. Room location and the number of windows in the room also play a part in creating classroom atmosphere; sunny rooms can be pleasant or excruciatingly hot. The outside weather alters the room's lighting as well as students' (and teachers') moods. Teachers need to adjust their curriculum and their expectations for student participation in that curriculum in terms of the physical conditions of the classroom.

The time of day, the time of year, and the length of the class period act implicitly upon the character/mood of the class. During first hour, students can swing between sleepy confusion and focused intensity. Just before lunch, students may be "antsy" and irritable. By the end of the day, they can be energetic or unruly. In addition, as vacations approach, students (and their teachers) find it more and more difficult to concentrate on their studies. The onset of winter or spring can precipitate changes of mood within the classroom. Annual events such as the prom and homecoming or an unusual event such as a basketball championship can affect classroom atmosphere. Changes in the class schedule—shortened periods, fire drills, special homeroom arrangements—even when anticipated or planned, can disrupt the teaching day. Other unanticipated outside events can transform classrooms. The arrival of a political candidate in a community, a tornado in the area, a sudden military action, or the death of a student or staff member set into motion undercurrents of concern and conversation never far from the surface. Teachers need to be flexible, ready to adapt lesson plans for different circumstances, different classes.

Group Dynamics in the Classroom

Though ability grouping or "tracking" is a common way of controlling certain aspects of group dynamics, the way students are grouped in any given classroom is generally a random process, with unpredictable consequences. The computer doesn't know the quirks, loyalties, and tensions between students. A class may (accidentally) turn up with twenty-two boys and six girls, every boisterous talker in the tenth grade, all of the student council officers. Of course, these scheduling accidents can have marvelous consequences, but they can also be disastrous and they are largely out of the teacher's control. Again, teachers need to adapt to the circumstances of individual classrooms. Lesson plans for first hour won't always work in second hour.

Although you may hear teachers raving or moaning about the configuration of third or fourth hour, such talk really does not address the important issues: Teachers must understand the dynamics of the particular classrooms they teach and must know how to conduct successful lessons nonetheless. Teachers need to discover answers to some critical questions: Who are the class leaders? To what activities do the students in this class respond? What are the cliques and groups within the class? What are some of the antipathies between class members? Have these students or some subset of them worked together before? Under what circumstances? What is the class "posture" toward reading and writing?

By knowing their classes, teachers can begin to anticipate their actions, reactions, and interactions. Teachers need to understand classroom moods and character in order to reach their students. Lesson plans are just that—plans. Few plans get executed exactly as written, nor should they. Teachers need to weave and bob, to shift gears when discussions die, to allow good conversations to continue, to pick up the pace when students show they understand. Most of all, teachers need to watch and listen carefully to their students. Sometimes teachers need to abandon their plans; on the other hand, teachers can choose to persevere with a plan in the face of resistance because they believe that the process or the end is so important. Above all, the choices teachers make, even when they seem spontaneous, should be based on prior knowledge of classes, contexts, and individual students.

Teacher Research Based on Kids and Classrooms

As we have suggested, reading kids and classrooms is a necessary condition of good teaching. Some educators (see Goswami and Stillman and Mohr and MacLean in Suggested Reading) have come to call this process "teacher research." We underscore the important relationship that exists between teaching and research in the classroom: Effective teachers must always be researching their own practice. Nancie Atwell talks about this process of research as the way teachers become "thoughtful practitioners." When she began teaching, she says, she "lacked a perspective essential to the teacher of the language arts: an awareness of language processes, of the wonderfully diverse, complicated, and idiosyncratic things that writers and readers actually do when they use language to make meaning; and knowledge of the individual writers and readers in my classroom."

To begin researching your own classroom, even on a very informal basis, you must begin to record your observations and to formulate questions that arise from your records. A teaching log—where you describe daily activities, your own evaluations of lessons, and student-teacher interactions—would be a logical basis for beginning to think like a teacher-researcher. For instance, if you found yourself commenting in several journal entries on the different ways male and female students respond during class discussions, you may want to pursue the issue of gender. You may ask yourself, "What kinds of questions am I asking during discussions? Are there times when the girls get really involved and the boys don't, or vice versa? Who interrupts whom? What are the implicit or explicit rules for turn-taking? What are my stated or unstated expectations for 'good' responses?"

If you find informal teacher observation exciting, you may want to pursue more formal teacher research, systematically investigating questions of practice. Some teacher-researchers conduct classroom studies for both personal edification and public dissemination. In other words, they research their classrooms to share their insights with others—teachers in their districts, teachers working in similar circumstances, even college faculty. They often publish their findings in professional magazines, such as *English Journal, Visions and Re-Visions, The Reading Teacher,* and *Language Arts.*

Formal teacher research entails much more than simply keeping a teaching log. Teacher-researchers incorporate detailed investigative strategies, such as video- or audiotaping class sessions, interviewing students, or creating surveys, into longitudinal studies. These studies are planned according to accepted research methodologies that interested teachers should investigate before they launch into a project. Many teacher-researchers conduct their studies as part of their graduate courses if they are working toward an advanced degree. Many others join informal research groups, benefiting from others' insights, examples, and suggestions.

Whether you are interested in your own formal teacher research or not, the publications resulting from others' projects will make useful reading for you as a teacher. Some offer informative accounts of actual teachers working in actual classrooms, experimenting with innovative teaching techniques. Others closely scrutinize individual students' growth. Still others explain both the project and the research methods used. Because these studies are intended for other practitioners, they tend to be well-written narratives rather than dry statistical reports.

When we talk about reading kids and classrooms, we're talking about a kind of critical, though informal, observation akin to the observations educational researchers make. In fact, we believe that some of the most important educational research these days is being initiated by classroom teachers. We also believe that researching one's own classroom is essential to becoming a responsive, reflective practitioner. By posing good questions about individual students, groups, and teaching methods, then recording their observations systematically, teachers can note their own growth as well as that of their students.

Suggested Reading

ATWELL, NANCIE. *In the Middle: Writing, Reading, and Learning with Adolescents.* Portsmouth, N.H: Boynton/Cook Heinemann, 1987.

Atwell's study, winner of the 1990 NCTE Distinguished Research Award, describes the growth of middle school students in a reading and writing workshop. With its publication, Atwell catalyzed the move toward student-centered classrooms, showing that students can learn to take responsibility for their own learning.

BISSEX, GLENDA, and RICHARD H. BULLOCK, eds. *Seeing for Ourselves: A Case-Study Research by Teachers of Writing.* Portsmouth, N.H.: Boynton/Cook Heinemann, 1987.

This text begins with a theoretical argument for teacher research, followed by six longitudinal classroom studies and four short-term studies. Each of these studies was conducted by classroom teachers as part of a graduate seminar.

CALKINS, LUCY. *Lessons from a Child: On the Teaching and Learning of Writing.* Portsmouth, N.H.: Boynton/Cook Heinemann, 1983.

Calkins focuses on a single child, Susie, and her early efforts at writing. Calkins chronicles Susie's development as a writer during the third grade, examining the history of an individual text and Susie's growth in revision. Both research methods and teaching techniques are discussed.

EVERHART, ROBERT B. *Reading, Writing and Resistance: Adolescence and Labor in a Junior High School.* Boston: Routledge and Kegan Paul, 1983.

A year-long study of junior high school, Everhart's text scrutinizes school life from the point of view of the students. The central chapters, which explore the students' "worlds" provide a fascinating perspective on adolescents, but the occasionally heavy-handed Marxist framework intrudes on the narrative.

GOSWAMI, DIXIE, and PETER R. STILLMAN, eds. *Reclaiming the Classroom: Teacher Research as an Agency for Change.* Portsmouth, N.H.: Boynton/Cook Heinemann, 1987.

This book contains a collection of position statements about teacher research by such well-known educators as James Britton, Garth Boomer, Shirley Brice Heath, Ann Berthoff, and Mina Shaughnessy. In addition, sample studies, methods, and the uses of teacher research are included.

GRAVES, DONALD H. *Writing: Teachers and Children at Work.* Portsmouth, N.H.: Boynton/Cook Heinemann, 1983.

Not strictly based on teacher research, this book presents suggestions for writing classrooms by one of our most important writing teachers. Graves shows teachers how to understand young writers' development and includes a section on documenting writers' growth.

HEATH, SHIRLEY BRICE. *Ways with Words: Language, Life, and Work in Communities and Classrooms.* New York: Cambridge University Press, 1983.

This landmark study documents children's language learning in and out of school. The children from two rural Carolina communities, Roadville and Trackton, distinguished by race, attend school together, but the language practices they bring to school are distinctly different. The implications for schooling are discussed in conjunction with the role of teacher research.

JAGGAR, ANGELA, and M. TRIKA SMITH-BURKE, eds. *Observing the Language Learner.* Urbana, Ill.: NCTE, 1985.

This collection of essays presents both theoretical and practical research centered on language learning. It includes useful suggestions for practitioners interested in understanding how students learn language and how teachers can facilitate this learning. Especially valuable is Yetta Goodman's essay, "Kidwatching: Observing Children in the Classroom."

KOHL, HERBERT. *Growing Minds: On Becoming a Teacher.* New York: Harper & Row, 1984.

A personal testament of one educator's efforts to cultivate the natural vitality of the learning process, Kohl's account is full of sage advice, stories about working with individual students and schools, and commitment to school and societal change.

LOPATE, PHILLIP. *Being with Children.* New York: Simon & Schuster, 1975.

A poet's inspiring account of his experience teaching during one year in a New York City school. A close look at students, it focuses on their experience of schooling and the creative writing they did in the author's classroom. The book is written from the perspective of the joy and wonder of being with children.

MOHR, MARIAN M., and MARION S. MACLEAN. *Working Together: A Guide for Teacher-Researchers.* Urbana, Ill.: NCTE, 1987.

Writing specifically for teachers, the authors argue that teacher research is an essential part of teaching: "As they begin to think of themselves as researchers, teachers are moved to redefine their roles as teachers, . . . their definition of teacher-researcher becomes teacher—a teacher who observes, questions, assists, analyzes, writes, and repeats these actions in a recursive process." The authors provide guidelines for teacher-research groups and for conducting teacher research.

PALEY, VIVIAN. *The Boy Who Would Be a Helicopter: The Uses of Storytelling in the Classroom.* Cambridge, Mass: Harvard University Press, 1990.

This book focuses on the challenge posed by one isolated boy in Paley's elementary school classroom. The story of Jason—the loner and outsider—is complemented by reflection on the meaning of events as they unfold. This book focuses on the moral dimensions of teaching, with particular emphasis on the importance of building on student differences in the classroom.

PERL, SONDRA, and NANCY WILSON. *Through Teachers' Eyes: Portraits of Writing Teachers at Work.* Portsmouth, N.H.: Boynton/Cook Heinemann, 1986.

Perl and Wilson narrate the stories of six teachers as they evolve over the course of a year. Based on the researchers' observations, the study also draws upon teacher journals, student writing, student journals, and excerpts from writing conferences, giving it a multivoiced character.

ROSE, MIKE. *Lives on the Boundary: The Struggles and Achievements of America's Underprepared.* New York: Free Press, 1989.

This is autobiography presented as research. The text describes Rose's own growing up as an underprepared student, his struggles through college, and his efforts to teach America's underprepared students. In documenting his work as a teacher, Rose also shares the stories of his students.

SCHWARTZ, JEFFREY, AMANDA BRANSCOMBE, and DIXIE GOSWAMI, eds. *Students Teaching, Teachers Learning.* Portsmouth, N.H.: Boynton/Cook Heinemann, 1991.

This is a collection of essays by teacher-researchers who have involved students directly in research into their classrooms. The accounts of this collaborative research are also, in some cases, written collaboratively with students.

SMITH, JENIFER. "Setting the Cat Among the Pigeons: A Not So Sentimental Journey to the Heart of Teaching." In *English Education* (May 1991): 68–126.

A British high school English teacher's retrospective "teacher research" of one year in her classroom, this essay discusses Smith's own growth in relation to her students' growth during this year. She also discusses the content of her classroom and gives examples of student writing and reading.

TAYLOR, DENNY, and CATHERINE DORSEY-GAINES. *Growing up Literate: Learning from Inner-City Families.* Portsmouth, N.H.: Boynton/Cook Heinemann, 1988.

The researchers document the stories of four inner-city families, exploring the uses of literacy in family life. Their findings call into question both stereotypes of inner-city life and the effects of education in urban settings.

3

Becoming an English Teacher: Theory into Practice

DAVE, WHO HAS just finished his pre-student teaching observation in a suburban high school, records his impressions in his observation journal:

I have just read over my journal notes and would like to add a few comments on the impressions I have left from my observations at Northern. One of the first things I saw was teachers doing things that would be condemned in our, or any, ed class and getting away with it. Mrs. Adams is brutally honest to her class about her opinion of their flaws. She does not compliment them often. She is often insulting and is always abrasive. But she gets away with it because the force of her personality is such that the kids respect her and like her anyway. They laugh in her class, they seem to try hard. Adams is not the only example of this I have come across, but she is the most obvious at Northern. I think what this might really say is that there is no set of rules governing teaching. Personality is such a determining factor of a teacher's classroom procedures that it is impossible to tell a group of education students what will work for them and what will not. Thus we arrive at perhaps a reason why it is so very difficult to teach teaching. Everyone is going to do it their own way, and yet they have to somehow learn what their own way is.

Dave is surely right that it is difficult if not impossible to "teach teaching," and he is also right that each prospective teacher must "somehow learn what their own way is." This chapter will concentrate on helping you to find your own way by suggesting how you can tap your own experiences as a learner; assess your potential strengths and weaknesses in a classroom; take into account the nature of the subject, the students, the schools; and then develop a theory of teaching and learning that accords with your beliefs and capabilities but at the same time allows you room to grow. The four following chapters present four different approaches to teaching and learning English, each grounded in a different perspective on language. Although there is some overlap among the four approaches, each assumes a distinctive position about how students best learn, develops a different focus for the classroom, and suggests a different way to organize the classroom and its activities.

Developing a Perspective

Preparing for teaching involves more than merely gaining technical expertise in classroom management, in discussion techniques, and in other pedagogical practices, as important as those issues might be. *What* and *why* things take place in classrooms should take precedence over *how* ends can be most efficiently accomplished. As teachers we should be able to articulate why we do what we do when we teach. The point is not that we must espouse a certain set of ideas or practices, but that we should reflect on certain issues and develop our teaching style on the basis of a consistent theory about language and language learning.

In his book, *How We Think: A Restatement of the Relation of Reflective Thinking to the Educative Process* (Chicago: Henry Regney, 1933), John Dewey made a distinction between *routine* and *reflective action*. Reflection, he said, "emancipates us from merely impulsive and routine activity . . . enables us to direct our actions with foresight and to plan according to ends in view of purposes of which we are aware. It enables us to know what we are about when we act." Developing a theory of language learning out of which you can shape your classroom and reflecting on that theory in practice keeps you an active learner in the continuing process of your own education; it also enables you to develop a questioning, critical posture about teaching. As Dave noted in his journal, "[I]t is impossible to tell a group of education students what will work for them and what will not. . . . Everyone is going to do it their own way, and yet they have to somehow learn what their own way is."

As we begin to find our way, we must *reflect* on our teaching practices so that we continually change and improve our theory. Theory and practice should exist in a reciprocal relationship in the process of learning about teaching. Certainly we learn best about teaching in the doing of it, and not through any objective understanding of philosophical principles. We best learn about teaching through teaching. But in that process, we must become what Donald Schon calls "reflective practitioners." We must reflect on our practice in such a way that we develop more useful theories in order to make choices consciously rather than unthinkingly.

How can you, with little or no experience as a teacher, learn to be a reflective practitioner? You can partly through becoming a more questioning learner and observer of classrooms, including your methods classes, but also by examining your own past experiences in the classroom. Your own experience is one place to start in thinking about your goals and in developing a perspective on teaching and learning. (See Box 3.1.) You can learn much from considering both the positive and negative aspects of your own experiences in English classrooms.

Think also about your observations of other students in English classrooms, for the experiences of others may not match your own. (There is really no such thing as a typical student, and even if there were, you would probably not fit that pattern: Because you are planning to be an English teacher, you surely have a greater interest in English than the majority of other students, and you probably have a greater "talent" for English than most of them. What worked for you may not have worked for less skilled or less motivated English students.) Questioning both your experiences and those of others in English classrooms can begin to give you answers to some larger questions: Which activities in English classes were most productive? Which were least useful? Which had the greatest impact on you and your knowledge and appreciation of English? What do the experiences that you and other students have had tell you about what it means to teach English?

The Teaching of Writing

As you will see in the following chapters, the question of goals for English teachers is a highly debatable one. It is a question you need to think about before you enter the classroom. Begin your process of reflec-

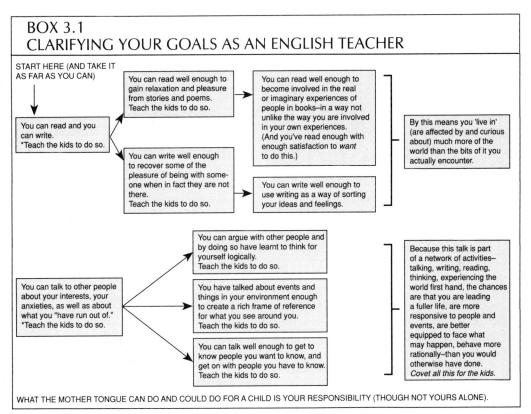

—From James Britton, "Attempting to Clarify Our Objectives for Teaching English," in *English Education* (October 1986):154.

tion by asking yourself the series of questions found in Box 3.2, all of which are directed at helping you to answer the general question, "How did I learn to write?" After you have answered the questions in Box 3.2, read these journal excerpts by three of Dave's fellow students in the English Methods class.

First Student

I remember the first time writing for me as trying to learn how to write cursive letters of the alphabet. Ironically, it is this very style of emulating and copying a formal style that continued throughout my writing education until college. Throughout junior high and high school writing was taught to me as a recipe with exact ingredients and careful measuring, resulting in a perfect apple pie. I would never have anything to say in my papers because I was not encouraged to think. The furthest thinking encouraged for me in

---

BOX 3.2
REFLECTING ON YOUR EXPERIENCE AS A WRITER

1. Can you remember the first thing you ever wrote?

2. What kinds of writing have you done for yourself (rather than for a school assignment)? Was the writing experience different? How?

3. What is the most satisfying school assignment you can remember?

4. Have teachers, their writing assignments, and their feedback helped or hindered you in learning how to write? In what ways?

5. Has feedback from friends, peers, or family members helped you learn to write?

6. Are there other writers—either professional or amateur—who have influenced you in developing a style or technique? Who? And how?

7. Under what conditions do you write best? Most happily? With the most frustration? With the most satisfying results?

8. Do you usually go through the same process when you write? What is it?

9. What metaphor(s) best describe your view of the writing process?

10. What do you think a good writer needs to do in order to write well?

11. Do you ever draw or doodle as part of the writing process?

12. How would you compare writing with other forms of communication and/or expression like dancing, using body language, sketching, doodling, painting, creating or performing music? Did you learn how to do any of these in similar ways? Do they sometimes serve similar purposes? Do they sometimes provide similar frustrations? Satisfactions?

13. What relationship do you see between the reading you do and the writing you do?

14. How important is writing in your life?

15. Why would it be important for students to learn to write?

16. Pose and then answer your own question(s).

Handwritten annotations:

2.) letters, journals, diary

3.) Scarlet Letter paper

4.) never paid much attention to written comments because paper was already graded. Verbal most memorable

5.)

6.) I pick up a little from every piece I read. I think my writing reflects the style of what I'm writing about.

7.) Happy - Journal letters. Best - when it's something I know about or grasp well. Frustration - something I don't know about or under time constraints. Satisfying - when I'm writing for myself

10. write, read, get others' opinion, edit

11. yes!

13. gives broader base of knowledge + vocab from which to write. gives vicarious experience of other people/places. models style

14. increasingly

15. express themselves in (, letters,

8.) write rough, crossouts, rewording, fast
Read
rewrite copy, reword, Thesaurus, add, delete, restructure
Type / careful reading, reword, thesaurus
Read Punct.
Type final draft Little or no change

Journal

letters: write more careful + thoughtful copy over neater + reword, Punct.

Paper

my writing would be to give supporting details (one-liners) to back up a thesis statement. Therefore, none of my creativity or analytical skills were ever utilized in my writing. Even writing the word "utilized" brings back memories of the way I learned to write. Each word I chose consciously to look impressive. My sentences were stiff, awkward, and often illogical. Writing a paper was a nerve-wracking, long, tedious process. It felt very much like I was pulling out my own teeth one by one. Yet I was a "successful" patient by [my] School District's measure. I believed I was a good writer.

9.) Knitting - taking a heap of yarn you know is all connected + using your own skills to make something orderly + new (although made of old). connecting one Part to another + making A fabric of knowledge - no longer just a string of facts.

having a sense of satisfaction at the end + a product either useful, decorative or both.

Second Student

> I think the first writing I did came when I was trying to get to know myself. I think it came when one English teacher made us keep journals—but left it open as to what we wrote about. At first I didn't find this exercise very comforting—I had usually been taught what to think, what to write, perhaps even what to believe—but to be left to write about anything with a presumption that it might have to do with your self-perception was rather scary. I suppose it's somewhat frightening to dissect yourself and see what you're really "made of " as you write. But at the same time, I think through keeping a journal, I discovered how wonderfully pleasurable it was.

Third Student

> In fact, the most satisfying writing assignment I ever had was in a seventh-grade English class. We had all been told to write a sonnet (metre was not taught at that level so it was basically a 14-line rhyming poem). I went home and spent all night constructing my masterpiece. The next day I read it aloud and everybody thought it was great. After class my best friend came up to me and told me that he knew it was about a fellow classmate of ours that I had a mean crush on. My secret was out.
>
> To this day, I believe that poem, which I can still recite by memory, was so good, in part, because it was something I really cared about. Writing is most effective when it is brutally honest and about something that we are really interested in or care a great deal about.

These three responses clearly reflect different perspectives on language and illustrate two common ways many of us have been taught to write: *by imitation* of forms and techniques and *by exploration and experimentation,* either encouraged by the teacher or self-sponsored by the student. The first way is apt to be found in a classroom where teaching style is based on the teacher as authority; the second is apt to be found in a classroom where teaching style is based on the teacher as facilitator. One of the main differences between the two teaching styles is in the degree of control students have over what and how they learn. As is made obvious in Box 3.3, Walker Percy saw the "sovereignty," or ownership of the learner as a crucial condition for true learning, as opposed to the kind of learning that takes place when the "educational packaging" obscures rather than illuminates the things to be learned. Seeing something as a "specimen" blinds us to its unique character. Imitation and experimentation may, of course, be combined, as in the third excerpt above, where the student assumed ownership in selecting a subject that he really cared about for his sonnet and spent "all night" finding ways to make it equally meaningful to others.

Imitation may also be indirect, as when writing grows out of the

---

BOX 3.3
OWNERSHIP IN THE LEARNING PROCESS

A young Falkland Islander walking along a beach and spying a dead dogfish and going to work on it with his jackknife has, in a fashion wholly unprovided for in modern educational theory, a great advantage over the Scarsdale high-school pupil who finds the dogfish on his laboratory desk. Similarly the citizen of Huxley's *Brave New World* who stumbles across a volume of Shakespeare in some vine-grown ruins and squats on a potsherd to read it is in a fairer way of getting at a sonnet than the Harvard sophomore taking English Poetry II.

The educator whose business it is to teach students biology or poetry is unaware of a whole ensemble of relations which exist between the student and the dogfish and between the student and the Shakespeare sonnet. To put it bluntly: A student who has the desire to get at a dogfish or a Shakespeare sonnet may have the greatest difficulty in salvaging the creature itself from the educational package in which it is presented. The great difficulty is that he is not aware that there is a difficulty: surely, he thinks, in such a fine classroom, with such a fine textbook, the sonnet must come across! What's wrong with me?

The sonnet and the dogfish are obscured by two different processes. The sonnet is obscured by the symbolic package which is formulated not by the sonnet itself but by the *media* through which the sonnet is transmitted, the media which the educators believe for some reason to be transparent. The new text-book, the type, the smell of the page, the classroom, the aluminum windows and the winter sky, the personality of Miss Hawkins—these media which are supposed to transmit the sonnet may only succeed in transmitting themselves. It is only the hardiest and cleverest of students who can salvage the sonnet from this many-tissued package. It is only the rarest student who knows that the sonnet must be salvaged from the package. (The educator is well aware that something is wrong, that there is a fatal gap between the student's learning and the student's life: The student reads the poem, appears to understand it and gives all the answers. But what does he recall if he should happen to read a Shakespeare sonnet twenty years later? Does he recall the poem or does he recall the smell of the page and the smell of Miss Hawkins?)

One might object, pointing out that Huxley's citizen reading his sonnet in the ruins and the Falkland Islander looking at his dogfish on the beach also receive them in a certain package. Yes, but the difference lies in the fundamental placement of the student in the world, a placement which makes it possible to extract the thing from the package. The pupil at Scarsdale High sees himself placed as a consumer receiving an experience-package; but the Falkland Islander exploring his dogfish is a person exercising the sovereign right of a person in his lordship and mastery of creation. He too could use an instructor and a book and a technique, but he would use them as his subordinates, just as he uses his jack-knife. The biology student does not use his scalpel as an instrument; he uses it as a magic wand! Since it is a "scientific instrument," it should do "scientific things."

The dogfish is concealed in the same symbolic package as the sonnet. But the dogfish suffers an additional loss. As a consequence of this double deprivation, the Sarah Lawrence student who scores A in zoology is apt to know very little about a dogfish. She is twice removed from the dogfish, once by the symbolic complex by which the dogfish is concealed, once again by the spoliation of the dogfish by theory which renders it invisible. Through no fault of zoology instructors, it is nevertheless a fact that the zoology laboratory at Sarah Lawrence College is one of the few places in the world where it is all but impossible to see a dogfish.

The dogfish, the tree, the seashell, the American Negro, the dream, are rendered invisible by a shift of reality from concrete thing to theory which Whitehead has called the fallacy of misplaced concreteness. It is the mistaking of an idea, a principle, an abstraction, for the real. As a consequence of the shift, the "specimen" is seen as less real than the theory of the specimen. . . .

If we look into the ways in which the student can recover the dogfish (or the sonnet), we will see that they have in common the stratagem of avoiding the educator's direct presentation of the object as a lesson to be learned and restoring access to sonnet and dogfish as beings to be known, reasserting the sovereignty of knower over known.

In truth, the biography of scientists and poets is usually the story of the discovery of the indirect approach, the circumvention of the educator's presentation—the young man who was sent to the *Technikum* and on his way fell into the habit of loitering in book stores and reading poetry; or the young man dutifully attending law school who on the way became curious about the comings and goings of ants. One remembers the scene in *The Heart Is a Lonely Hunter* where the girl hides in the bushes to hear the Capehart in the big house play Beethoven. Perhaps she was the lucky one after all. Think of the unhappy souls inside, who see the record, worry about scratches, and most of all worry about whether they are *getting it*, whether they are bona fide music lovers. What is the best way to hear Beethoven: sitting in a proper silence around the Capehart or eavesdropping from an azalea bush?

However it may come about, we notice two traits of the second situation: (1) an openness of the thing before one—instead of being an exercise to be learned according to an approved mode, it is a garden of delights which beckons to one; (2) a sovereignty of the knower—instead of being a consumer of a prepared experience, I am a sovereign wayfarer, a wanderer in the neighborhood of being who stumbles into the garden.

—Excerpt from "The Loss of the Creature" from THE MESSAGE IN THE BOTTLE by Walker Percy. Copyright © 1975 by Walker Percy. Reprinted by permission of Farrar, Straus and Giroux, Inc.

experience of reading. "I guess for me writing is very closely tied to reading," another of the students in Dave's English Methods class wrote. "That's why I know it's true that writing is improved, in part, by reading. I've always loved reading, maybe that's why I like to write." Another classmate echoed the sentiment: "I learned to write by osmosis, by absorbing the words and culture of the books I read."

Writing as Related to Reading

The connections between reading and writing are important, although—as the next two excerpts suggest—it isn't always teachers who help students make the connections most usefully:

Fourth Student

I remember in middle school and high school, writing research papers as the main writing exercises, and God, were they stupid: I got little from them. Sure, I learned what lots of critics thought of Flaubert or Salinger, but what did I think? That part was never tested in my school. I was always taught that my personal opinion should never enter into my papers. To me that's one of the most counterproductive ways to learn. I want to know what others think; I want to encourage students' own thinking and ideas as valid and extremely important.

Fifth Student

Now. Look at how I began this paragraph. That is a stylistic device, trick, characteristic, whatever, of Mitch Albom, lead sports columnist for the *Detroit Free Press*. I have read almost everything he has written in the last four years or so, and I admire his work to the extent that bits and pieces of his style filter out through my pen. And that is natural for me; I was not consciously trying to imitate his style. It just felt right that I should write "Now."

Now. (Okay, that one was on purpose.) There is another strong influence on my style (whatever that is)—author John D. MacDonald, who wrote 78 books, about 40 of which I have read. Echoes of his voice no doubt come through my work . . . just as echoes of Jimmy Breslin's voice come through Mitch Albom's work. This does not mean we are all evil plagiarists. What I think it means is that art feeds on art. That is, everyone's work (writing, painting, music, whatever) is influenced by whatever collage of previous artists the current artist has studied. Throw in some individual experience, and individual identity, and you come up with each writer's unique style. Make sense? That is how I think I have developed my writing. . . . So reading has a lot to do with my development as a writer.

The fourth student was asked by the teacher to summarize what critics had thought of the things she was reading, while the fifth student discovered for himself, in his reading outside class, things that influenced the development of his own writing style. The books he read are not likely to be studied in classrooms, yet he apparently gained more from his reading than the fourth student did merely by learning what other people thought about what she was reading. He asserted ownership as a learner; she was not encouraged by her teachers to develop ownership. A prospective teacher can thus usefully think about his or her experiences with English and about the degree of ownership a teacher might allow or encourage students to attain in their use of language. The teaching style adopted by the teacher helps to determine the writing style the student will develop.

The Teaching of Reading

While we have been talking about the teaching of writing and connections between reading and writing, the same kinds of questions might profitably be asked about reading itself. The approach to reading that a teacher adopts influences the "reading style" a student develops. Think about this as you answer the questions given in Box 3.4; try to recall the things that teachers have done that have helped you and other students to read with greater pleasure and understanding. Try to recall also the things that teachers have done that have hindered you from achieving those goals. Explore the relationship between approaches to reading and approaches to writing that your teachers followed: Is one consistent with the other?

The foundation for a teacher's approach to reading and writing is a set of beliefs about language and language learning. What is language, and how can it best be learned? What part does control of language play in learning other things, and how can students enhance that control? How does a teacher's theory of language help to determine approaches in a classroom?

Consider the questions in Box 3.5. After you have answered them, look back at the five excerpts from student journals quoted above and try to determine what the perspectives on language of students and teachers were in each case. Were they the same? Which ones agree with your view of language? What things about language do you want your students to learn, and what attitudes toward language will you try to foster in your classroom?

The perspective on language that a teacher embraces determines, in part, his or her approach to teaching reading and writing and is reflected in everything from the way a semester is organized; to the way a particular book, film, poem, essay, or principle of writing is taught; to the way the directions for a reading or writing assignment are given. It is often crucial in determining not only what students learn, but what attitudes toward

---

BOX 3.4
REFLECTING ON YOUR EXPERIENCE AS A READER

[handwritten notes in margin: Isl. of the Blue Dolphins 3rd Grade? | off/on half-day | Dick+Jane | wisdom | arguing w/ segan]

1. Can you remember being read to by parents, babysitters, others? If so, can you remember what they read?

2. What can you remember about the process of your learning to read?

3. Can you remember the first thing(s) you read on your own? What kinds of books did you like to read after you could read them for yourself? What did you especially like about those books?

4. Were the books you read on your own different from those you read in school? If so, how were they different?

5. Do you read for pleasure now? What kinds of books? What do you especially like about them?

6. What books have you read in school that you enjoyed? What was it that you enjoyed about the experience of reading them?

7. Has a teacher or another adult ever recommended a book to you that you found boring or unsatisfactory? Did you feel a little guilty about your reaction?

8. Do you sometimes gain additional insight into a book during a class discussion of it? If so, what kind of discussion?

9. Do you sometimes gain additional insight into a book while writing about it? If so, what kind of writing?

10. Do you sometimes gain additional insight into a book by discussing it with a friend?

11. Do you read different kinds of books in different ways? What are the differences?

12. Do you see similarities in the ways that information or narratives are presented in books and in movies or on TV? What are some of the differences?

13. Is it important for students to read literature? Why? If yes, then what kind of books? How will the choices for what to read in your classes be made? On what criteria will those choices be made?

14. Pose and then answer your own question(s).

---

learning they develop. (Box 3.6 discusses how "teacher stance" is reflected in language.)

Perspectives Personified

Listen now to two teachers, Doris Ballinger and Amy Slavak (you'll meet Amy again in Chapter 6) as they assign a character sketch to their ninth graders. First, imagine yourself in Doris Ballinger's class as she says:

BOX 3.5
DETERMINING YOUR PERSPECTIVES ON LANGUAGE

1. What is your definition of language?

2. Can you remember anything about the process by which you learned to use language?

3. What were your first words? Did you learn how to speak sentences in a way different from the way in which you later learned to read and write in school?

4. What have you learned about language in school? Outside of school?

5. Have you ever caught yourself using language dishonestly?

6. In what circumstances does language give you pleasure? What kinds of pleasure?

7. In what circumstances does language give you pain? *Truth, sometimes.* – *hearing* – *use of negative words/labels*

8. What are the most important differences between your uses of spoken and written language? *more comfortable w/ spoken. less formal w/*

9. Are you satisfied with the way you use language? Why or why <u>not?</u> *never will be*

10. What does it mean to use language *appropriately*? Give examples of appropriate and inappropriate use.

11. How can language best be learned?

12. If you see language learning in that way, how will you teach reading and writing?

13. If you view language learning in that way, what will your classroom look like?

14. Pose and then answer your own question(s).

---

limits areas where students may have more than 3 things to say, where they have less

Pleasure where than 3.

limits categories to 3

defines + for them

sounds more daunting u/ some

like an assignment. wants to be waded through

The assignment for this week is to write a character sketch. What I want you to do is first choose either someone you know or an imaginary person and write down three complete sentences describing what that person looks like. Then you must write three complete sentences telling what your person does. Then I want you to write three complete sentences, pretending each sentence is written by a different friend of your person, giving the friend's impression or opinion of your person. What you must do next is to look at your nine sentences and come up with a thesis sentence that describes the person's personality or characteristic traits or actions. Be sure your thesis sentence is a complete sentence. Then you must write an outline. . . .

Now imagine yourself in Amy Slavak's class as she says:

Think of a person you know, or an imaginary person. If it's a real person, it might be someone you're curious about and want to know better or it might be someone you know well. You'll probably want to begin by making some rough notes about your person: appearance, likes, dislikes, habits, hobbies. How would this person walk across the room? What do other people think of him or her? What might he or she do when confronted by a screaming baby? By a homeless person asking for a quarter? What are this person's

BOX 3.6
TEACHER TALK

[handwritten note: "she was an egoist"]

Let me give an example of stance in teacher talk, one drawn from Carol Feldman's work. She was interested in the extent to which teachers' stances toward their subject indicate some sense of the hypothetical nature of knowledge, its uncertainty, its invitation to further thought. She chose as an index the use of modal auxiliary markers in teachers' talk to students and in their talk to each other in the staff room, distinguishing between expressions that contained modals of uncertainty and probability (like *might, could,* and so on) and expressions not so marked. Modals expressing a stance of uncertainty or doubt in teacher talk to teachers far outnumbered their occurrence in teacher talk to students. The world that the teachers were presenting to their students was a far more settled, far less hypothetical, far less negotiatory world than the one they were offering to their colleagues.

Stance marking in the speech of others gives us a clue about how to use our minds. I recall a teacher, her name was Miss Orcutt, who made the statement in class, "It is a very puzzling thing not that water turns to ice at 32 degrees Fahrenheit, but that it should change from a liquid into a solid." She then went on to give us an intuitive account of Brownian movement and of molecules, expressing a sense of wonder that matched, indeed bettered, the sense of wonder I felt at that age (around ten) about everything I turned my mind to, including at the far reach such matters as light from extin-guished stars still traveling toward us though their sources had been snuffed out. In effect, she was inviting me to extend *my* world of wonder to encompass *hers.* She was not just *informing* me. She was, rather, negotiating the world of wonder and possibility. Molecules, solids, liquids, movement were not facts; they were to be used in pondering and imagining. Miss Orcutt was the rarity. She was a human event, not a transmission device. It is not that my other teachers did not mark their stances. It was rather that their stances were so off-puttingly and barrenly informative. . . .

Each fact we encounter comes wrapped in stance marking. But now take the next step. Some stance markings are invitations to the use of thought, reflection, elaboration, fantasy. . . . And if the teacher wishes to close down the process of wondering by flat declarations of fixed factuality, he or she can do so. The teacher can also open wide a topic of locution to speculation and negotiation. To the extent that the materials of education are chosen for their amenableness to imaginative transformation and are presented in a light to invite negotiation and speculation, to that extent education becomes part of what I earlier called "culture marking." The pupil, in effect, becomes a party to the negotiatory process by which facts are created and interpreted. He becomes at once an agent of knowledge making as well as a recipient of knowledge transmission.

—From Jerome Bruner, *Actual Minds, Possible Worlds,* pp. 126–7. Reprinted by permission of the publishers from *Actual Minds, Possible Worlds* by Jerome Bruner, Cambridge, Mass.: Harvard University Press, Copyright © 1986 by the President and Fellows of Harvard College.

friends like? The next step would probably be to look over your notes and see if you can sum up this character in a single sentence. Then if you look at your notes again, you can separate those things that tell more about the summing up sentence that you wrote. You might think next about what order to put these things in. What would a friend who was reading your character sketch want to know first?

Notice that Doris's use of language reflects a different idea than Amy's of what a teacher's language should do. Doris's words command students to go through a very specific series of steps and do not invite them to exert ownership. Amy's use of language, in contrast, is much more tentative and invites students to make more choices in working out their own approach to the topic. The very language that Doris uses in giving the assignment implies the view that language is to be used in her classroom only to command or to inform, while Amy's directions imply that language is to be used to negotiate and to explore possibilities. Although some students may be reassured by the precise expectations with which Doris defines the task, others will respond more positively to the freedom and the choices that Amy encourages. Neither approach to the assignment will reach all students equally well, though if the goal is to give the learner as much ownership as possible, Amy's style will come much closer to accomplishing that goal.

As you read Doris's and Amy's assignments for their classes you probably imagined each speaking in a somewhat different tone of voice, one that matched in each case the stance suggested by the language she used and stemming from a different conception of what a teacher's language should do. Both tone of voice and body language, along with words, can convey teacher attitudes toward students and toward language, and will, in turn, influence student attitudes toward learning. A teacher's impatient gesture, an edge of sarcasm in a voice, a warmly approving tone in a compliment, a challenging tone in a question, laughter—all these can make a significant difference in a student's response to a learning task. Comparable signals like these from a student can also alert a teacher to what is going on in a student's mind and can give clues to the student's attitude toward learning.

Students are all unique individuals, and though they sometimes respond collectively to what is going on in a classroom, more often than not, different students may have very different responses to any classroom event. (You can prove this by a simple experiment: Ask students or some of your colleagues in a class to doodle or write down everything they are thinking about during part of a class period; the results will give you an insight into the very different things that are going on in their minds while you might have assumed they were all concentrating on the same things in the lesson being taught.) Each student will also have a slightly different learning style, a different writing style, a different reading style,

BOX 3.7 (continued on facing page)
IN THE CREATIVE MODE: COLLAGES AND MAPS

COLLAGE OF LESLIE MARMON SILKO'S *CEREMONY*

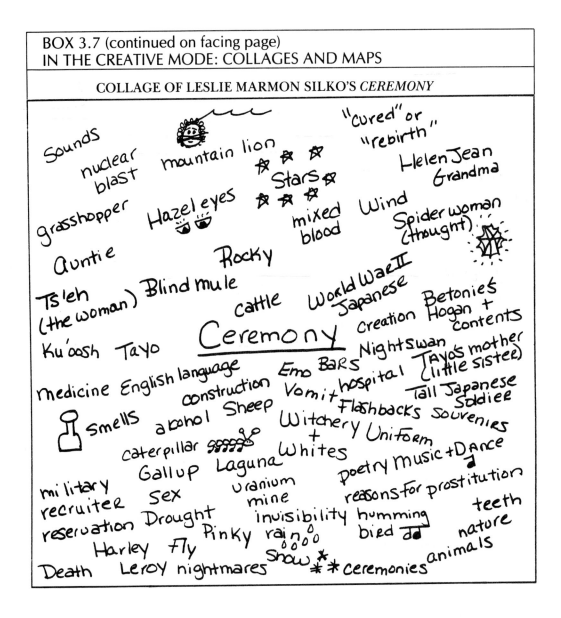

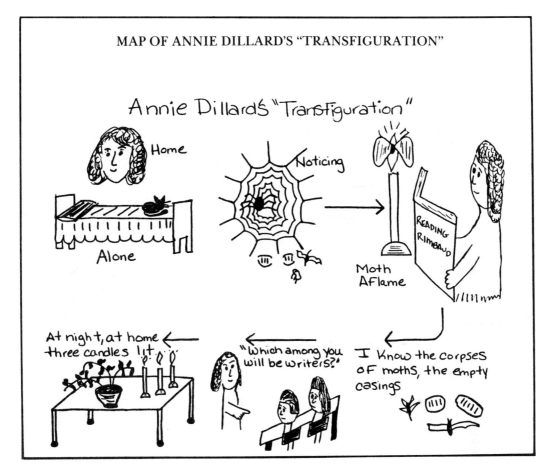

MAP OF ANNIE DILLARD'S "TRANSFIGURATION"

just as your approach to teaching and your teaching style will differ somewhat from those of other teachers.

Styles of both teaching and learning—for students and teachers—are developed over the course of time; they are not things that can be learned as you might learn a scientific principle or the facts in a history lesson or the conjugation of a French verb. Thus the job of the English teacher is to help students find the ways of learning, writing, reading that work for them, rather than to impose "ideal" ways on them. Likewise, the beginning teacher will need time to work out a consistent theory of language and develop effective teaching practices from that theory. This isn't something that can be acquired all at once. A perspective on teaching, a teaching style, a consideration of what is best for one's own particular students in any given school or class develop over time, in part from trial and error and in part from continuing reflection upon alternatives.

Modes of Learning and of Teaching

As you reflect, you should take into account what both teacher and students can and should do; you can then decide whether your classroom will be predominantly student-centered or teacher-centered. This decision will be partly informed by the perspective on language that the teacher adopts. A related decision concerns which modes of learning to stress. Some teachers tend to assume that an analytical mode (reflected in linear forms like outlines, summaries, and chronologies) is the most efficient kind of learning, but other teachers would insist that less organized, more creative ways of learning (like brainstorming; creating clusters, maps, or collages; and developing metaphors) produce more fruitful results. Actually, each kind of learning produces a different kind of insight: A plot summary or outline of a novel, for example, gives a linear view of the progression of events in the book, but a collage containing significant elements from the novel can give a more holistic view of the book, which makes it easier to bring it all before the mind at once. Each kind of insight may have its place in achieving your overall goals for a class. Collages and maps can also help to show the range and variety of responses in a class. Box 3.7 presents a collage based on Leslie Marmon Silko's novel *Ceremony* and a map based on Annie Dillard's essay "Transfiguration.") In general, analytical modes of learning are more likely to be appropriate in a teacher-centered classroom; creative modes of learning are more likely to be appropriate in a student-centered classroom.

Modes of teaching and learning follow from attitudes toward language and result in various classroom organizations. Different teaching modes likewise are appropriate for different purposes: They send different implied messages to students and set up different expectations. Lecturing usually suggests that there is information to be recorded by students and eventually repeated in written assignments or tests, recitation suggests that the class will answer very specific questions with definite and predictable answers, discussion suggests that the class and the teacher will explore a topic together, and group activities suggest that each student is being asked to take part of the responsibility—either through independent work or in conjunction with others—for what the group as a whole will explore.

Thus the teacher and the text (or the material presented) are the central focus during lectures; the text is the likely focus during recitation; in discussion—whether in large or small groups—the focus is likely to alternate between student responses and the text itself; and in other group activities the focus might be on the students, individually or collectively. In all modes the teacher plays an important role in orienting students to the particular approach. Subject matter may well dictate different modes of classroom discourse. The particular conditions of any given day or classroom might also call for different approaches. Which are you most comfortable with? Which seem consistent with your perspective on language and language learning, as you see it now?

Implementing a Perspective: Practical Aspects

In addition to considering modes of teaching and learning and the central focus for your classroom, you also choose—consciously or unconsciously—ways to organize your room. The more conscious the choice, the better chance that it will fit with the perspective on language you are developing as a beginning teacher. There are some important considerations in deciding how best to achieve a balance between routines and variations that allow for novelty and surprise: how to run a middle course between formal structure and serendipity, how to work toward well-defined goals and at the same time take advantage of genuine student interests that you couldn't have predicted.

At this point, you should perhaps consider your personality—what you feel comfortable or uncomfortable doing. At the same time remember that forcing yourself to do something you are not entirely comfortable doing may be a step toward your growth, toward development of your potential. It is, of course, important to know your limits. How much noise, how much clutter can you tolerate in your classroom? How large is your store of patience? How much structure do you need to give you the necessary confidence as a beginner? How much will you depend upon established procedures that can be repeated? How fast can you think on your feet? One might sum up this process by saying that you want to become conscious of yourself and your actions without becoming self-conscious. In other words, you should watch yourself and evaluate what you do without letting that process cause you to become so nervous that you act less naturally. (A certain amount of nervousness obviously goes with the territory of being a beginning teacher.)

Planning will help give you confidence and allow you to work toward meaningful goals. Planning simply enables you to foresee what you want to have happen in a class and what other things might happen. What do you want students to learn? What will help them reach that goal? What may hinder them from reaching it? What difficulties can you foresee? What modes of instruction will work best for the particular material you want to teach? What predictions can you make about the amount of time specific activities may require? How might writing contribute to the students' learning process? How will you be able to evaluate how well you and the students have succeeded in reaching your goals?

Unit Plans

Though it is natural that beginning teachers are concerned about daily plans, experienced teachers spend time planning on a larger scale, at the unit or course level. Unit plans reflect individual philosophies of teaching and learning to a greater extent than daily plans do. In fact, day-to-day planning becomes quite easy, even automatic, once you have a good unit plan—and some teaching experience. (See Box 3.8.)

In the following four chapters we have included sample unit plans that reflect various philosophies of language. However, because good English teaching in the 1990s necessarily acknowledges the communities and cultures of American students as well as current movements in education, you may notice underlying similarities in the sample unit plans and deduce some cautionary notes from those similarities:

1. *A novel is not a unit.* We are not teaching books, we are teaching students about reading, writing, communicating, and connecting. There is a corollary to this dictum: A list of books is not a curriculum. We have tried to build units that aren't merely aiming to teach a book.

2. *English teachers should teach strategies, not mere facts.* In this century, since information multiplies and changes dramatically every few years, students must be able to evaluate, to analyze, and to create for themselves, not simply to memorize. We have tried to create activities that foster higher-order thinking.

3. *Students need many opportunities to practice writing, reading, and talking about their ideas.* They also need opportunities to practice risk taking, decision making, cooperating, and integrating. The key word here is *practice*; teachers needn't grade every attempt students make. We have tried to build in many opportunities for such practice.

4. *Each learner has unique struggles, experiences, and ways of knowing, and a teacher must find ways to reach each one.* Teachers must learn to "read" students, to know them well enough to build bridges. By varying methods, media, and classroom arrangements, teachers can engage students with various learning styles. We have tried to employ a range of media, activities, and group sizes so that students can tap into their strengths at some point during a unit or semester.

Daily Plans

Assuming your school does not require a specific format for lesson plans, what form of written reminder will be most helpful for you to bring to class? (Too detailed and rigid a plan will distract your attention from the class itself and prevent you from capitalizing fully on useful but unforeseen student responses, while too vague a plan may leave you with nothing really accomplished or an awkward and empty fifteen minutes at the end of a class.) Whatever planning you do, it is wise to allow for contingencies and to have serviceable activities or materials on hand that you can turn to when the projector breaks down or the film doesn't arrive or the class has not done the assignment.

Finally, don't assume that any plan can possibly cover (or predict) all that goes on in a classroom. Listen again to Dave (whom you met at the beginning of this chapter) as he continues the summary in his observation journal:

> I think there is so much a teacher is doing at once, we [as pre-student teachers] don't see half of it. A teacher is not just executing a lesson plan. She or he is also maintaining control of the class, making a thousand split-second decisions to compensate for the unexpected, and always adapting the lesson plan to the direction in which the class is moving. Remember learning to drive a car? It was so easy to watch Mom or Dad

---

BOX 3.8 (continued on pages 78–80)
A TEACHER DISCUSSES PLANNING

When I first began teaching, I think I wrote down every word I thought I might utter in front of kids. No matter how many words I put down on paper, I managed to run a little short—I'd have five, ten minutes at the end of a period. I began to stash filler activities for those little moments of emptiness, and I began to use that time to talk with my students. Second time through any course, I ran out of gaps and silences. I have so many proven activities and new ideas, I could probably use another week in any semester.

I do keep daily plans, usually a brief list of activities for each class, and reminders about students I need to talk with, projects that need checking. At the beginning of the semester, when I'm a little nervous, not really knowledgeable enough about my students, I have more detailed lists, but once I know the students and everything is underway, my memory seems to improve.

There have been classes . . . one class had such an unpredictable attendance record and volatile mix of personalities

that I'd go in with Plan A, Plan B, and Plan C—three plans every day, different modes depending on who was there and what the prevailing mood seemed to be. Believe me, it was easier to make three plans than to go in there with a bomb.

Some of the best moments are, of course, unplanned. The first snow, my kids clamoring to play in it—some of the best writing and memories came out of that spontaneous trip outside.

Unit planning matters most to me these days, because I am finally much clearer about my role and purposes. I try to imagine my students' questions and concerns, and try to articulate my own. I brainstorm about texts in various genres, about topics of discussion, about outside resources like guest speakers, about classroom projects and activities. Daily planning seems obvious, almost incidental, once the unit planning is done.

Here's my brainstorming about a unit on teacher-student relationships, as well as a list that typically serves as my daily plan.

9th Grade English — Teacher-Student Relationships

Key Questions/Concepts:

What kinds of relationships do you and others form with teachers?
How do you and others best learn?
What qualities do "good teachers" possess?
What responsibilities do students have?
What responsibilities do teachers have?
In your view, what knowledge is most worth having?
What arguments do others make about worthwhile knowledge?
What purposes do schools serve?
What should schools look like in the future?
How did schools look in the past?

Possible texts:

Short stories – "Gryphon", "The Kid Nobody Could Handle", "French
  Lessons", "Turning", "The Kind of Light That Shines on Texas"
Novels – Catcher in the Rye
Poems – "The Blue Dog", "The Slow Classroom", "M. Degas", "On My Own"
Articles – censorship, excerpts from Hunger of Memory, Teacher,
  Small Victories
Plays – Inherit the Wind
Other – Dead Poets' Society (film), The Paper Chase (film), history of
  ed, Inherit the Wind (film)

Alternate texts:

I heard the Owl Call My Name, Roll of Thunder, Hear My Cry,
Helen Keller, Teacher, Goodbye, Mister Chips more...

Topics:

Censorship, class structures/inequity, the nature of knowledge,
problems & possibilities of schools, depression/loss and school
performance, Darwinism/creationism, mentoring, broader
notions of teaching/lifetime learning.

Teacher-Student Relationships, continued

Learning strategies:

how to approach a poem, an article, a novel, a play
making thematic connections between texts
making connections between personal experience and texts
finding evidence from texts; making inferences based on evidence
reacting informally out loud and in writing to ideas and texts
drafting and revising
responding to others' work

Possible activities:

Character sketch of memorable teacher (preceded by conversation,
  mapping, notes, increasingly formal drafts)
informal responses to short stories, novel, thematic ties
Small groups, gathering evidence, making inferences
Critical paper on some aspect of Catcher in the Rye and/or stories
written reflection on self as a learner; comparison of styles
Story or sketch in Holden's voice
drawing or written piece on future schools
debate - over what really happened at Mr. Antolini's, or over
the Darwinism/creationism/what should be taught issue

Plan, Tuesday, March 3

1) Discuss Charles Baxter's "Gryphon".
  - Miss Ferenczi desirable as a teacher? Ethical?
  - World of 4th grade classroom created by author

2) Brainstorming for character sketch or fictional piece based on school life.
  - map classroom
  - concretely describe classmates, self, teacher, etc.

  Rough draft by Friday

Sara R. - makeup assignment for last week
Pete M. - move closer to board to see

cruise down the street, and it was equally easy to think they should be able to avoid accidents or getting a ticket or whatever. But when you get behind the wheel for the first time, all of a sudden you have to learn to do the things you don't even notice an experienced driver doing. Touch the accelerator ever so lightly, let the clutch . . . out and press down on the gas simultaneously, and with just the right timing and coordination. . . . I think the analogy is becoming clear. It will probably take some time before we as young teachers get a handle on these basics, before we can start making our theories and innovative ideas work.

Planning won't automatically make you an "experienced driver," but it's a start.

Metaphors for Teaching

Listen now to Wil, Dave's classmate, as he looks for metaphors to describe what a teacher does. Wil gives himself some advice in a summary of his observations:

> I saw how the job of "teacher" is not the job of "imparting knowledge." Rather . . . [it] is similar to the job of an architect in that the teacher must create an atmosphere that fosters discovery and motivates learning. Or, maybe considering a teacher as a gardener may be better (as long as no one takes the vegetable analogy too far). A successful gardener must prepare the soil, carefully plant seeds, provide water and nutrients, and carefully tend [plants] so as to encourage growth in positive directions. . . . Remember there are at least a million ways to access any work of literature. . . . Don't fall into the rut of any one teaching style. You will be bored to death and wish you were doing something else. You owe your students and yourself more than that.

We have said that a useful first step in developing a perspective on teaching and learning is to review and assess your own education, taking into account your personality. We emphasized the importance of beginning to develop a theory about the nature of language and language learning through that reflective process. The next step for you in developing a perspective on the classroom might well be to decide what you think it is important for students to know, that is, to decide the content of your curriculum. Even though you may be teaching in a school with a rigidly defined curriculum, you will still have some freedom to determine how you teach that curriculum and what you think is important to emphasize. Which skills are most important? How important is it to relate classroom study to students' lives, and how can these connections best be made? What factual material is really important? How important, in contrast, is an understanding of contexts and frames of reference apart from facts? (See William Perry's remarks in Chapter 9, Box 9.1.)

Your answers to questions like these will depend, directly or indirectly, on your overall perspective on language and language learning. Those answers will lead you to answers for the more global questions: What is English? and Why teach English? To begin to answer these important questions, we suggest that you, like Wil, develop a metaphor for the classroom and explore its implications. Consider Wil's metaphors. What do you think of them? Do they square with your experiences with English teachers and English classrooms? Are they similar to what yours might be? What kind of classroom would you like to have? (The questions posed in Box 3.9 may help you in developing your own metaphor or metaphors.) Your metaphor should be consistent with your perspective

---

BOX 3.9
DEVELOPING A METAPHOR FOR THE CLASSROOM

---

1. What is your metaphor for the classroom? If one metaphor doesn't quite seem adequate, think of more than one.

2. Extend and develop your metaphor. Consider your role as teacher, your relationship to the students, and what your classroom would look like. How would you teach reading and writing in terms of your metaphor?

3. Choose a work of literature or a particular social issue. How might you approach it in terms of your metaphor?

4. What concerns (that you can now think of) does your metaphor fail to address?

5. In what way is your metaphor consistent with your view of language?

6. In what way was your choice of metaphor influenced by your experiences in the classroom, the way you yourself learned to read and write?

---

on language. Share your metaphor with teachers and classmates; have them respond to it and share theirs with you. Reshape your metaphor or develop another as your understanding evolves.

Compare your metaphor(s) periodically with the explicit or implicit metaphors connected with the teachers and the approaches discussed in the following four chapters. These chapters will enable you to explore some of the many options English teachers have. Though each of the four overall approaches discussed is quite different from the others, there is some overlap in activities, and you may also find that you can combine elements from more than one approach without losing consistency. As you read these chapters, prepare to be eclectic even as you maintain consistency in your approach to developing your own metaphor(s) for your own classroom.

Looking Ahead

In the following four chapters we highlight teachers—good teachers, we think—who embrace different perspectives on teaching, who create different classroom environments because of their fundamentally different views of language. (We have titled the chapters in terms that reflect a particular perspective on language.) Through specific examples of individual teaching styles we illustrate the importance of developing a consistent theory about language as a foundation for one's classroom practices.

In each chapter we have tried to create a brief though vivid portrait of a teacher who exemplifies one approach, and in each chapter we suggest ways of implementing this approach in a high school classroom and a middle or junior high classroom. We discuss typical teaching units that these teachers have or might have taught, and we consider why those teachers might have taught their units in this way. We give serious attention to theoretical considerations by which we can analyze and assess various perspectives—and by which, we hope, you will be able to develop your own perspective. But we also give you some very practical advice on what you can do within this perspective should you choose that particular alternative. We discuss potentials and limitations of each perspective as we see it, and attach an annotated bibliography that can be a starting point to explore this perspective for yourself if it seems useful to you.

We have created these portraits as composites of teachers whom we have observed and interviewed. We do not intend by these portraits to suggest that there are teachers who actually conform neatly at any one time to the language perspective in caricature, or that any teacher merely chooses a perspective and teaches according to that perspective for the rest of his or her career. Developing a perspective on teaching and learning is a process, which in some respects is always affected by one's own practice. Most teachers combine some aspects of these four perspectives in their teaching philosophies, and philosophies will change over the years in terms of changing student populations and a changing society.

In the process of developing a perspective, it is important to reflect on one's own experience and important to read about how teachers have variously organized their curricula and classrooms. But there are other ways to develop this perspective, of course; it is important, if possible in your area, to observe English teachers in action and to discuss with them why they believe what they believe. Perhaps this can take place through a practicum arranged by your Office of Field Experience (or a similar office in your school). Regardless, it is important to spend as many hours as possible in a classroom, sometimes observing, but also getting involved with students and getting some opportunity to teach—whether working with small groups, tutoring, or leading a discussion. In that way, all these theoretical considerations will begin to be real for you.

It is also very useful to observe a variety of teachers in other disciplines, to see other perspectives, other styles, other classroom environments. And again, it is important to take the opportunity to interview teachers about their teaching practices. Usually teachers are more than willing to discuss with prospective teachers why they do what they do.

In addition to observing and talking with teachers, it is also important to talk with students. We might suggest that you spend a day with one particular student in the school in which you will student teach in order to get a sense of the kind of schooling experience that one student has. We recommend that you talk with students, ask them about their feelings about their school experiences. That's one way of informing yourself about viable classroom design. Getting a sense of the varieties of ways of learning, of student interests and concerns, can only make you a better teacher.

Finally, it is important, we believe, to share your evolving perceptions with each other, with your supervising teacher, with your methods teacher, with your classmates. We think it is important that you have the opportunity to write about and talk with others about your concerns, your hopes, your fears about teaching. Get help from others with more or different classroom experiences in developing your perspective on the English classroom. You must develop a theory of your own, but in the process of developing that theory it is important to learn from others. With that in mind, we offer our four different perspectives in the four succeeding chapters. We hope that you will discuss and analyze these perspectives with each other and with experienced teachers as well.

Suggested Reading

BRUNER, JEROME. *Actual Minds, Possible Worlds.* Cambridge, Mass.: Harvard University Press, 1986.

A leading educational philosopher and psychologist outlines a perspective on learning that emphasizes the social and creative aspects of the mind.

GREENE, MAXINE. *Landscapes of Learning.* New York: Teachers College Press, 1978.

This collection of essays by a noted educational philosopher basically asserts the need for the arts in developing the imagination and inspires teachers to develop curricula in terms of notions of social justice and equality.

KNOBLAUCH, C. H., and LIL BRANNON. "Philosophy in the Writing Class: Teaching with a Purpose." *Rhetorical Traditions and the Teaching of Writing.* Portsmouth, N.H.: Boynton/Cook, 1984, 1–21.

This essay underscores the need to make philosophical choices about language and learning when becoming an English teacher.

SCHON, DONALD. *The Reflective Practitioner: How Professionals Think in Action.* New York: Basic Books, 1983.

A social scientist focuses on the theory that most professionals develop and adapt in action. Planning here emphasizes imagination and improvisation.

ZEICHNER, KENNETH. "Alternative Paradigms of Teacher Education." *Journal of Teacher Education* 34(1981): 7–24.

This article examines alternative perspectives in teacher education and advocates a reflective approach in shaping a theoretical foundation for teaching and learning.

4

Language as Artifact

"LET'S TALK ABOUT Hester's letter sweater. We'll have a guilt-trip day," Beth Goldman announces, leaning against the lectern at the front of the classroom, prodding her tenth- and eleventh-grade American Literature students in this middle-class suburban high school to open their books. Beth, short, energetic, and casually dressed, is forcefully brilliant, and her students know it. She drives home her points: "How does one arrive at theme? A bad definition of theme is 'the idea behind the story, the moral.' I think theme is the author's insight into a human being. What was Golding saying about human nature?"

Students who sit in rows facing Beth's podium raise their hands in response to her question. After a nod from Beth, Karen replies, "Humanity is evil, even demonic."

"What did Steinbeck think of us humans?"

Bill speaks: "That we are weak and vulnerable?"

"What do you think, Linda? Are we merely to be pitied for our weakness?"

"Well, Steinbeck's characters are weak, I guess, but I don't think that means we just pity them. I think Steinbeck likes his characters and sort of respects them in some ways."

"Yes," Beth says, "Steinbeck holds a socialistic view—that there is a certain human dignity, that we are basically good. Now if *I* were to write a book . . . ."

The discussion continues, with students listening intently to Beth's animated talk, struggling to figure out the worldviews of various authors they've studied. Then Beth circles back to Hawthorne: "*The Scarlet Letter* is a story of human sorrow; Hawthorne believes we are all weak. Pity is in order."

She offers a loose formula to determine the theme of a writer's work: The nature of the characters + the nature of the conflict + the outcome of the novel = the theme. Once Beth has given her students something neat to copy down in their notes, however, she undercuts its simplicity. She talks about the differences between human beings as characters and as literary figures: "Your parents cannot control what you are, ultimately. But the writer controls everything the character is. The writer plays God." Beth uses characters from *The Scarlet Letter* to make her point; she also uses her own students and fellow teachers to make her point.

"A novel is like an onion: The variations peel off and there is a core theme. . . . Writers make their own worlds. A good writer is careful how he or she peoples that world. Hester, Hawthorne's main character, is driven by imagination in a world that doesn't value it . . . . This passage says Hester 'issues forth.' Who on this staff issues forth? No, not Mrs. Petry . . . she skips, she bounces. Miss Howarth? Yes, she's tall and stately and fully capable of issuing forth."

Beth's talk is mesmerizing, peppered with examples from the lives of her students as well as from complex literary texts. She confesses she teaches her "self"; she stands centerstage and models her way of thinking, reading, and writing. Yet her students do not sit idly by; Beth involves them, even challenges them to try out their ideas in conversation and in writing. Both discussion and written texts are subject to revision in the world inside her classroom.

Beth's success depends upon several aspects of her personality and background. She has taught for thirty years, working with students from the elementary grades to college. Her rich background allows her to gauge the levels of her students, to devise strategies for helping them learn what she feels they must, and to draw on a wealth of texts. Additionally, she wholeheartedly subscribes to traditional notions of curricula, so the survey courses she teaches are to her liking. Since she regards writing as a way of thinking, she focuses on a student's meaning before leading the student to consider forms and structures of expression. More importantly, she is an astute reader of human beings and of herself; without this gift, she would not dare risk personal critiques of students and staff, because they would backfire, alienating her classes. Finally, Beth is charismatic, even egotistical. She believes she *should* be at the center of her classes, helping her students to come closer to her under-

standing of the texts she teaches, because she is brilliant, ruthlessly honest, and absolutely devoted to her students' education.

This devotion translates into very high expectations for her students. Beth acts as if she is preparing future English majors for college. She wants her students to know a good deal about literature, and she also wants them to be able to write effectively. Most of Beth's writing assignments ask students to write in response to texts they have read. Her essay exams, which she distributes the day before the test so students have an opportunity to prepare, are famous in the high school where she teaches. Frequently a full page in length, they pose complicated questions and challenge students to think carefully and write insightfully about what they read.

Analysis of the Approach

Beth concentrates on the text, whether the specific activity is reading, writing, or speaking, and keeps herself, as an expert on the text, at the center of the classroom. The text is regarded as an artifact to be looked at closely; the class, under the teacher's guidance, reaches a common understanding of it. This approach—language as artifact—is probably the most familiar one, because it has been common in high schools for a long time. It assumes that when students read they should find the meanings encoded in the text and that when they write they should produce texts that demonstrate their ability to think clearly and well.

Beth sees literary texts as vehicles for authors to express their views on the human condition. She believes that by the comparison of one text with another our understanding of both is enhanced. Although she draws a sharp distinction between characters as literary creations and characters in life, she believes that literature may comment in significant ways on life. In order to help her students understand the relevance of literature to life she gives them critical tools for understanding the themes and the worldviews of writers. She considers the issue of quality relevant, as she suggests what a "good writer" does.

Beth tries to get her students to see writing "as a way of thinking." Accordingly, she gives writing assignments that challenge students to read texts critically and to develop their capacity for independent thought. Finally, though she is firmly in control of the class, she involves students actively in the ongoing structure that she has devised.

The concern with the text as focal point arose with the "new critics" and their mid-twentieth-century movement toward regarding the text as autonomous and self-contained. Reacting against a tradition that tended to view literature as merely illustrative of literary history and biography, the new critics, in contrast, started with the question, What is *this* text about? Answers to the question were drawn from the evidence of the text itself (and expectations derived from its genre), not from authors' statements about purposes or speculation by critics about background or influence or intention.

This concern with the text, applied most directly to the reading and discussion of literature, also complemented a much older rhetorical tradition that informed the teaching of writing. Derived from classical rhetoric, this tradition classified kinds of discourse into narration, description, exposition, and argumentation and translated the classical concepts of invention, arrangement, and style into schoolroom advice about ways to find a subject, develop and organize it, and present it through effective language. Student writing was seen as sharply different from professional writing. Emphasis was placed on formulating thesis statements and finding ways to prove points. The success of communication was traced to the effect of specific elements and devices in the text. Although this tradition continues, it has been undercut in some classrooms by the development of new views of rhetoric that emphasize communication between reader and writer as a cooperative, two-way process in which writers aim to convey their ideas to readers. The modes of discourse—exposition, narration, description, and argument—have also been undercut by contemporary writing that fails to fall neatly into such categories as "narration" or "exposition."

Another tradition, epitomized by Matthew Arnold's belief that it is the function of the critic (and by implication, of the teacher) to transmit "the best that is known and thought in the world," usually determined the specific texts to be studied—the "canon," which would guarantee exposure to many of the most significant literary artifacts in the Judaeo-Christian cultural tradition. This ideal has been restated and espoused by E. D. Hirsch as recently as 1987 in his discussion of "cultural literacy." (See Suggested Reading at the end of the chapter.) Though this goal sometimes degenerated into "knowing about" rather than truly experiencing the great cultural artifacts of the past, there was merit in its aim to bring students into contact with the best in this heritage.

Debates among teachers over what should be included in the canon, as well as whether the very idea of a canon is viable, have occurred with increasing frequency and have been stimulated in part by the explosion of literature in new directions in the twentieth century and in part by the availability of paperback books, which enable teachers to supplement or replace the canonized selections in anthologies. (See Box 4.1.)

Phase-elective programs with a greater variety of literary materials multiplied in the late sixties and early seventies, placing more emphasis on genre than on literary history and also including multicultural and multimedia materials, although the survey course—in British literature, American literature, and world literature and usually tied to an an-

---

BOX 4.1
THE GREAT CANON DEBATE

Beowulf; Chaucer's *Canterbury Tales*; Spencer's *Faerie Queene*; Sidney's sonnets; Shakespeare's plays; Milton's *Paradise Lost*; the poems of Keats, Shelley, and Byron; the novels of D. H. Lawrence and Henry James—familiar works, all, to any English major. This English canon, "the best that has been thought and said" in the English language, along with its American equivalent—Hawthorne, Emerson, Thoreau, Melville, Dickinson, et al.—has long been the foundation for literary study in American colleges and schools. Critics and scholars once argued over the relative merits of these authors' works. Current debate has grown more heated, perhaps because harder questions are being asked: How does a literary work become part of the canon? Who makes these decisions? What are the political, economic, and social ramifications of being included or excluded? To what extent is there such a thing as a common culture, and must all citizens be familiar with it?

The debate over the literary canon has taken on great importance because it embodies most of the key educational issues of our time: the knowledge that is most worth teaching, the teacher's role in fostering independent thinking, the extent to which schools will reproduce the social order or create a new, more equitable order. There are four main positions in this debate:

- *Leave the English/American canon as it is.* This position tends to be taken by politicians or community members who don't really believe that the canon, or any institution, for that matter, continues to evolve. William Bennett is an outspoken proponent of this view.

- *Broaden the canon somewhat.* By acknowledging the contributions of women, African Americans, other minorities, and non-Western cultures, some believe a balance can be achieved. Supporters of this position allow that exclusion from the canon may occur because of political considerations, but they accept the notion of a hierarchy based on quality.

- *Deconstruct the canon.* This radical position is held by those who view any sort of canon as a tool for oppression, for maintaining inequity. At a minimum, they believe that the idea of a canon and the works included in one should undergo rigorous, politically charged scrutiny.

- *Deemphasize the canon.* Supporters of this position choose to emphasize the acts of reading and writing and critiquing, rather than the works themselves. The organization of courses and programs around canonical booklists is called into question.

thology—survived and is still a fixture in many curricula. In classrooms today that focus on language as artifact, however, one may find more texts by women writers and minority writers, as well as films to be studied as texts, examples of "new journalism," and experimental literature. Likewise, teachers may modify the new-critical approach by emphasizing the social contexts and political implications or "relevance" of a text, rather than regarding it as an isolated aesthetic object.

If the teacher makes the text the focus of the classroom, certain kinds of activities are likely to take place. Teachers are apt to become performers—experts initiating students into the text's mysteries and guiding them past the difficulties. Teachers are more likely to lecture than are teachers adopting other approaches, though, like Beth, they may construct their lectures in part as dialogues with their students, who participate actively in the exploration of new material and of new contexts for material already learned. This exploration assumes that the answers to questions lie in the text itself, which contains a knowable reality, and thus that training students to become better and more sophisticated readers is a major goal. Finally, the language-as-artifact approach tends to assume that helping students become better readers—and writers—depends upon an understanding of the processes that supposedly all students go through in learning, though there is not complete agreement on what these processes are or how they can best be analyzed or guided.

One useful description of the learning process was provided by Alfred North Whitehead as early as 1922. (See Suggested Reading at the end of this chapter.) Whitehead saw the educational process as consisting of repeated cycles with identifiable stages, which the student goes through both in approaching any single learning task and in his or her overall development. "Romance," Whitehead's first stage, involves "first apprehension," when the "subject matter has the vividness of novelty . . . [and] holds within itself unexplored connection with possibilities half-disclosed by glimpses and half-concealed by the wealth of material." In this stage of initial exploration, the learner's interest in the subject is aroused, but "knowledge is not dominated by [the] systematic procedure" that becomes appropriate for the next stage, "precision." In this second stage students strive for "exactness of formulation" and analysis of facts, with the addition of facts not discovered during the romance stage. The final stage, "generalization," is a synthesis, a "return to romanticism with the added advantage of classified ideas and relevant technique." This last stage should bring together what has been learned in the previous stages and leave a permanent legacy of "a few general principles with a thorough grounding in the way they apply to a variety of concrete details." It is the goal of the whole process, since Whitehead believes that learning is "useless to you till you have lost your textbooks, burnt your lecture notes, and forgotten the minutiae which you learnt by heart for the examination" (Alfred North Whitehead, *The Aims of Education and Other Essays*, New York: Macmillan, 1955, p. 75).

Whitehead's first stage reminds us of the importance of securing the student's interest in a subject before proceeding to a closer look and more detailed analysis. The third stage is equally important, since it enables students to pull things together, make comparisons with other things they have learned, and reexperience some of the pleasure and excitement of their initial view of the subject, only now with a deeper and more complete understanding. Students who think they "hate" poetry, for example, may be led to give a poem a chance if analysis doesn't begin before they have gained an initial interest in the subject of the poem. Students who complain that analyzing a poem "spoils" it for them are less likely to feel that way if the teacher "puts it back together" in a third stage, which relates it to other things they have known or experienced. Though the text is the focus of the language-as-artifact approach, that text is best seen against the background of other texts and other knowledge that students possess—in other words, as fitting into the larger concepts and frameworks that Beth stresses when she talks about "worldviews."

Language Study

In the language-as-artifact approach, language study may range all the way from the formal grammar unit prescribed in some school curricula, to a selective study of key grammatical concepts, to a functional treatment of whatever usage problems students may be having. It may also include vocabulary enrichment and the study of logic, of the nature of language, of the history of the English language, of connotation and denotation, and of the political and social power of language. Imaginative teachers often succeed in integrating the study of language with the reading and writing that students do.

If language is regarded as an artifact, it follows that the study of it will focus on its qualities and characteristics, either through grammatical analysis or through analysis of other sorts. Unfortunately, grammar is often studied for the wrong reasons and by the wrong students. The popular myth that a study of grammar will improve a student's writing has never been fully dispelled in spite of a large body of evidence to the contrary, and hence some school systems require formal grammar units in the hope of improving student writing. Actually, the formal study of grammar should probably be undertaken only with the best students and in a more challenging way than that provided by drill in recognizing grammatical forms in grammar workbook exercises. Seeing how language works is potentially a fascinating study for some students. At the same time, specific students' problems in usage and grammatical construction can easily be dealt with—either individually or in a group—

through a highly selective, functional approach involving a few key grammatical concepts.

In order to talk about key grammatical concepts more efficiently, students need to learn basic terms for the parts of speech and the parts of a sentence, not because these are important in themselves, but because they are a necessary tool in discussing such questions as: What distinguishes a *sentence* from a *fragment*? What is the difference between *coordination* and *subordination* of the elements in a sentence? How may the different parts of a sentence be *expanded* or *modified*? How does the particular *point of view* (personal, temporal, spatial) in a sentence determine the need for *agreement* among its elements? How can *transitions* help to connect sentences or larger units with one another in a piece of writing?

Other purposes for studying language are equally important in helping students with their reading and writing. Among these, vocabulary enrichment is likely to be most effective when it stems from what students are reading rather than from separate lists of words they "ought to know," and a study of key words in a text can enlarge students' working vocabularies at the same time that it deepens their comprehension of the literary text itself. Teachers may ask leading questions: What is the significance of the word "shrewd" in Hawthorne's "My Kinsman, Major Molineux?" How is Marc Antony's repetition of "honorable" in his speech at Caesar's funeral in *Julius Caesar* both central to his ironic method of argument and a reminder of one of the issues of the play? Students may also be asked to pick their own examples of key words for a piece and relate them to the theme, point of view, or tone of the piece as a whole. This exercise might lead in turn to consideration of connotation and denotation and to the ways that language can indirectly express attitudes, emotions, and prejudices.

Literature Study

In the language-as-artifact approach, literature study picks up easily where language study leaves off, as students come to appreciate how language functions both directly and indirectly through their close reading of literary texts. Close reading is perhaps most successful with poetry (see Box 4.2), where texts are shorter, richer, more dense, and hence repay close scrutiny, but it may also be applied to drama and longer works of fiction (see Box 4.3).

Study of a poem may begin with an oral reading and move on to consider words and phrases, metaphors, symbols, and the themes suggested by these. Other elements that teachers may emphasize through close reading in texts of all sorts include point of view, tone, and style. Close reading may also lead to focus on elements or characteristics of genres that are relevant to texts: Is Willy Loman a tragic hero? How is this poem representative of the sonnet? Close reading, in other words, ex-

---

BOX 4.2
CLOSE READING OF POETRY

PORTRAIT

Buffalo Bill's
defunct
      who used to
      ride a watersmooth-silver
               stallion
and break onetwothreefourfive pigeonsjustlikethat
                               Jesus

he was a handsome man
                               and what i want to know is
how do you like your blueeyed boy
Mister Death

This poem essentially deals with a very usual theme and treats that theme simply. Death claims all, even the strongest and most glamorous. How does the poet in treating such a common theme manage to give a fresh and strong impression of it? He might have achieved this effect, of course, in a number of different ways, and as a matter of fact, the general device he employs is not simply one device; it is complex. In this case, however, the most prominent element is the unconventional attitude that he takes toward a conventional subject. And in this particular poem, the matter of tone is isolated sufficiently for us to examine it rather easily (though we must not forget that there are other matters to be examined in this poem and that tone is a factor in every poem).

In the first place, what is the difference between writing

    Buffalo Bill's

    defunct

and

    Buffalo Bill's
    dead

The first carries something of a tone of conscious irreverence. The poet here does not approach the idea of death with the usual and expected respect for the dead. He is matter-of-fact, unawed, and even somewhat flippant. But the things that he picks out to comment on in Buffalo Bill make a strong contrast with the idea of death. The picture called up is one of tremendous vitality and speed; for example, the stallion is described as "watersmooth-silver." The adjective contains not only a visual description of the horse that Buffalo Bill rode but implies a kinetic description too. How was the horse "watersmooth"? Smooth, graceful in action. (The poet, by running the words together in the next line, is perhaps telling us how to read the line, running the words together to give the effect of speed. The way the poem is printed on the page is designed probably to serve the same purpose, the line divisions being intended as a kind of arrangement for punctuation and emphasis. But the odd typography is not of fundamental importance.)

The "portrait" of Buffalo Bill given after the statement that he is "defunct" is a glimpse of the man in action, breaking five clay pigeons in rapid succession as he flashes by on his stallion—the sort of glimpse one might remember from the performance of the Wild West show in which Buffalo Bill starred. The exclamation that follows is exactly the sort of burst of approval that might be struck from a child seeing him in action or remembering him later. And the quality of "handsome" applies, one feels, not merely to his face but to his whole figure in action.

The next lines carry on the tone of unabashed, unawed, slangy irreverence toward death. Death becomes "Mister Death." The implied figure of the spectator at a performance of the Wild West show helps justify the language and manner of expression used here, making us feel that it is in character. But the question as asked here strikes us on another level. It is a question that no child would ask; it is indeed one of the old unanswerable questions. But here it is transformed by the tone into something fresh and startling. Moreover, the dashing, glamorous character of the old Indian fighter gets a sharp emphasis. The question may be paraphrased: Death, you don't get lads like him every day, do you? The way the question is put implies several things. First, it implies the pathos of the idea that even a person of such enormous vitality and unfailing youthfulness has to die. But this sense of pathos is not insisted upon; rather, it is presented indirectly and ironically because of the bantering and flippant attitude inherent in the question, especially in the phrases, "Mister Death" and "blueeyed boy." And in this question, which sums up the whole poem, we also are given the impression that death is not terrible for Buffalo Bill, for "Mister Death" stands in some sort of fatherly and prideful relation to the "blueeyed boy."

plores the details of texts not only to determine all the nuances of *what* is being said but also the significance of *how* it is being said. Its ultimate aim is not only to understand the meaning but to take pleasure in the form of a text.

Study of the characteristics of genres and forms gives another insight into literary texts. As with the study of grammatical concepts, here definitions or lists of characteristics are not important in themselves, but merely as aids to understanding a text. Realizing that plays are intended to be seen on a stage rather than merely to be read, for example, affects the way

BOX 4.3
CLOSE READING OF FICTION

For the rate at which bodies fall in a vacuum, it is perfectly irrelevant to science whether the bodies might be feathers or men, ostrich feathers or feathers of a Chinese nightingale, politicians or plumbers. . . . But for fiction the particular body that a thing has is of the very greatest importance to the whole fictional structure. Does it squeak, is it scared, is it brown, is it round, is it chilly, does it think, does it smash? Questions of this kind fiction has to be constantly concerned with in order to have any formal existence at all.

The procedure of the novel is to individualize. As with other art forms, what it has to say that is of collective value is said by inference from individual concrete things. History, on the other hand, proceeds by generalization. It treats people as groups; and when individuals appear they appear as catalysts of large collective actions or as representatives of groups, their significance being that of the group forces, the collection, the sum. . . .

"After the death of Frederic the Second," Gibbon says,

> Germany was left a monster with a hundred heads. A crowd of princes and prelates disputed the ruins of the empire: the lords of innumerable castles were less prone to obey, than to imitate their superiors; and according to the measure of their strength, their incessant hostilities received the names of conquest or robbery. Such anarchy was the inevitable consequence of the laws and manners of Europe; and the kingdoms of France and Italy were shivered into fragments by the violence of the same tempest.

Let us place beside this passage, describing a state of anarchy, one from *Vanity Fair*, also describing a state of anarchy. Jos Sedley has just heard the rumor of British defeat at Waterloo.

> Such is the force of habit, that even in the midst of his terror he began mechanically to twiddle with his hair, and arrange the cock of his hat. Then he looked amazed at the pale face in the glass before him, and especially at his moustachios, which had attained a rich growth. . . . They *will* mistake me for a military man, thought he, remembering Isidor's warning as to the massacre with which all the defeated British army was threatened; and staggering back to his bed-chamber, he began wildly pulling the bell which summoned his valet.
>
> Isidor answered the summons. Jos had sunk in a chair—he had torn off his neckcloths, and turned down his collars, and was sitting with both his hands lifted to his throat.
>
> *"Coupez-moi, Isidor,"* shouted he: *vite! coupez-moi!"*
>
> Isidor thought for a moment he had gone mad, and that he wished his valet to cut his throat.
>
> *"Les moustaches,"* gasped Jos; *"les moustaches—coupy, rasy, vite!"*

In the passage from Gibbon all is plural and collective. We need to know nothing specific about any prelate or lord or about any act of hostility or violence: the sum of all the individual situations is sufficiently communicative. In the passage from Thackeray, all is singular and particular, from particular gesture and thought down to the gasp of the voice and Jos's individually bad French. Communicated by this passage in its context are more than specific images of gestures and sounds, although it is all made up of the specific. In Jos's anarchy of soul is read with horrifying vividness the anarchy of a city, and still more, the anarchy of a culture. And yet the complex general meaning of the scene is dependent wholly upon particularity, or "embodiment," and would disintegrate without such embodiment.

—From Dorothy Van Ghent, *The English Novel: Form and Function* (New York: Harper & Row, 1961), pp. 4–5.

one reads (or teaches) them. The concepts of the tragic hero and the tragic flaw help one see what happens to Macbeth as a human being; knowing the formal pattern of a sonnet helps one to follow the development of its thought.

Knowledge of one genre can help to throw light on a text in a different genre, and writing based on a text can increase understanding. In the course of preparing a film or TV adaptation of a poem, for example, students can come to better understand the point of view of the original as they make decisions about what the camera will "see." Or attempting to turn a brief dramatic scene into prose narrative may help them see the potentials and limitations of both forms and give them a better understanding of the text of each. Similarly, reading or writing a parody may help to clarify for them the characteristics of the original text.

Writing Instruction

In the language-as-artifact approach, writing can thus go hand in hand with reading, and much of the writing students do is likely to be on topics arising directly or indirectly from the literary texts they are reading. They may be asked to examine an element in the text closely or to relate parts of the text to each other, to discuss the motivation of characters, to deal with themes arising from the text. They may also be asked to make applications of the text to universal or contemporary problems or to compare it with other texts. In some classes students may also be given opportunities to write about controversial social or political issues, or about personal experiences, the latter particularly at the lower grade levels. Literature nearly always, however, serves as the springboard for writing in a language-as-artifact classroom.

Whatever the topic or the kind of writing students do in a language-as-artifact class, the ultimate goal is likely to be to produce as polished, correct, and "professional" a product as possible. (This is somewhat ironic, since writers in the classroom are likely to be thought of in an entirely different category from professional writers, with an entirely different set of problems.) Teachers often specify the process for reaching the goal of a polished product; they teach in terms of rough outlines, rough drafts, and revisions. At one extreme they may even specify such forms or formats as the five-paragraph essay or the formal outline. Though designed to help students, these more rigid specifications stifle independence and creativity, and they do not reflect the way individual writers actually work. Human beings don't really think in five-paragraph essays, nor does the five-paragraph theme appear in writing done outside the school. A series of "laundry lists" in which elements and ideas can easily be switched around and tried out in different arrangements and combinations is much closer to representing the process of thought in organizing a paper than is the formal outline with its Roman numerals, letters, and careful parallelisms. A period of free-writing may be more useful in turning up ideas for a paper than a period of agonizing over devising a B to go with an A in a formal outline. Finally, the kind of revision a teacher expects may vary all the way from a mere correction of errors to a complete rewriting of the paper to an exploration of alternative approaches to the subject.

Although in many language-as-artifact classrooms the activities connected with language, literature, and writing are sharply separated—a short story on Monday and Tuesday, a vocabulary quiz and a grammar lesson on Wednesday, a writing assignment on Thursday, and so on—the subject of English makes more sense to students if its parts are brought together and integrated. The study of point of view in a poem or a novel becomes more meaningful when students are asked to take a particular point of view in their own writing. The teacher's comment that the tone in a student paper is inconsistent or inappropriate will register more firmly when the student is reminded of the successful handling of tone by a short-story writer.

Potentials and Limitations of the Approach

Many of the potentials and limitations of the language-as-artifact approach to teaching English should already be apparent, including those associated with its extremes. The most important of these might be summarized as follows:

Potentials

1. *It develops a cultural literacy.* Students are exposed to a common body of knowledge, usually including some of the best of the Western cultural tradition.

2. *It permits measurement against a standard.* Focus on the text tends to produce results that are easier to measure and that can be held up against a common standard. Student understanding of a literary text is easier to evaluate when it is compared with that of the teacher and

professional critics. Since student writing is frequently on common questions or topics and is likely to be expository, teachers find it easier to rank-order results and arrive at evaluations that are seemingly more objective.

3. *It teaches close reading.* Intensive training in close reading gives students a useful skill that will serve them in good stead in college or in other contexts where understanding both the central meaning and the nuances of a text is useful. It may also provide them with aesthetic pleasure from the perception of the literary features and the subtleties of a text—its patterns, symbols, themes.

4. *It imposes intellectual discipline.* Focusing on the text and being forced to measure up to a common standard in turn provides intellectual challenges for students and helps them to acquire intellectual discipline.

5. *It prepares students for college.* Learning the language of formal literary analysis, the skills of close reading, and some of the modes of instruction common to college classes helps to prepare students for success in college.

6. *It affords flexibility.* Finally, since the boundaries between this and other approaches are blurred, the language-as-artifact approach can readily incorporate many elements from other approaches, making possible the kind of eclecticism that is crucial in developing an individual teaching style. A language-as-artifact teacher, for example, may ask students to do some free-writing and extensive drafting (normally associated with the expressive or developmental approaches) or to consider what the text of *Julius Caesar* says about political power or political processes that may be relevant to contemporary situations.

Limitations

1. *It neglects the individual learner.* The language-as-artifact approach tends to assume that all students learn in the same way. Putting teacher and text at the center of the classroom often means that the individual learner is neglected, and differences in learning styles are ignored even when teachers take different rates of learning into account. In particular, students who favor participatory or visual styles are neglected.

2. *The <u>product</u> is privileged over the process.* Focus on the text also leads to stress upon achieving the final error-free product—whether it is a piece of writing or an oral interpretation of reading—at the expense of consideration of the whole process of learning. "Right" answers may thus be prized above true understanding and intellectual growth. Students are not encouraged to learn from their mistakes through experiment.

3. *Student writing is seen as mere exercises.* Language-as-artifact teachers often tend to draw sharp and artificial distinctions between the writing

Tremendous emphasis upon Conformity

a tendency to teach to formula

students do in classrooms and the writing that writers (both amateur and professional) do in the real world. This leads to "writing for the teacher" rather than for a wider audience, and writing becomes a mere exercise rather than a truly meaningful activity. It may also result in missed opportunities to tie reading and writing together and reinforce a student's understanding of such concepts as point of view, tone, and style, since these are not likely to be stressed in "schoolroom" exercises.

4. *Analysis is stressed over other activities.* Focus on text and product can often lead to an exclusive concentration on analysis and to the neglect of other kinds of activities, especially those involving the affective dimensions of both reading and writing.

5. *Texts become static.* When analysis of texts is the sole focus, the texts—and language itself—tend to become static objects rather than representations of dynamic processes. A short story or a lyric poem becomes a collection of literary devices rather than an account of people interacting or thinking or feeling. Students see their papers as merely words on a page, not as attempts to communicate with other people.

6. *Formula and format are stressed over creativity and individuality.* In its extreme form, this approach stresses formula and format and discourages creativity in students. Works of literature may be forced into rigid descriptive patterns; and the five-paragraph essay, the five-sentence paragraph, or other gridlike writing forms may be taught as a series of rigid rules rather than as possible heuristics.

7. *It can present problems in motivation.* The stress on text, on product, and on analysis to the neglect of students' reactions and feelings tends to make the whole process of learning less intense, less exciting, less meaningful, and hence makes it much harder to motivate students. Students don't get excited about tasks they see as trivial, needlessly exacting, or distanced from themselves.

8. *It places demands on the teacher as performer.* If teachers are at the center of the classroom as final authorities on the text, they have an extremely demanding role to play. They must be very skillful performers (as Beth is), if they are to keep students actively engaged in the learning process. Otherwise students may become passive sponges, absorbing teacher wisdom from lectures, and discussion sessions tend to turn into recitations in which students have little room for exploration and intellectual growth, since they are always so painfully aware that there is one "right" answer to be given.

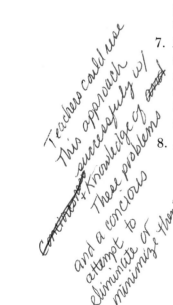
Teachers could use this approach w/ successfully w/ control + knowledge of these problems and a concious attempt to eliminate or minimize them

IMPLEMENTATION
TEACHING SHIRLEY JACKSON'S "THE LOTTERY" IN JUNIOR HIGH

Classic modern short stories such as Richard Connell's "The Most Dangerous Game," Frank Stockton's "The Lady or the Tiger?" and Shirley

Jackson's "After You, My Dear Alphonse" are often included in middle school literature textbooks. Shirley Jackson's "The Lottery" is another common selection, perhaps because it meshes rather neatly into the canon of American literature, with its Gothic flavor and ironic tone.

"The Lottery" would fit nicely into a unit on the short story, into a thematic unit touching upon inhumanity and injustice, into one dealing with customs and rituals, or into one focusing on social change. As a model for student writing, the story demonstrates how a writer methodically reveals key information for a surprise ending and how plot can be emphasized over character.

Desired Student Outcomes:

Proficiency in reading literary texts closely

Understanding of the notion of irony

Understanding of themes significant in American fiction

Understanding of notions of justice and injustice

Possible Whole-Class Activities:

Listen to Rosemary Timperley's short story, "Harry" (*Roald Dahl's Book of Ghost Stories*, pp. 33–46).

Discuss situations and events where the everyday becomes horrifying.

Discuss irony; try to elicit examples of irony in students' lives.

Discuss fairness/unfairness.

Discuss the history of stoning as punishment. (Be sure to delay this until students have read the story.)

Watch the film version of "The Lottery."

View episodes of *The Twilight Zone* or *Star Trek*, which can serve as critiques of unexamined social rituals.

Possible Small-Group Activities:

Discuss unexamined social rituals students may have participated in (for example, making fun of certain people or hazing).

Rework "The Lottery" into a skit or play.

Perform plays for rest of class.

Read and discuss a poem that reveals its shocking subject slowly, such as Poe's "Annabel Lee."

Possible Individual Activities:

> Write a response to the discussion of fairness. What does it mean to be fair? Have you ever been treated unfairly?
>
> Read Virginia Woolf's short story "A Haunted House," which uses irony just as "The Lottery" does.
>
> Compare and contrast Woolf's story with "The Lottery," making a list of similarities and differences.

Resources:

Friedman, Lenemaja. *Shirley Jackson*. Boston: Twayne Publishers, 1975.

Graves, Donald H. *Experiment with Fiction*. Portsmouth, N.H.: Heinemann, 1989.

Jackson, Shirley. *The Lottery, or the Adventures of James Harris*. New York: Farrar, Straus, 1949.

Oppenheimer, Judy. *Private Demons: The Life of Shirley Jackson*. New York: Putnam, 1988.

Woolf, Virginia. "The Haunted House." In Milton Crane, ed., *Fifty Great Short Stories*. New York: Bantam, 1962.

Organization of the Unit:

Typically, teachers would not build an entire unit around a single short story—they would probably build it around the genre of short story or around a particular theme; thus, the following should be seen as a segment of a larger whole.

Day 1

There are several ways to introduce the short story "The Lottery." The teacher might open a discussion on the notion of fairness, a subject that middle school students can speak about with passion, particularly in terms of relationships with parents, teachers, and friends. It would also be appropriate to begin with talk about social rituals, such as initiation ceremonies or hazing. Students would then be asked to read "The Lottery," aloud or silently. Depending on the time spent in discussion, the teacher might assign an informal piece of writing for homework—a response to reading or to in-class discussion.

Day 2

Discussion of the short story would likely center on the final scene, where Tessie is stoned. However, the setting and introduction of characters is worth a closer look because of the expectations evoked in readers. Students might discuss their understanding of the term "lottery" and compare that with its use in the story. They could be asked to reread for the exact point when they began to see that something was amiss. Additionally, the teacher might want to explain stoning's history or talk about fertility rituals.

It would probably be desirable (from both the teacher's and the students' perspectives) to shift into a less discursive, more interactive mode before the end of the period. Students could adapt the short story for the stage, making changes in setting, dialogue, or characterization as needed. Another option would be to have students brainstorm with their classmates about subjects for their own short stories.

Day 3

Whether "The Lottery" would still be the focus of your class period would depend on the choices you made; obviously, if students are working on scripts or short stories, the text would be used as a model. Perhaps you would introduce other texts for purposes of comparison—the Stephen King short story, other short stories in your unit, poems that followed a similar pattern of revelation, or episodes of a specific television series or a film.

Evaluation:

The teacher can evaluate students on the following activities:

Students read another short story and make a list of its similarities to and differences from "The Lottery."

Students lead a class discussion of another short story based on a list of discussion questions to be submitted to the teacher in advance.

Teacher selects a passage from "The Lottery" and asks students to do a close reading of it and then write a paragraph explaining what they see in the passage.

Students write on this essay question: The narrator explains that much of the ritual has been forgotten, but the tradition of the lottery continues just the same. What does this combination of forgetting and continuing tell you about the nature of tradition? (The students are given the question the day before the exam.)

IMPLEMENTATION:
TEACHING NATHANIEL HAWTHORNE'S *THE SCARLET LETTER* IN HIGH SCHOOL

Hawthorne's *The Scarlet Letter* often serves as the "centerpiece" for high school American literature courses. A typical American literature survey course would include works by Melville, Hawthorne, Emerson, Thoreau,

Whitman, Poe, Dickinson, and Steinbeck, among others. Usually survey courses are organized in chronological order, mirroring college survey courses, although the reading requirements are not usually as demanding because of the use of excerpts and abridged editions.

The tenth, eleventh, and twelfth graders who are asked to read *The Scarlet Letter* usually find it quite a stretch, in terms of prose style and subject matter. Teachers have to help students establish connections between the text and their own lives. Teachers may find that their students have little sense of the geography or cultural milieu; Hester's "sin" may not seem particularly sinful. Even the concept of sin itself may seem distant.

One way to help students enter *The Scarlet Letter* is to begin with one of Hawthorne's short stories such as "Young Goodman Brown," where much of the same cultural context is developed. Another alternative is to work with a social studies teacher who is teaching American history and develop a plan for discussing colonial America in both English and history classes.

In thinking about how to approach a book such as *The Scarlet Letter*, you may want to consider questions such as these:

1. *How closely do you want to monitor student reading?* While most college professors would simply give a deadline for completing the novel because they can count on their students' extensive reading experience, high school teachers must consider their students' experience, motivation, and persistence, and help them plan their time during the reading of the novel. If students find the book difficult, the teacher will probably want to run interference, prompting, explaining, and drawing explicit connections with the students' lives. In addition, most high school students find the openings of novels such as *The Scarlet Letter* perplexing; it might make sense to help students determine the main characters, the basic story line, and the emerging themes through early chapters, then monitor less closely as the students become more familiar with the text.

2. *What thematic issues in the novel seem most pertinent for your particular class at this point in the semester?* Teachers must consider the texts, concepts, themes, and terminology that have been introduced previously. *The Scarlet Letter* could serve to reinforce prior examples or to introduce new ideas. For instance, if the class already understands the notion of tone, the teacher might point to this passage in the first chapter:

> The founders of a new colony, whatever Utopia of human virtue and happiness they might originally project, have invariably recognized it among their earliest practical necessities to allot a portion of the virgin soil as a cemetery, and another portion as the site of a prison.

The irony, the sly suggestion of humor in this sentence would challenge students to apply their theoretical understanding. Students could be pushed to extend their understanding of tone to get a handle on the narrator of the novel.

3. *To what extent do you need to provide a context for the work or a series of ties with contemporary life?* If students have read several short stories by Hawthorne, have read other works from this period, and have fairly extensive understanding of American life in 1650 and in 1850, little will need to be done. However, if students don't have much to draw upon and are struggling with their reading, the teacher should consider designing activities that help students find meaningful, interesting information that could illuminate the reading for them.

4. *What genres of writing seem important for your students to practice at this point?* Again, students' previous writing experiences should guide your choices. Students who have been writing formal critical papers for several semesters may need to attempt informal "writing to know" activities such as writing reactions or responses to the text or keeping a reading log. Perhaps students could attempt their own "hellfire" stories, modeling their efforts on particular passages of *The Scarlet Letter*, or perhaps they could write scripts dramatizing brief scenes.

Desired Student Outcomes:

Understanding the role of the complex hero in American fiction

Increased recognition of metaphor's part in conveying the text's meaning

Improved ability to read literary texts closely and analytically

Understanding of *The Scarlet Letter's* significance as a work of American fiction

Possible Whole-Class Activities:

Read "Dr. Heidegger's Experiment" aloud.

View the film version of "Dr. Heidegger's Experiment."

Discuss the narrator's style in the short story.

Read complex passages of *The Scarlet Letter* aloud.

Listen to a lecture on the world of Salem, circa 1640, as contrasted to Hawthorne's world, circa 1840.

Read two other Hawthorne stories that characterize Puritan life, "The Maypole of Merrymount" and "Endicott and the Red Cross." The latter contains the germ for *The Scarlet Letter* (see Box 4.4); compare this with Hawthorne's later treatment of Hester and Puritan society in the novel.

BOX 4.4
THE GERM OF *THE SCARLET LETTER*

[The Puritan leader John Endicott] was a man of stern and resolute countenance, the effect of which was heightened by a grizzled beard that swept the upper portion of his breastplate. This piece of armor was so highly polished that the whole surrounding scene had its image in the glittering steel. The central object in the mirrored picture was an edifice of humble architecture, with neither steeple nor bell to proclaim it—what nevertheless it was—the house of prayer. A token of the perils of the wilderness was seen in the grim head of a wolf, which had just been slain within the precincts of the town, and according to the regular mode of claiming the bounty, was nailed on the porch of the meeting-house. The blood was still plashing on the doorstep. There happened to be visible, at the same noontide hour, so many other characteristics of the times and manners of the Puritans, that we must endeavor to represent them in a sketch, though far less vividly than they were reflected in the polished breastplate of John Endicott.

In close vicinity to the sacred edifice appeared that important engine of Puritanic authority, the whipping-post— with the soil around it well trodden by the feet of evil doers, who had there been disciplined. At one corner of the meeting-house was the pillory, and at the other the stocks; and, by a singular good fortune for our sketch, the head of an Episcopalian and suspected Catholic was grotesquely incased in the former machine; while a fellow-criminal, who had boisterously quaffed a health to the King, was confined by the legs in the latter. Side by side, on the meeting-house steps, stood a male and a female figure. The man was a tall, lean, haggard personification of fanaticism, bearing on his breast this label,—A WANTON GOSPELLER,—which betokened that he had dared to give interpretations of Holy Writ unsanctioned by the infallible judgment of the civil and religious rulers. His aspect showed no lack of zeal to maintain his heterodoxies, even at the stake. The woman wore a cleft stick on her tongue, in appropriate retribution for having wagged that unruly member against the elders of the church; and her countenance and gestures gave much cause to apprehend that, the moment the stick should be removed, a repetition of the offense would demand new ingenuity in chastising it.

The above-mentioned individuals had been sentenced to undergo their various modes of ignominy, for the space of one hour at noonday. But among the crowd were several whose punishment would be life-long; some, whose ears had been cropped, like those of puppy dogs; others, whose cheeks had been branded with the initials of their misdemeanors; one, with his nostrils slit and seared; and another, with a halter about his neck, which he was forbidden ever to take off, or to conceal beneath his garments. Methinks he must have been grievously tempted to affix the other end of the rope to some convenient beam or bough. There was likewise a young woman, with no mean share of beauty, whose doom it was to wear the letter A on the breast of her gown, in the eyes of all the world and her own children. And even her own children knew what that initial signified. Sporting with her infamy, the lost and desperate creature had embroidered the fatal token in scarlet cloth, with golden thread and the nicest art of needle-work; so that the capital A might have been thought to mean Admirable, or anything rather than Adulteress.

Let not the reader argue, from any of these evidences of iniquity, that the times of the Puritans were more vicious than our own, when, as we pass along the very street of this sketch, we discern no badge of infamy on man or woman. It was the policy of our ancestors to search out even the most secret sins, and expose them to shame, without fear or favor, in the broadest light of the noonday sun. Were such the custom now, perchance we might find materials for a no less piquant sketch than the above.

—From Nathaniel Hawthorne, "Endicott and the Red Cross" (1837) in *The Complete Novels and Selected Tales of Nathaniel Hawthorne* (New York: Modern Library, 1937), pp. 1014-18.

Discuss contemporary notions of sin.

Read newspaper clippings and articles regarding contemporary incidents of punishment for moral offenses.

Discuss the purpose of the novel's preface, "The Custom-House" (though in some classes you might want to have students skip this).

Read the first chapter of *The Scarlet Letter* aloud.

Discuss the relationships between the three main characters.

Stage a mock trial of the three main characters. What are their crimes? What should be their punishments?

Examine critical responses to the novel. How do the critics' interpretations vary? Where do students stand in relation to the critics' views?

Become familiar with conflicts between critics through teacher-led discussion of Jane Tompkins's article in *Sensational Designs* (see Resources below) on the construction of the novel as canonical text.

Examine contemporary novels that respond to *The Scarlet Letter* in some sense. Toni Morrison's *Beloved* and John Updike's *S.* come to mind.

Read a noncanonical novel such as *Hope Leslie* by Maria Sedgwick, which was published before *The Scarlet Letter*, and compare the two.

Possible Small-Group Activities:

Find all references to and descriptions of a particular character; discuss the nature of the character on that basis.

Respond to peers' drafts of critical essays.

Share copychanges. (See Box 4.5.)

Possible Individual Activities:

Keep reading logs, responding informally to specific passages in *The Scarlet Letter*.

Read assigned passages of *The Scarlet Letter*.

Do a copychange of a selected passage. (See Box 4.5.)

Write a brief character sketch based on one of the novel's main characters.

Write a critical essay describing the isolating effects of sin on one or more of the novel's characters.

Resources:

Bradley, Sculley, Richard Croom Beatty, and E. Hudson Longedis. *The Scarlet Letter* (Norton Critical Edition). New York: Norton, 1962.

Colacurcio, Michael J., ed. *New Essays on The Scarlet Letter*. New York: Cambridge University Press, 1985.

Crews, Fredrick C. *The Sins of the Fathers: Hawthorne's Psychological Themes*. New York: Oxford University Press, 1966.

Fiedler, Leslie. *Love and Death in the American Novel*. Cleveland: World Publishing, 1962.

Gross, Seymour L., ed. *A Scarlet Letter Handbook*. Belmont, Calif.: Wadsworth Publishing, 1960.

Lynn, Kenneth S. *The Scarlet Letter: Text, Sources, Criticism*. New York: Harcourt, Brace & World, 1961.

Murfin, Ross C., ed. *The Scarlet Letter: Case Studies in Contemporary Criticism*. New York: Bedford Books of St. Martins Press, 1991.

Tompkins, Jane. "Masterpiece Theater: The Politics of Hawthorne's Literary Reputation." In *Sensational Designs*. New York: Oxford University Press, 1985.

Updike, John. *S*. New York: Ballantine Books (Fawcett Crest), 1988.

Organization of the Unit

Week 1

The teacher's first job is to help students become familiar with Hawthorne's style so that it does not prove to be too much of an impediment for them. The short story "Dr. Heidegger's Experiment" (also available in film) is more immediately accessible to students in subject and style; thus, it could serve as a place to begin discussing a typical Hawthorne narrator.

BOX 4.5
COPYCHANGE

Imitation is the basis for much of our learning. We learned to walk, to speak, to brush our teeth, and to clean our plates by imitating our parents and other adults. Young dancers, artists, and musicians learn craft and style through imitation, reminded constantly about the value of practice—limbering up, sketching, and doing finger exercises—by their teachers. "Leap like Gelsey Kirkland does, make the canvas shimmer like Monet did, aim for technical perfection like Zukerman does," they say, and their pupils struggle to match their idols' attainments.

Likewise, apprentice writers rely on other writers' good examples. Thus, teachers of English may choose to build many of their lessons upon imitation. However, simply inviting students to "imitate" a piece of writing may not be enough; the few students who will be able to do the assignment are probably teaching themselves to write on their own, with or without your help. Better to introduce imitation as "practice," preceded and followed by explicit conversation on what exactly is being imitated and to what effect.

One strategy for introducing students of all abilities to the concept of imitation is through a method Stephen Dunning, a former president of NCTE, calls copychange. First, you must select a model passage of appropriate length that manages to achieve something you would like your students to do. For example,

> I bent over my desk, trying to make fat vowels sit on the line like fruit, the tails of consonants hang below, and colored the maps of French and German empires, and memorized arithmetic tables and state capitals and major exports of many lands,

---

Other short stories such as "Endicott and the Red Cross," "The Maypole of Merrymount," "The Birthmark," or "Young Goodman Brown" might provide a counterpoint to a discussion of contemporary definitions and responses to "sin" or immorality. Students might begin with written explanations of their own views on sin: What is sin? What do you consider as "sinful behavior"? In your own estimation have you ever sinned? Newspaper clippings or articles about fallen televangelists and politicians, the Amish concept of shunning, and the Puritan notion of sin could spur student talk. The first chapter of *The Scarlet Letter*, "The Prison Door," might be read aloud by the teacher, then discussed in class. Nightly homework assignments of several chapters each would follow, along with in-class discussions of the reading to establish characters, setting, and conflict.

Week 2

Students, now immersed in the novel, likely would benefit from a closer look at Hester, Pearl, Dimmesdale, and Chillingworth. By focusing discussion time or small-group work on specific passages of the novel where characters act or speak or are described, the teacher can help students

and when I was stumped, looked up to see George Washington's sour look and Lincoln's of pity and friendship, an old married couple on the wall. School, their old home, smelled of powerful floor wax and disinfectant, the smell of patriotism. (From Garrison Keillor, *Lake Wobegon Days*, New York: Viking, 1985, p. 211.)

Copychange, the practice of substituting words and ideas into another writer's structures, should then be modeled by the teacher:

> She leaned over the bathroom sink, trying to make soap bubbles swirl in even patterns like strings of pearls, the water tepid below, and stirred the handwash, the pantyhose and scarves, and recited the Apostle's Creed and Girl Scout Oath and Pledge of Allegiance, and when she was winded, looked up to study her own smirking face and her mother's photograph, the whole family in the mirror. The bathroom, their most used room, smelled of Lysol and Woolite, the smell of suburbia.

Students may change as few or as many words as they want to, but once they have committed to characters and ideas they should try to follow through, making sense. By attempting copychange, students will probably generate ideas they may not have otherwise. But more importantly, they will have to pay close attention to the model text. By rewriting it, they will notice the way the sentence stretches out, the way Keillor uses conjunctions and appositives and similes, even if they don't know those terms.

When students understand the basic premises of copychange, they may want to choose their own texts to imitate, they may stray far from the original, or they may use copychanged pieces to begin more substantial essays. Of course, it is important to teach students to credit their influences and triggering sources; for example, "After Garrison Keillor's essay 'School' in *Lake Wobegon Days*."

learn to analyze literary characters. Students could be asked for written reactions to characters. Students with artistic abilities might be asked to create drawings of characters and scenes.

Another dimension of this unit could be introduced during the second week (or, optionally, during the first week): research into the actual historical period Hawthorne fictionalizes and research into the world of the writer. Students should have the opportunity to explore the conflicts and issues of these historical periods, as well as to gain background knowledge about Puritanism and Salem's place in history. Either teacher lecture or hands-on research would be appropriate as students explore why a writer like Hawthorne would choose to write about a different era. Discrepancies between historical fact and Hawthorne's fiction should be highlighted, so that students can see the problems and possibilities inherent in historical fiction.

Reading assignments could perhaps be lengthened during the second (or third) week, depending on the students' level of comfort with the text.
Week 3
At this point, students should be nearing completion of the novel. They

should be familiar with the main characters and their relationships; they should have a good sense of the novel's setting and style. If the teacher intends for students to write a formal paper of some kind, the assignment should be introduced if it hasn't been already. (For an example of a student paper on *The Scarlet Letter*, see Box 9.6.) Most of the less formal writing that has occurred during the previous couple of weeks can be used as a basis for the formal effort. Students could be asked to sort through their reading logs for pertinent concerns, and the character work of the small groups could be another source of ideas. Mid- or late week, drafts should be ready for in-class response groups or for the teacher's reactions. Brief, focused lessons might well be given in order to address specific problems students are having as they write.

In discussion, the week's talk might well center on the final scenes, where Dimmesdale reveals his secret. Other increasingly complex topics might include the device of the explained supernatural. The second paragraph of the concluding chapter would be an appropriate paragraph for students to copychange, partly because it would cause them to scrutinize it so closely. By having students substitute their own words and meanings into Hawthorne's structures, the teacher can guarantee a close reading. Copychange also introduces the potential power of syntax in an inductive fashion. The lesson on copychange could provide a basis for a more sophisticated discussion of narrative intrusion.

Week 4

Whether the unit extends through a fourth week depends on several factors: the students' progress with the novel, the time you have, and your own style. The week would surely include concentrated work on the students' critical essays. This would be a natural place to study other critical responses to the novel.

Evaluation:

Issues such as those listed below might be assigned as questions in essay examinations or as topics for papers to be written outside of class.

> Consider the metaphorical significance of the green letter A in Chapter 15 of *The Scarlet Letter*.

> Explain the relationship among Dimmesdale, Hester, and Chillingworth.

> Consider Hester's behavior in the final scaffold scene. In what ways can she be described as a heroine here? In what ways is she not a heroine?

> Compare contemporary attitudes toward children born to unmarried women with those expressed in *The Scarlet Letter*.

Select another nineteenth-century American novel and write
an essay comparing it with *The Scarlet Letter*.

Explore the concept of isolation as it is represented in the
novel.

Explain the relationship of the introductory chapter, "The
Custom-House," to the rest of the novel.

⁓ Explain why students in high school today should be required
to read *The Scarlet Letter*.

Suggested Reading

ARNOLD, MATTHEW. "The Function of Criticism at the Present Time" (1864). In
Essays in Criticism: First Series. New York: Macmillan, 1893.

Arnold asserts that criticism should be "a disinterested endeavor to learn and
propagate the best that is known and thought in the world, and thus . . . establish
a current of fresh and true ideas." He further asserts that criticism should remain
aloof from social and religious issues and should aim "to see the object as in itself it
really is."

BLOOM, ALLAN. *The Closing of the American Mind*. New York: Simon & Schuster,
1987.

Although Bloom's critique focuses on higher education, it has galvanized
critics of the American educational system at all levels. Bloom argues that American intellectual and spiritual life is ebbing away while social insitutions mouth
platitudes.

BOOTH, WAYNE C. *The Rhetoric of Fiction*. Chicago: University of Chicago Press,
1961.

This book treats "technique as rhetoric" and analyzes rhetorical methods by
which the author of fiction controls the response of the reader. Especially useful
are the distinctions Booth suggests between "showing" and "telling," and the
discussion of different types of narrators.

BROOKS, CLEANTH, and ROBERT PENN WARREN. *Modern Rhetoric* (3d ed.). New
York: Harcourt, Brace & World, 1970.

An updating of classical rhetoric that attempts to teach students "to write well
. . . through the cultivation of an awareness of the underlying logical and psychological principles, an awareness to be developed in the double process of constantly analyzing specific examples and constantly trying to write against a background of principle."

——. *Understanding Poetry*. New York: Holt, 1938.

Brooks and Warren provide the most famous example of the application of
new-critical theories to the study of poetry.

CHRISTENSEN, FRANCIS. *Notes Toward a New Rhetoric*. New York: Harper & Row,
1967.

This book presents a modern rhetoric based upon a study of actual practices in contemporary American prose and concentrating on stylistic principles.

EAGLETON, TERRY. *Literary Theory.* Minneapolis: University of Minnesota Press, 1983.

The author provides a survey of contemporary critical theories, many of which have not yet had a noticeable impact on secondary English classrooms.

ELIOT, T. S. "Tradition and the Individual Talent." In *Selected Essays* (new ed.). New York: Harcourt, Brace, 1950.

This essay develops Eliot's "impersonal theory of poetry," which holds that "the poet has, not a 'personality' to express, but a particular medium, which is only a medium and not a personality, in which impressions and experiences combine in peculiar and unexpected ways."

FRYE, NORTHRUP. *The Anatomy of Criticism.* Princeton, N.J.: Princeton University Press, 1957.

Frye attempts to give "a comprehensive view of criticism" and to eliminate the "barriers" between the various methods of different critics.

HIRSCH, EDWARD D. *Cultural Literacy: What Every American Needs to Know.* Boston: Houghton Mifflin, 1987.

In *Cultural Literacy,* Hirsch claims that American schools are failing to impart a body of common knowledge that would mark citizens as literate. He traces the decline of public education; his arguments have subsequently captured the imagination of critics in government and industry.

MARTIN, HAROLD C., and RICHARD M. OHMANN. *The Logic and Rhetoric of Exposition* (rev. ed.). New York: Holt, Rinehart and Winston, 1963.

This book is a modern rhetoric, designed for use with advanced students.

OHMANN, RICHARD. *Politics of Letters.* Middletown, Conn.: Wesleyan University Press, 1987.

This series of essays explores the relationship of "literature" and literacy in a capitalistic, market-oriented society. How the literacy canon is formed and how it interacts with mass culture are some of the topics Ohmann takes up.

RICHARDS, I. A. *Practical Criticism.* New York: Harcourt, Brace & World, 1929.

This book, central to "new criticism," outlines a way of reading that focuses on texts themselves.

VAN GHENT, DOROTHY. *The English Novel: Form and Fiction.* New York: Harper & Row, 1961.

Van Ghent gives sensitive close readings of a number of novels; the techniques of analysis she uses can easily be applied to the reading of other fiction.

WELLEK, RENE, and AUSTIN WARREN, *The Theory of Literature.* New York: Harcourt, Brace, 1956.

Based on "new critical" theories, this book provides a rationale for reading literature from that perspective and raises important critical questions about literature.

WHITEHEAD, ALFRED NORTH. *The Aims of Education and Other Essays.* New York: Macmillan, 1959.

Whitehead discusses the cycles in the learning process and proposes a combination of freedom and discipline that best promotes learning.

5
Language as Development

"QUENTIN, THAT'S SOME HAT you have on," Rich says as his third-hour Language Arts students file into the room. Quentin, gangly for an eighth grader, chuckles as he saunters toward the cluster of desks in the back of the room. He knows that it's against school rules to wear hats in class. He whips off the bright orange Chicago Bears baseball cap and hangs it on the hook Mr. Chapin has installed for just that purpose. Even though it's only October, this interchange has become a ritual.

Kevin enters the room with less drama. He pauses at the door to ask Mr. Chapin for help with his social studies homework. "Can you stop by during lunch hour?" the teacher asks. When Julie comes in with a group of other girls, she shows Mr. Chapin the new book she's taken out from the library. "Hey, Mr. Chapin. I started reading Stephen King's *Different Seasons* last night."

"Oh yeah? Is that the collection of short stories?"

"Yeah. The one I was reading is called 'The Body.' It's the one they made the movie *Stand by Me* from."

"I think I saw it on HBO this summer."

After the bell rings, Rich continues to walk around the room, chatting with students for several more minutes. An experienced teacher with a master's degree in reading, <u>Rich believes that when he shows interest in his students' lives, he can use such personal connections to motivate them.</u> Snippets of conversations, anecdotes, and subject matter from these informal talks pepper the formal lessons, bridging the distance between students' prior knowledge and the new skills they are acquiring.

"Hey, guys. Listen up." Rich rallies student attention to the front of the room. He leans on the corner of his desk, looking to the blackboard where the day's lesson plan is neatly listed:

October 14—3rd Hour Language Arts

"Teens and Their Parents: Learning How to Talk"

Before you read:

Make your journal entry. From the title of the article, what do you think it will be about? How do you talk to your parents? What problems do you have talking to your parents? How could your talk be better?

While you read:

Make a list of the similarities and differences between your descriptions of parent-child talk and the article's descriptions. At the beginning of each page, stop and jot down the things you like about the article and the things you disagree with.

"Let's get out paper and pencils. We're going to read an article about the way parents and their children talk to each other today. I've got two things I want you to do before you read: Let's guess what kinds of information you might get from this article. Remember when we read the article about Ellis Island? We looked at the title and flipped through the text. We wanted to find out what we might learn by reading this article. Where was Ellis Island? Why was it an important place? What happened there? This time, we're going to read about teens and their parents. You are all becoming teens, you have a pretty good idea what it's like to talk to your parents or other adults. So, we're going to write about your ideas, then compare them with what we find in the article. Take about five minutes to write your responses in your journals, then we'll talk about what you've written."

Rich surveys the room. Everyone has settled in, heads bent over books, pencils scratching. Everyone, that is, but Quentin. Rich catches his

Predict

Journal

eye. "I don't know what I'm supposed to do, Mr. Chapin." Rich rolls his eyes. It's not the first time that Quentin has missed the directions. A good reader who scores well on the school's standardized tests, Quentin landed in Language Arts, the school district's euphemism for remedial English, because he spends most of his time daydreaming or fidgeting.

"Just read the directions on the board, Quentin," Rich sighs. He recognizes the pattern in Quentin's schoolwork: lots of potential and little motivation. Quentin requires different teacher strategies than most of the other students in this class. For instance, Julie, who suffers from petit mal epilepsy, needs to find ways to compensate for her occasional lapses of attention. She has yet to develop several key reading skills, especially retaining information and inferring from text. Rich has noticed that she is rather withdrawn, but he's not sure how much her recent transfer to the class has affected her behavior. Kevin, on the other hand, is not shy at all. In fact, he's quite eager to learn, joining discussions and answering questions at every available opportunity. He is probably the least proficient reader in the group. He seems to enjoy writing his own stories, but finds expository writing difficult. So far this year, Kevin has made little progress, despite after-school tutoring. Rich has decided to investigate Kevin's problems further by observing his tutoring sessions. In this way, Rich can observe closely how Kevin reads and writes, what patterns his errors take; and by interacting with Kevin he can get a sense of the strategies most likely to help him progress. Then, both he and the tutor can use these strategies in their respective teaching sessions.

Rich's careful, but informal, assessment of each student embodies his philosophy of teaching English. By gauging a student's repertoire of skills, he can tailor his instruction to individual needs. Rich believes that students develop more complex reading and writing skills sequentially, building upon past learning experiences. For learners who struggle with schoolwork, he believes that it is especially important that the goals of learning be made explicit. Posters listing steps of the writing process, strategies for reading textbooks, and study-skills checklists cover the bulletin boards in his room. His conversations with students also push them to examine their thinking processes directly.

Rich monitors closely the educational plans of his students, especially those placed in special programs. He frequently confers with the educational support staff—counselors, reading specialists, teacher-consultants—but believes that all students should remain in the general education program. His teaching responsibility extends to all students, regardless of their previous achievements, and he makes every effort to accommodate all the students in his classroom. His colleagues at Riley Middle School respect him, although they often wonder why such a talented teacher would choose to teach low-skilled and underachieving students.

Analysis of the Approach

Language-as-development classrooms embrace a theory of language learning consistent with cognitive and developmental psychology. Learning, from this perspective, proceeds through a progression of stages, from the simple to the complex. Students learn best when they build upon previously learned skills toward more advanced skills. For example, English teachers working from this perspective make sure students understand the literal interpretation of a text before taking up its figurative interpretation. They draw on students' past life experiences, reading experiences, or writing experiences, using questions to help students connect past and present activities. In moments of misunderstanding, the teacher compares previous experiences, showing students how they can apply what was learned before to this new reading or writing situation.

In the above scenario, we see Rich reminding students of the strategies they have used earlier. He encourages them to apply a similar reading strategy to a new story, but this time for a different purpose, to gain different skills or insights. He adopts these teaching methods because he, like other language-as-development teachers, believes that underlying our language abilities (which include reading and writing) are cognitive structures that can and should be taught directly. These structures can be generally described for all students, even though they are dynamic processes that individuals acquire and apply idiosyncratically.

According to cognitive theorists, children learn language by using it in a variety of situations. They are actively involved in its acquisition, by testing the implicit language rules they learn in interaction with others, by imitating what others say and do with language, and by expanding their repertoire of skills as their cognitive abilities develop. For example, as students are gradually exposed to more difficult and varied reading materials, they increase their vocabularies and their knowledge of sentence and rhetorical patterns.

Learning and development are intertwined; as students develop new cognitive abilities, they also acquire new language abilities. New language abilities in turn foster cognitive development, since students use language as a means of discovery. For example, language-as-development teachers often use questions to guide students' journal writing. Through these questions they help students sort out the meanings of a text.

Above all, language learning occurs in goal-oriented situations. The language learner is always trying to solve some problem with language: understand an event or a text, organize and remember new information, or complete some task. Box 5.1 outlines the essential elements of learning from the language-as-development perspective.

It may also be useful to describe the specific models of reading and

---

BOX 5.1
THE LANGUAGE-AS-DEVELOPMENT PERSPECTIVE

1. Learning is goal oriented.
2. Learning is linking new information to prior knowledge.
3. Learning is organizing information.
4. Learning is acquiring a repertoire of cognitive and metacognitive structures. *learning about how to learn.*
5. Learning occurs in phases yet is non-linear. *Recursive*
6. Learning is influenced by development. *Physical + mental*

—From Beau Fly Jones et al., eds., "Learning and Thinking," in *Strategic Teaching and Learning: Cognitive Instruction in the Content Areas* (Elmhurst, Ill.: North Central Regional Educational Laboratory, 1987), p. 4.

writing that the language-as-development perspective espouses. Generally speaking, developmental theorists see both reading and writing as composing processes. (See, for example, Flower and Hayes, and Baker and Brown in Suggested Reading at the end of this chapter.) Individuals engage in both activities to generate meaning, whether from a received text as in reading or in creating a text of one's own. Among language-as-development researchers, Linda Flower and John Hayes have laid out the most commonly accepted model of this composing process. According to their model, writers (and readers) follow a recursive path that includes the following types of activities:

1. *Planning:* In both reading and writing, students decide what the topic or assignment is about, who they are completing it for, and what they can bring to the task in the way of past experience or prior knowledge. In order to do this, they must generate ideas and set goals, thereby planning how they will complete the task.

2. *Translating:* Writers, as they decide what to write, continually translate these ideas into the words and phrases that will make up their compositions. Similarly, readers, using the graphic cues of the text, translate these cues into meaningful information: They imagine characters, picture settings, and make sense of events based on what appears in the text and their understanding of the terms and phrases a writer has used.

3. *Monitoring and revising:* Both readers and writers monitor their activities while they are enacting them. We have all experienced the feelings of misunderstanding or miscommunication as we read and write. These miscues lead us to reread and revise our writing or our com-

prehension of a passage. In an attempt to create meaning, we systematically check our interactions with texts.

All of these processes are contingent upon both the task environment—the assignment, the course, the teacher—and the learner—his or her prior experiences, motivations, and personal goals. It is also important to remember that learners do not follow these processes in a lockstep fashion. English teachers using this approach often model their own processes, showing students how they use context clues to determine a word meaning or how they compose an essay. For example, the teacher might show students samples of his or her own free-writing, explaining how to select specific ideas for further development. The teacher might also demonstrate revision strategies by putting a draft essay on an overhead projector and then having students observe the process. In this way, the language-as-development teacher can show how processes interact; rereading can and often does contribute to the creation of new ideas.

This model of composing relies on two strands of cognition: the actual strategies, skills, and knowledge readers and writers possess and the knowledge of how to use them in various contexts. Knowing how and when to apply specific strategies is called *metacognition,* and it is an essential part of effective learning in the language-as-development perspective. Researchers have identified six fundamental metacognitive strategies: *checking* the outcome of the problem, *planning* one's next move, *monitoring* the effectiveness of any attempted action, and *testing, revising,* and *evaluating* one's strategies for learning. (See Linda Baker and Ann L. Brown in Suggested Reading at the end of this chapter.) Note that these terms are in many ways similar to the terms used to describe the composing process outlined above, evidence of influence from cognitive theory.

Language-as-development teachers provide students with opportunities to practice these metacognitive skills in conjunction with the study of literature, writing, or other English tasks. For example, these teachers believe that it is not enough for students to possess a knowledge of various writing genres. Students must also be able to select specific genres for appropriate tasks or be able to adapt a genre to suit the occasion. Similarly, knowledge of grammatical rules will not help writers unless they can apply these rules in checking their own work. As a result, teaching in language-as-development classrooms involves teaching students to develop monitoring and evaluating strategies such as peer review, discussions of the methods others use while reading or writing, and development of flexibility in the use of strategies.

English teachers adopting this perspective encourage students' language learning by continually introducing them to new, more sophisticated opportunities to use language. A new genre of literature may be introduced by collecting samples of it from everyday sources. (See, for example, the unit on satire for high school students outlined later in this chapter.) Reading assignments often begin with prereading activities that ask students to list what they already know about the topic of the reading. Students may also be asked to examine their own learning: What new information have they acquired? How can they put new ideas or strategies into practice? Can they compose their own texts, like the ones they have studied? In all of these instances, the teacher begins with what students have already acquired, adding to it through the discovery of new ways to use language.

Language learning as a process of discovery has applications to the ways students learn in subject areas beyond English as well. Language use is seen as a rule-governed, intentional process, and each discipline possesses its own conventions that students must acquire in order to participate successfully in that discipline. Reading, writing, and talking about science is different from reading, writing, and talking about literature. Moreover, reading and writing are ways of learning more about any subject. According to this perspective, students need to be able to test out their responses to what they read by writing, making connections to their own lives and adding new information to what they had previously understood. Through writing, students can internalize what they are learning about as well as practice using the conventions of each discipline. Some schools have specific writing-across-the-curriculum programs, but individual English teachers can also work out arrangements with colleagues in other disciplines for cooperative or joint assignments.

More generally, schooling itself is viewed as a complex set of skills to be mastered or of problems to be solved. Teaching from this perspective thus tends to include instruction in study skills, critical-thinking skills, and problem-solving strategies. Students need to learn the differences between preparing for an essay test and preparing for a multiple-choice test. They also need to apply different strategies when they read their biology textbook and when they read *To Kill a Mockingbird*. Direct instruction in these skills helps students learn to learn the subject matter of schooling, and so becomes a part of the language-as-development curriculum.

Language-as-development teachers design a number of methods to help individual learners acquire the skills and strategies necessary to become effective in English classrooms: The emphasis on the individual is one of this perspective's important characteristics. The methods described below are geared toward the development of individual learners who come to class with varying abilities.

Language-as-development teachers make decisions about what skills or strategies should be taught on the basis of mistakes their students make. Analyzing student errors tells the teacher what skills or strategies students have yet to learn. These teachers see errors as diagnostic information rather than as evidence of sloth or stupidity; they assume that students would write grammatically correct sentences if they knew how. There are many tools available to language-as-development teachers to discover the nature of student error. Listening to the responses students make to a reading selection and observing the patterns of error in student texts help teachers identify what students need to learn. As these patterns emerge, teachers can design lessons to teach the skills students need. If students' written stories consistently reflect errors in punctuating dialogue, the teacher might develop a mini-lesson that would teach students how to punctuate dialogue correctly.

Language-as-development teachers also use patterns of error to work with individuals, setting specific goals with specific students. A teacher using this perspective might work with a student having trouble drawing conclusions from a text by explaining writers' uses of signal words, such as *therefore, consequently, as a result,* and so on. Using sample passages, the teacher might then model how a reader can use these signal phrases to locate conclusions within a text.

Consistent with the developmental orientation of this perspective, teachers expect that students will be able to complete some tasks with little difficulty but will need instruction to complete others. The instructional format used in this approach follows a step-by-step pattern usually called *scaffolded instruction:* modeling → guided practice → independent practice → feedback.

These two concepts, "modeling" and "scaffolding," are the central elements of language-as-development instruction. Teachers regularly model for students how a task is completed, then assist students, whenever needed, to complete the task themselves. For example, to teach students to revise their writing to make it more descriptive, a teacher might list sentences from students' texts on the board and then make revisions on a few of them by adding sensory details, such as colors, smells, or sounds. The students would then try to revise the rest of the sentences, experimenting with sensory details of their own. Another day, the same teacher might repeat this process, this time focusing on more descriptive actions. These lessons would also be applied to the compositions the students were working on and might form part of the criteria for evaluation of the students' papers.

Scaffolding is an instructional process similar to modeling, but in it the teacher's role is defined in greater detail. Based on the idea that students need assistance at first with new tasks, scaffolded instruction begins with modeling and ends with the gradual withdrawal of teacher support until students can complete the task on their own. One well-known example of scaffolded instruction is reciprocal teaching, a method developed by Annemarie Palincsar and Ann Brown. (See Box 5.2.) Designed to improve reading comprehension, it is a method where small groups of students focus on some specific reading strategies: summarizing, question generating, clarifying, and predicting. Initially the teacher plays his or her usual role, directing the activities of the students. Gradually the students take turns leading the reading groups, asking

---

BOX 5.2
RECIPROCAL TEACHING

---

1. The teacher introduces or reviews the text and the reading strategies to be learned:

   Summarizing: Identifying and paraphrasing the main idea;

   Question generating: Self-questioning about the text;

   Clarifying: Identifying and resolving problems in comprehending the text;

   Predicting: Hypothesizing about what will come next in the text on the basis of its structure and its content.

2. The students in the group discuss their predictions about the text and what they might learn through reading.

3. A student is selected to lead the discussion for the first segment of the text.

4. Students and teacher read the segment.

5. The leader asks a question to which others respond, summarizes and invites elaborations.

6. The group discuss any clarifications or difficulties encountered in the reading.

7. The group makes predictions about what will happen in the next segment of the text, and a new teacher is appointed.

8. While the teacher is initially responsible for modelling and retaining the dialogue, the students are encouraged to assume increasing responsibility each day of instruction.

—From "Metacognitive Strategy Instruction" by Annemarie Sullivan Palincsar, *Exceptional Children* 53(2)(1986):118–124. Copyright 1986 by The Council for Exceptional Children. Reprinted with permission.

other students to summarize the text, explain a passage, or predict what will happen next. The teacher provides individual student/teachers with assistance in leading the discussion as they need it. The purpose of such instruction is twofold: Students learn to use strategies to improve their reading comprehension, and they internalize strategies through their role as teacher. (For examples of classroom applications of reciprocal teaching, see Helfeldt and Henk in Suggested Reading at the end of this chapter.)

Instructional methods such as reciprocal teaching can be adapted for more advanced reading strategies. The language-as-development teacher might establish literature circles, small discussion groups that meet to analyze reading selections. At the beginning of the year, the teacher might give each group interpretive questions as models to increase the students' critical reading abilities. As the groups become more practiced in analyzing texts, they can also begin to shape discussion questions of their own. The point is not so much the nature of the activity as it is the sequence of the learning. In language-as-development classrooms, teachers use their greater experience as a model for their students, coaching the students in the strategies of successful learners.

English teachers adopting a language-as-development perspective have also developed a number of strategies to help students learn metacognitive strategies. Planning and brainstorming activities to enhance students' reading and writing proficiency lend themselves well to the English classroom. To begin reading a new text or writing a new essay, students need opportunities to decide the purposes of their activities and to plan their own strategies. Teachers can use a variety of techniques: generating lists of ideas or concepts on the board related to the topic, listing prereading questions to guide students' reading, and free-writing about the topic all help students understand what they will be doing and why they are doing it. (See Box 5.3 for general principles for directed reading activities.)

Throughout the composing process (which includes both reading and writing), language-as-development teachers instruct students in metacognitive strategies. "Mapping" and "clustering" are two teaching methods that these teachers use to help students comprehend what they are reading. Mapping a story presents students with a visual picture of a story's structure. It can take the form of a chart, diagram, or picture that describes both events and the connections between them. (See Box 5.4 for an example.) Clustering most commonly takes the form of a collage where students generate all the significant information they have gathered from a text on the board; gathering this information helps students form an impression of the work as a whole, and elements can then be grouped into selected topics or compared and contrasted with each other. (See Box 5.5.) These two activities make the process of reading more concrete; students can use the visual diagrams to make connections and inferences about relationships between elements in the text.

Teaching the writing process in language-as-development classrooms follows similar lines. Teachers use a variety of techniques to teach each of the steps in the process. Brainstorming and free-writing have already been mentioned. Directed peer review, where students read each other's texts for specific traits, is another. In this procedure, the teacher identifies specific grammatical, structural, or content items that students use to evaluate and respond to other students' papers. The items chosen for evaluation are generally consistent with the genre or grammatical concepts taught in previous lessons.

One method of teaching grammar—sentence combining—deserves mention because it is so closely affiliated with developmental language learning. Sentence combining introduces students to complex sentence patterns by demonstrating the ways simple sentences are combined to make more complex ones. For example, the three sentences below can be combined into one sentence using a relative clause and noun modification:

BOX 5.3
DIRECTED READING ACTIVITY: GENERAL PRINCIPLES

1. Sequenced tasks: One activity should build upon another. Free-writing or brainstorming helps activate students' prior knowledge, which will then be used as the basis for making inferences as students read.

2. Teacher- or student-defined goals: Students should have some purpose for their reading; for example, looking for images and finding their patterns, acquiring new information about a topic, detecting rhetorical devices and their uses.

3. Open-ended responses: Students should be encouraged to generate their own creative responses to a text. The responses should lead to more than just identifying information; they should also lead to interpreting the significance of information in the text.

4. Preparation for a final project: Reading and writing activities should build toward some project that synthesizes and integrates strategies and content.

5. Systematic use of inference strategies: Instruction should push students beyond the literal interpretation of a text toward evaluations and judgments based on connections students make about events or characters.

6. Tasks organized according to text structures: Because texts are used as models of genres, attention to the specific structures making up a genre should also be included in instructional activities.

7. Reviewing and self-monitoring: Students should frequently review what they have done and what they have learned from the activities. Throughout their learning, they should also be encouraged to take notice of their difficulties.

8. Relating knowledge, attitudes, and experience to the text: Students can use their own past experiences to help them understand and respond to the reading. Similarities and differences between the characters in a text and the students' own experiences are a rich source for understanding individual responses to literature.

9. Built-in examples: Modeling is based on examples of a strategy in use. In discussions, teachers can and should draw on ready-made examples, highlighting student use of strategies.

10. Collaborative efforts: Group work helps students learn by example from their peers. It also provides more opportunity for individuals to share insights and successful methods.

11. Variations according to different expectations for different students' abilities: This can take the form of variations in assignments. However, teachers should be cautious about overrestricting the learning opportunities of less able students.

—Adapted from Richard Beach, "Strategic Teaching in Literature," in Beau Fly Jones et al., eds., *Strategic Teaching and Learning: Cognitive Instruction in the Content Areas* (Oak Brook, Ill.: North Central Regional Educational Laboratory, 1987), pp. 146–7.

BOX 5.4
MAPPING "THE TELL-TALE HEART"

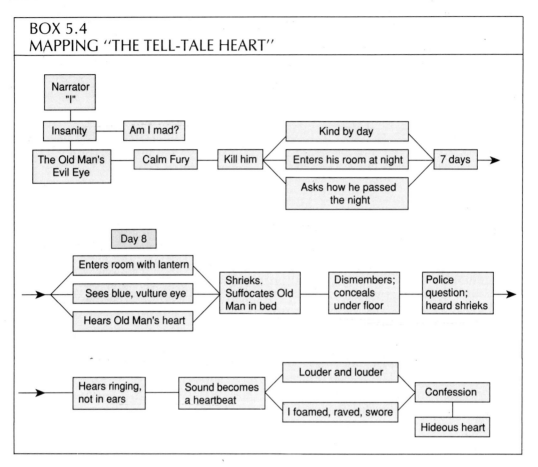

1. Jan is a restaurant manager.
2. She works a regular schedule.
3. The schedule is from 5 to midnight.

Sentence combining yields: Jan is a restaurant manager who works a regular 5-to-midnight schedule.

Beginning with simple patterns using conjunctions, adjectives, or adverbs, sentence-combining instruction moves through various syntactic options. Language-as-development teachers usually provide students with opportunities to use these patterns in their own writing. Oftentimes, they introduce specific patterns in conjunction with texts that students are

BOX 5.5
A CLUSTERING STRATEGY WITH *CATCHER IN THE RYE*

Piano player   Stradlater   coat + gloves   "fuck you"   Biltmore
Sally Haye's Christmas tree   taxis   Grey hair   morrow's mother   Mr. Antolini
Little Shirley Beans   Grand Central Station   James Castle   bodies   Showercurtain
hunting hat   Too good   "it made me depressed"   Calling Jane   -Kings in back
intellectual   broken hand   Pencey   scotch + soda   Perverts   Ed Banky
types   "God damn"   coke   Sunny   Phoebe - PJs   Ackley
museum   morons   suitcases   Girls   D.B.   Loneliness   Movies   not in the mood
impotence   carousel   crazy   Yellow   Phony   You   Deaf mute   Stinking Drunk

"Boy"   THE CATCHER IN THE RYE   affluence

cigarettes   Peter Pan   Allie   "bastard"   bullets   boring
"One thing I can't stand is.."   baseball   "so what I would do, I would.."   cowardice
good luck   "that killed me"   Central Park ducks   Cobin teachees   leaving
"that really annoys me"   digression   iceskating   Crumby   Fear of change
very sexy   "very, very big deal"   Old man Spence's   Psychotic introversion
Chronic liar   dancing   "a minor"   in rebellion   Knotty chest + nose   picking + bed   death
messages   corny   Ivy League   leaning   exaggeration   "if you want the truth"
zoo   Prince   "giving her the time"   secret goldfish   "Grow up"
"he was the type of guy that would"   grand
repetition   Holden   madman   "you would have liked him…"

---

reading, using the authors' sentence patterns as models for students to imitate. (See Box 5.6.)

Instructional practices such as sentence combining draw upon modeling to help students become sensitive to the structures of language. The language-as-development perspective takes the view that students need to be introduced systematically to such structures and to the processes by which we learn to apply them. Teachers using this approach see their role as that of assessor and guide, identifying what students need to learn, providing them with appropriate models, and scaffolding instruction to ensure they can use them independently.

BOX 5.6
SENTENCE COMBINING

A language-as-development teacher might use a sentence like the one that follows (from Mildred Taylor's *Roll of Thunder, Hear My Cry*) to teach students a new sentence pattern:

Papa sat on a bench in the barn, his broken leg awkwardly stretched before him, mending one of Jack's harnesses.

The teacher (with the help of students) would extract the simple sentences embedded in the longer one:

Papa sat on a bench in the barn.

His broken leg was awkwardly stretched before him.
He was mending one of Jack's harnesses.

Then students might use these sentences as a model to create their own long one:

Mary walked to the store.
Her eyes were focused on the ground.
She was eating an apple.

Sentence combining gives:

Mary walked to the store, eating an apple, her eyes focused on the ground.

Potentials and Limitations of the Approach

Potentials

1. *It assumes that all students can learn.* More than any other approach, the language-as-development perspective contends that, given enough time and adequate instruction, all students can learn to succeed in school.

2. *It accepts the developmental stage of the learner.* Teachers working from a language-as-development approach attribute students' difficulties in school to the lack of skill or experience, not to the lack of innate capacity. They target the current proficiencies of the students, then attempt to build on students' strengths to help them acquire necessary academic skills.

3. *It makes learning strategies explicit.* Teachers using a language-as-development approach do not expect that students will necessarily understand learning processes unless these processes become a subject for classroom discussion. These teachers believe that metacognitive strategies such as self-testing and monitoring comprehension can and should be taught as a part of the English curriculum.

4. *It promotes successful imitation by students.* Modeling is the foundation of a developmental theory of language. To learn to write a new type of paragraph students need to see many, many examples and even watch a more experienced writer attempt the same task. By watching a teacher solve a reading or writing problem, students acquire valuable clues they can use to solve similar problems on their own.

Limitations

1. *Its view of sequencing is too often rigid and excessively linear.* Recent criticisms of developmental theory have pointed out the fuzzy boundaries between developmental stages. Students learn in fits and starts, not always obeying a strict sequence or a smooth progression. Similarly, complex cognitive tasks like reading and writing are often grossly oversimplified by developmental models. These tasks are more recursive and organic than evenly sequential.

2. *Strategies are too often isolated from content.* Developmental exercises such as prereading questions and sentence combining do not necessarily transfer to other academic and real-world situations. Instructional packages designed to teach critical-thinking skills frequently lack adequate references to the subject matter; learning to find the main idea in isolated paragraphs may not help students discover the themes of a novel.   *will use in curriculum not in addition to*

3. *It privileges the literal over the interpretive.* The emphasis on specific skills and teachable strategies tends to limit the focus to the details of a text, ignoring the larger conceptual or thematic issues. Testing and perpetual assessment rely on easily measurable aspects of reading or writing that appear to be objective. By contrast, reader response, critical analysis, and creative writing do not lend themselves to objective measurement and are frequently omitted from the curriculum in language-as-development classrooms.

4. *It privileges reading over writing.* The language-as-development approach has its roots in remedial and compensatory education. Because of governmental and institutional concerns for functional literacy, more resources have been directed toward reading instruction than toward instruction in writing. (But as definitions of literacy are broadened to include writing, the role of writing in language-as-development classrooms will increase.)   *every student lacks some skill. why not approach higher level classes w/ practical methods to make learning easier*

5. *It is apolitical and nonaesthetic.* This approach fails to acknowledge the political forces that influence the way students get labeled, texts are ordered, and tests are administered to define students' abilities. It is naive to believe that all students can succeed merely with enough effort and good instructional programs in spite of poverty, discrimination, and educational inequity. Teachers who adopt the language-as-

I intend to make writing a central focus of my classroom.

So we shouldn't try?

Just because they've come this far w/o them, dosn't mean they can't use them to become even better learners.

development approach may also accept texts uncritically. Since they see themselves as teachers of strategy, it makes little difference to them to which text the strategies are applied or whether students enjoy the reading. *entirely teacher attitude.*

not appropriate criticism for a method?

IMPLEMENTATION:
TEACHING JOAN BLOS'S *A GATHERING OF DAYS* IN THE SEVENTH GRADE

The unit that follows emphasizes three important aspects of teaching from a language-as-development perspective. First, it demonstrates to students the need for background information specific to the reading. Second, it relies on modeling, both teacher- and text-centered, to introduce students to the diary as a genre of writing. Third, it asks students to predict, on the basis of their prior knowledge and their own experiences in writing diaries, the events of the text as a way of learning about text structure. The unit focuses on historical knowledge, both early American and contemporary, introducing students to the notion that words have histories, too. It is not very likely that most students will have firsthand experience of sugaring or even of weaving. Teaching them about the customs of early America lays a foundation for their understanding of the text.

The language-as-development approach also frequently makes use of young-adult literature, because it focuses on the students' developmental levels. These books and stories are written specifically for a teenage audience, taking up issues of interest to adolescents. There are a number of young-adult novels set in historical periods suitable for this unit. In fact, it would be possible to alter this teaching unit to allow students to select their own books to read and research. Teachers can also make use of the many reference books that list titles by subject and that usually provide plot summaries. (See Resources for this teaching plan.)

Desired Student Outcomes:

Increased knowledge of early American history, especially terms, phrases, and customs that have since disappeared, or that the students have not encountered themselves

Greater skills in predicting events and in applying prior knowledge to reading

Increased vocabulary through historical research

Development of questioning techniques to set purposes for reading

Comparison of the students' experiences with the characters' experiences

Using the text as a model, creation of a diary-story of one's own

Possible Whole-Class Activities:

Read *A Gathering of Days* by Joan Blos.

Participate in classroom discussions.

Possible Small-Group Activities:

Prepare and present group projects.

Participate in peer-review groups.

Possible Individual Activities:

Keep a double-entry journal.

Keep a personal diary.

Write a diary-story.

Compare early American and contemporary American dictionaries.

Resources:

Berger, Allen, and H. Alan Robinson, eds. *Secondary School Reading.* Urbana, Ill.: ERIC and NCTE, 1982. (See especially Chapter 7, "Learning from Text," and Chapter 8, "Assessment: Responses to Literature.")

Blos, Joan. *A Gathering of Days.* New York: Aladdin, 1979.

Broderick, Dorothy M., ed. *The Voya Reader.* Metuchen, N.J.: Scarecrow Press, 1990.

Davis, James E., and Hazel K. Davis. *Your Reading: A Book List for Junior High and High School Students,* 7th ed. Urbana Ill.: NCTE, 1988.

Gillespie, Joanne S. "The Life of a Seventh Grader: Writing a Memoir." *English Journal* 80 (1991):48–51.

——. "Reliving the Depression: Integrating English and Social Studies." *English Journal* 79 (1991):64–8.

Miller, Suzanne. "Planning for Spontaneity: Supporting the Language of Thinking." *English Journal* 80 (1991):51–6.

Paris, Scott G., Marjorie Y. Lipson, and Karen K. Wixson. "Becoming a Strategic Reader." *Contemporary Educational Psychology* 8 (1983):293–316.

Peterson, Bruce T., and Jill N. Burkland. "Investigative Reading and Writing: Responding to Reading with Research." *College Composition and Communication* 37 (1986):236–40.

Organization of the Unit:

Week 1

The first week serves primarily as an introduction to the texts, activities, and skills students will learn. The teacher explains to the students that they will be reading *A Gathering of Days* by Joan Blos, that it is the fictional diary of a 13-year-old girl who lived during the 1830s, and that they will also explore the history of that period in order to better understand the story.

To elicit from students what they already know about early American life, the teacher has several options. Students might free-write about the time period: What do you think life was like in the 1830s? How did people get around? What did they do for fun and entertainment? How did a family make its living? What was school like? The teacher could also collect period pictures, asking students to describe what the pictures tell them about early American life.

This perspective works to build upon student knowledge, expanding and increasing it. Seventh graders' understanding of history, even their own national history, will be incomplete. Using the resources of the school library, students can work in small groups to prepare class presentations on a variety of topics: transportation, schooling, clothing, work, family life, religious practices, and pastimes, for example. The teacher should consult with the school librarian so that historical texts and encyclopedias are made easily available to students. This kind of small-group project generally spans more than a single week, but can be started during the first week of the unit. Generally speaking, students complete such projects prior to reading, since the projects themselves are intended to increase the store of knowledge students bring to the text.

The teacher also starts students writing their own diaries during the first week. Because the students will use their diaries as the basis of their own creative writing, they need to have ample time to generate material from which they will draw. Again, the teacher might ask students if they already keep diaries, what they might want to write about in a diary, and why people like to keep diaries. It might be interesting to explain that much of our knowledge of history comes from individuals' diaries that have been preserved.

Week 2

The second week of the unit is spent working on small-group projects. The teacher might provide suggestions about working in small groups and about designating tasks and might give instructions in note-taking skills and in presentation formats. The specific skills presented will depend largely on the collaborative work or library research students have previously done. Toward the end of the week, student groups will give their presentations. Middle school students have frequently not had much experience working in groups, so issues like dividing tasks, setting group and individual goals, and achieving cooperation will occupy much of the teacher's time during the week.

Each of the group presentations will provide opportunities for vocabulary development. As the students explain the facets of early American life, they will also introduce the specialized vocabulary relevant to the period. Presentations about transportation will likely introduce students to terms such as *hansom* and *tram*; reports about farming will likely introduce terms such as *thrasher* and *scythe*. The teacher might have students list the new words and their definitions in their journals, creating a dictionary of early American terms, categorizing the terms according to the topics (farming, transportation, clothing, for example) they describe.

Week 3

In preparation for reading *A Gathering of Days*, this week starts with sharing from individual students' diaries. Volunteers read excerpts from their writing, paying special attention to the vocabulary that identifies the historical period for the listener (or reader). Alongside their early American dictionary, the students begin a dictionary of contemporary terms— words, phrases, activities that are specifically associated with their own lifetimes, such as CD, videogame, and microwave.

By way of beginning, the teacher might ask the students to read the letter that opens the book. (See Box 5.7). Who is writing the letter? Why is she writing it? What do you learn about the writer from the letter? What do you think the rest of the book will tell us? These questions guide students' reading by helping them establish a frame of reference for the book and setting a purpose for their reading. Prediction, guessing what will come later in the text, is an important aspect of reading comprehension in the language-as-development perspective. Throughout the reading, students will be asked again and again to predict what will happen next on the basis of what they have read so far. This strategy also helps students focus on the relationships between events in a story.

The teacher should give students regular reading assignments. This week they might read the first six chapters. While reading, they will keep a double-entry journal. One entry should respond to the text, telling how they feel about characters and what happens to them, what impressions they have of the book, and/or how their life experiences are similar to or different from the characters' experiences. The other entry is used to note historical references: new vocabulary and new things they learn about early American life. The teacher might give students time to read during class, while assigning further reading and journal writing as homework. Classroom discussion will draw on the students' predictions about the text, students' responses to the text, and their historical observations. The teacher might also set aside class time to troubleshoot any difficulties students are having with the reading.

Week 4

The students continue to read *A Gathering of Days*. This week the teacher might set out specific questions for students to answer as they are reading:

1. What things does Catherine tell us about? What does she report to her readers?

2. How do the things she writes about compare with your own diaries? Are there any similarities? What are the differences?

BOX 5.7
OPENING OF *A GATHERING OF DAYS*

Providence, Rhode Island
November 20, 1899

To my namesake, Catherine:

I give you this book on your fourteenth birthday, as I turned fourteen the year of the journal; the year that was also my last on the farm tho' I did not know it then. It was also the year that my father remarried, and my best friend, Cassie, died. Cassie lives in my memory still, of all of us the only one never to grow old.

Once I might have wished for that: never to grow old. But now I know that to stay young always is also not to change. And that is what life's all about—changes going on every minute, and you never know when something begins where it's going to take you.

So one thing I want to say about life is don't be scared and don't hang back, and most of all, don't waste it.

Your loving great-grandmother,
Catherine Hall Onesti

—From Joan Blos, *A Gathering of Days* (New York: Aladdin Books, 1979), p. 3. Reprinted with permission of Charles Scribner's Sons, an imprint of Macmillan Publishing Company from *A Gathering of Days* by Joan Blos. Copyright © 1979 by Joan W. Blos.

These questions should stimulate response entries in the students' journals. During class discussions, students might read from both the book and their own diaries, illustrating the similarities and differences they have discovered.

A second activity this week could deal with historical information and how it helps readers better understand the text. Students should search the text during their reading for items they have learned about through their own historical research, items they did not know before. In addition, they could explore the ways that writing their own diaries has shaped their predictions about the text. For example, have they looked for resolutions to events that appeared in earlier entries? Have they seen why entries contain the record of several events? What do diaries tell us about characters' lives? Are events always connected to each other? Why do we choose to record some daily events, but not others? Why isn't every day recorded in a diary? These questions will serve to enhance the students' understanding of story structure as well as to anticipate the writing project they will begin the next week.

Week 5

Students will finish reading the book this week and begin their own writing projects, modeled on the text. Classroom discussion might center on the themes that have emerged from both reading and journal writing. From the diaries they have been keeping throughout the unit, students might construct their own stories, selecting and revising journal entries. They can review their journals in order to devise a writing plan. This plan, shared in small groups, should define the themes they see in their diaries, which then shape their revisions. The students might work on their drafts, participating in peer-review groups whose primary tasks would include examining theme development, historical references, and realism. (Does the diary seem to portray events accurately?) Final drafts are then handed in to conclude the unit.

Evaluation:

The teacher can evaluate students on the following activities:

Small-group presentations. All students in the group should receive the same grade, which is to be based on the thoroughness, clarity, and organization of their presentation.

Double-entry journals. Students should receive grades for each entry category. The journal, which the teacher will check periodically during the reading, should provide the teacher with evidence that the student has, indeed, completed the reading assignments, as well as indicate the student's comprehension (or lack of comprehension).

Daily entries in the personal diaries. Students may request that the teacher not read every entry, since they may choose to record personal information, but they must also provide evidence that they have completed all entries.

The early American and contemporary American dictionaries.

Peer review. Students' assistance to their peers in the form of constructive criticism or suggestions is important to the development of critical-thinking skills. As such, it is also an important aspect of students' performance.

Completed diary-stories, including drafts. The teacher should look specifically for attempts to incorporate historical references as well as for the development of themes.

IMPLEMENTATION:
TEACHING SATIRE IN HIGH SCHOOL

Desired Student Outcomes:

Identification of specific qualities and strategies of satire

Application of strategies satirists use in the students' own satirical writings and drawings

Reading and understanding of a range of satirical texts, including cartoons, films, novels, and short prose works

Identification of aspects of the students' own worlds that are worthy of satire

Ability to think critically and to reflect upon that thinking process

Possible Whole-Class Activities:

View clips from *Saturday Night Live, The Simpsons,* or a Monty Python work, discussing the meaning of satire and ways to satirize a subject.

Brainstorm subjects in students' lives that would make for good satire.

Discuss satirical techniques in *Mad* magazine and other parody magazines such as *National Lampoon* and *Dogue.*

View satirical film. Many titles are available (see Resources); all contain elements of satire. The choice would depend on school guidelines and student viewing habits.

Read Swift's "A Modest Proposal" aloud and discuss the subject of its satire, exploring techniques the writer used to create his ironic tone.

Discuss the satirization of human behavior in *The Mouse That Roared* and/or *Animal Farm.*

Discuss the satirization of political situations (nuclear proliferation, power mongering) in *The Mouse That Roared* or *Animal Farm.*

Dr. Seuse – for a shorter work – Bitterbutterbattle (neuclear war)
Shel Silverstein poems — some are satirical.

Possible Small-Group Activities:

Discuss sample political/satirical cartoons, pooling knowledge about current events.

Write and act out satirical skits (à la *Saturday Night Live*).

Discuss and evaluate the process of writing the skit: How did you settle on your idea? How was the work divided? What were the strengths and weaknesses in your group's skit?

Search for descriptions of, chunks of dialogue from, and other characters' reactions to an assigned character from *The Mouse That Roared* or *Animal Farm.*

Prepare for an essay exam on the satire unit, predicting exam questions and searching for possible answers.

Possible Individual Activities:

> Write a rough draft of an analysis of a political cartoon.
>
> Revise the analysis in response to teacher or small-group critique.
>
> Design a satirical cartoon; revise it, taking peer suggestions into consideration.
>
> Read chapter assignments in the assigned novel.
>
> Write an essay exam.

Resources:

Orwell, George. *Animal Farm.* New York: New American Library, 1954.
Satirical film (for example, *Airplane, Being There, Brazil, Caddyshack, Gremlins, The Naked Gun, Who's Harry Crumb?, Young Frankenstein*
Satirical magazines (for example, *Dogue, Mad, National Lampoon*)
Saturday Night Live (TV series)
The Simpsons (TV series)
Swift, Jonathan. "A Modest Proposal."
Wibberley, Leon. *The Mouse That Roared.* Boston: Little, Brown, 1955.

Organization of the Unit:

The genre of satire is an appropriate though potentially controversial subject of study for high school students. Although students are immersed in satirical entertainment options, they find written satirical texts to be challenging, in part because the detection of tone requires rather sophisticated reading skills. Teachers can use satire's humorous appeal to motivate students to think deeply and critically. However, new teachers would be wise to choose materials and texts for this unit in collaboration with experienced teachers who are familiar with community attitudes. In addition, students must understand the difference between satirical humor and sheer vindictiveness as they construct their own sketches and cartoons.

Week 1

Teachers working out of a language-as-development approach would generally begin a unit by tapping students' prior knowledge or by taking an angle on material that renders it relevant to students' lives. *Mad* magazine, *Saturday Night Live,* or other politically motivated comedy is familiar territory for most high school students. By teasing out comedic aspects of familiar texts, the class could begin to construct a definition of satire. The first class session or two could include the viewing of several satirical television sketches and a discussion of students' understandings of satire.

Students might then be asked to bring in satirical cartoons they find in magazines or newspapers. Cartoons, which are slightly less familiar to students, could first be analyzed through small-group discussion. The teacher could ask students to reflect upon the processes they used to "read" the cartoons. Students should begin to understand the need for at least a cursory knowledge of the satirized subject. Once students feel fairly comfortable with the oral analysis of cartoons, the teacher could ask them to attempt a written analysis of a cartoon on their own or to base a written analysis upon their group's discussion.

The language-as-development teacher would feel comfortable asking students to create their own satirical cartoons, based on their own school or home experiences. He or she would hold that the task draws upon visual and aesthetic abilities while requiring analysis and language skills. In addition, the planning, drafting, and revising students do while creating cartoons parallels the process they go through when writing; by reflecting on the similarities and differences, students can gain a greater understanding of creative acts.

During the first week of the satire unit, the teacher would likely choose to have students begin reading a satirical novel such as *Animal Farm* or *The Mouse That Roared*. The teacher should anticipate students' difficulties with the texts. For instance, many students have trouble tolerating the confusion and uncertainty they feel when beginning a novel; by discussing this problem and strategies to address it, the teacher can help students begin to work out ways to read beginnings. Also, while relatively few high school students would have difficulty following the plot of the suggested novels, many would have trouble detecting tone and understanding narrators' intrusions. Those places could be looked at closely over the course of the unit.

Week 2

Students would continue reading the novel. Early in the process, it might be helpful to divide the class into small groups and assign a character to each group. Group members could scan chapters for description and dialogue connected with their character, then begin to make inferences about the character's nature and purpose in the novel. Observations and inferences could be shared with the class as a whole.

Once students are progressing with the reading, daily discussion of the novel can be supplemented with other activities. Collaborative satirical sketches generate strong student interest and utilize abilities that are sometimes ignored in the English classroom—dramatic abilities and social skills. A classwide brainstorming session about topics for skits may facilitate students' writing in small groups. Students should be encouraged or required to perform their sketches for other class members. Again, the links between the collaborative writing process and other creative processes should be explicitly discussed.

Week 3

The third week of the satire unit may concentrate on high-level discussions of the novel(s). In large- or small-group discussions, students could talk about aspects of human nature and the larger society being satirized in the text(s). Supplementary newspaper articles and essays on the same issues could be introduced to class members. In addition, the teacher could ask students to reflect on satire's social uses.

During the third week, it might be appropriate to introduce a brief text that students might find especially challenging—Swift's "A Modest Proposal" meets that criterion. By modeling the process of making meaning from a complex, seemingly remote text, the teacher can show students how to approach other such texts in the future.

Students might begin to note differences in sophistication between various satirical works. They might notice that various levels of prior knowledge are required, depending on the writer's intent and audience.
Week 4
The structure of the fourth week depends on the students' progress with previous tasks. Students might view a satirical film (preferably one that challenges and amuses them) during this week. Also, class time might be spent in preparation for an essay exam. Students working in small groups could begin to outline themes and patterns, then transform them into appropriate essay questions.

Evaluation:

Students would submit for evaluation a written version of their group's skit and the exam questions from their group discussions. Although all students in a group would be generally assigned the same grade, the teacher would want to monitor an individual student's participation in group work. Students would be individually evaluated on their cartoon analysis and the revisions they make, their original cartoons, and the essay exam covering the readings. Throughout the unit, the teacher should have ample opportunity to assess individual progress by having students submit their drafts, by working with small groups as they prepare their skits, and by monitoring participation in discussions of the reading.

Suggested Reading

BAKER, LINDA, and ANN L. BROWN. "Metacognitive Skills and Reading." In P. David Pearson, ed. *The Handbook of Reading Research.* London: Longmans, 1985.

The authors discuss the relationship between metacognition and reading. They distinguish between reading for meaning (comprehension) and reading for remembering (study skills). In both cases research findings and instructional strategies are presented.

BRUNER, JEROME. *The Process of Education.* Cambridge, Mass.: Harvard University Press, 1960.

Growing out of the Woods Hole Conference (1969) of scholars from many different disciplines, this book presents views about the processes of learning and the nature and sequence of a curriculum that are applicable to all subjects.

———. *The Relevance of Education.* New York: Norton, 1973.

Bruner considers the tension in education between the need to teach traditional skills and at the same time to consider subject matter that is directly relevant to students' lives and interests.

———. *Toward a Theory of Instruction.* Cambridge, Mass.: Harvard University Press, 1966.

This text implements the educational theory put forth in *The Process of Education* by translating it into examples of curricular strategies and units in various fields, including English.

FLOWER, LINDA. *Problem-Solving Strategies for Writers.* New York: Harcourt Brace Jovanovich, 1981.

Flower presents a step-by-step description of the writing process as characterized by cognitive researchers, including suggestions, tips, and ideas for each phase of the process.

FLOWER, LINDA, and JOHN R. HAYES. "The Dynamics of Composing: Making Plans and Juggling Constraints." In L. W. Gregg and E. R. Steinberg, eds., *Cognitive Processes in Writing.* Hillsdale, N.J.: Lawrence Erlbaum Associates, 1980.

This chapter outlines the Flower and Hayes model of the writing process.

GOODMAN, KENNETH, ed. *Miscue Analysis: Applications to Reading Instruction.* Urbana, Ill.: NCTE, 1973.

This volume provides teachers with descriptions of miscue analysis, the kinds of information it yields, and its applications for the classroom.

GOODMAN, MARSHA, and JIM HAHN, eds. *Visions and Re-visions.* Davis, Calif.: University of California—Davis.

A journal published three times a year by the University of California—Davis Department of University and School Programs, this publication contains first-person teacher-research articles, examines classroom-based research and current theories of writing and writing instruction, and applies these theories to classroom practice.

HELFELDT, JOHN P., and WILLIAM A. HENK. "Reciprocal Question-Answer Relationships: An Instructional Technique for At-Risk Readers." *Journal of Reading* (April 1990): 509–14.

This article describes practical applications growing out of Palincsar and Brown's work with reciprocal teaching. Although they are geared for at-risk students, the strategies could be applied to other students as well.

JONES, BEAU FLY, ANNEMARIE PALINCSAR, DONNA SEDERBURG OGLE, EILEEN GLYNN CARR, eds. *Strategic Teaching and Learning: Cognitive Instruction in the Content Areas.* Elmhurst, Ill.: North Central Regional Educational Laboratory, 1987.

This text describes cognitive and metacognitive theories of learning as well as their applications in various content area classrooms.

SHAUGHNESSY, MINA. *Errors and Expectations: A Guide for the Teacher of Basic Writing.* New York: Oxford University Press, 1977.

Originally published for teachers of college writing, *Errors and Expectations* provides a thorough examination of the various kinds of errors beginning writers make. It is a sympathetic text, viewing error as diagnostic.

6

Language as Expression

THE STUDENTS FILING INTO Amy Slavak's third-period sopho-more English class push the movable desks into an irregular circle before they sit down. The previous class has left desks scattered in clusters throughout the room, and before they leave at the end of the hour, the third-period sophomores will also have pushed their desks together. But at the beginning of the hour they want to be able to see everyone in the class. Amy's desk is pushed against the back wall, and it is covered with the folders that help Amy keep her classes organized. As the students move desks, she moves among them asking one about the status of a rough draft, checking on the reading log of a second, and handing a paper to another.

A bookshelf filled with paperbacks stands in one corner, and a piece of carpet covered with cushions sits in the other. Several bulletin boards are filled with collages made by the students, and on one side of the room there is a large piece of blank paper with the heading "Found Poems." Roger takes a felt marker and writes a found poem on the paper:

> Girls Just Want
> Time After Time
> All Through the Night
> Primitive

Several of the other students watch him write, smiling with recognition as they see how he has transformed the titles of Cindy Lauper's songs into a poem.

Students choose much of their own reading in Amy's class. They select books from the shelves in the classroom, or they borrow from the school library, or they buy their own paperbacks. At the beginning of each marking period Amy announces a theme, and she encourages students to read texts that deal with this theme. This term's theme is "Growing Up," and the list of recommended texts includes some excellent titles:

Charles Dickens, *Great Expectations*

Charlotte Bronte, *Jane Eyre*

Mark Twain, *The Adventures of Huckleberry Finn*

Ernest Hemingway, *The Nick Adams Stories*

Anne Frank, *The Diary of a Young Girl*

Langston Hughes, *Not Without Laughter*

John Knowles, *A Separate Peace*

Alexei Panshin, *Rite of Passage*

William Golding, *Lord of the Flies*

Maya Angelou, *I Know Why the Caged Bird Sings*

J. D. Salinger, *Catcher in the Rye*

Jamake Highwater, *Legend Days*

William Demby, *Beetle Creek*

Yukio Mishima, *The Sound of Waves*

Richard Rodriguez, *Hunger of Memory*

Toni Morrison, *The Bluest Eye*

James Baldwin, *Go Tell It on the Mountain*

Paule Marshall, *Brown Girl, Brownstones*

Frank Conroy, *Stop-Time*

Dylan Thomas, *Quite Early One Morning*

Susan Allen Toth, *Blooming: A Small-Town Girlhood*

Russell Baker, *Growing Up*

Tobias Wolff, *This Boy's Life*

A member of NCTE, Amy regularly purchases copies of *Books for You* (see Suggested Reading at the end of this chapter) to learn about new books that may interest her students. In cases where Amy feels that some element of the book may concern parents, she uses a form to request parental permission for students to read the book. (See Box 6.1.)

Students may also propose books for Amy's approval; this gives her one way of adding to her list from year to year. Each student is required to read three books during the ten-week term, and students may read more for extra credit. They also have the option of watching a movie or play that fits with the theme and writing about that. Among the films students have chosen this term are *Stand by Me* and *Ferris Bueller's Day Off* and film versions of *Jane Eyre, The Adventures of Huckleberry Finn, Our Town, The Learning Tree, Oliver Twist* (both the David Lean version and *Oliver!*), *A Separate Peace, Member of the Wedding, The Red Pony,* and *Lord of the Flies.*

Once they have made a selection, students fill out a form indicating title and author and expected date of completion. As they are reading, they write about their impressions in a journal that Amy checks as she circulates among students. Sometimes journal entries are merely triggered by ideas in the books they are reading, and these ideas are then developed in other directions. (The journals, of course, are also used for writing on other topics such as self-exploration, school issues, and current events.) When they have completed a book, students have the option of doing a "book talk" for the class, writing a book review, or creating a piece of art such as a collage or a drawing. Amy keeps a log of what each student is reading at any given time, and twice a week she asks students to bring their books to class and gives them a half-hour period of sustained silent reading (SSR).

Amy also assigns a few texts to the whole class each term; the current class text is *To Kill a Mockingbird.* On this October day the students have just finished reading to the end of Chapter 24, the chapter in which Scout attends her Aunt Alexandra's Missionary Society tea and learns of Tom Robinson's death. Amy asks Emily to read the last two pages of Chapter 24 aloud and then says: "I'd like you to write in your journals about how you feel about the experience of growing up shown here. You might want to start with the last sentence of Chapter 24, Scout's statement, 'After all, if Aunty could be a lady at a time like this, so could I.' What is your reaction to this? Can you think of a time when you felt that you had to act grown up even though you didn't feel like it?"

Amy suggests that students might want to think about Scout's growing definition of "background" and consider how background influences one's maturing, or that they might want to look back at Chapter 13, at the description of Aunt Alexandra's arrival and her explanation that Scout was growing up. The students write for about ten minutes; some stop to stare into space while others write without interruption. Then Amy invites a few volunteers to read from what they have written. After each volunteer reads, Amy puts a check beside that person's name in her grade

---

BOX 6.1
PARENTAL PERMISSION FORM

Dear Ms. Slavak:

    I understand that _____ (insert name of student) will be reading
_____ (insert name of book) as part of the optional work for your
course. I have discussed this book with _____ (insert name of student)
and s/he has my permission to read this book.

Sincerely,

_____
Parent/guardian

---

book. She does not require students to read on any particular day, but
they must read at least five times during the grading period. Some of
them write about how Scout begins to appreciate Aunt Alexandra even
though she doesn't like her initially, and they make comparisons with
stepparents or parents' friends whom they have finally grown to appreciate. Others write about Scout's growing awareness of the meanings underlying the ladies' conversation, and they note the similarities to their
own experiences of beginning to understand adults' euphemisms and
innuendos. Still others write about how Scout's maturing differs from
Jem's, how gender shapes definitions of growing up. Angela, in particular, reads what she has written about how her parents have always allowed
her brother to do things she is forbidden to do. "It's not fair," she con-
cludes. Amy encourages students to respond to one another's writing,
and they spend about ten minutes listening to and talking about their
reactions to this portion of the novel.

    Amy acknowledges her students' various responses and then focuses
on the issue of gender. "Why does Aunt Alexandra insist that Scout needs
a 'feminine influence'? What *is* a feminine influence anyway?" she asks.

    "It seems to me that all Aunt Alexandra cares about is good man-
ners," Demetrius responds.

    "Yeah, that's probably true," says Kari, "but I think something else is
going on here. I remember seeing a movie called *Steel Magnolias*. Dolly
Parton was in it. It was about this girl who died, and her mother and her
mother's friends. Those women were, like, well, made of steel. They were
the ones who took care of everything, but they wouldn't let on. They'd
pretend to be all weak and fragile."

    "Do you think Aunt Alexandra could be described as a steel magno-
lia?" asks Amy. Another student responds, and the discussion continues
for several minutes as students explore the connections between man-

Sounds wonderful for these students to come up w/ these ideas unassisted! Suspicious!

ners, background, and personal strength. Then she shifts the discussion back to the question of gender.

"What does it mean to grow up female?" she asks. "How is that different from growing up male? What does *To Kill a Mockingbird* tell us about growing up female and male? There are many sections in this book that say something about the relationship between gender and growing up. You could look at the end of Chapter 4 where Jem rebukes Scout for acting like a girl, or you could look at Chapter 8 where Jem finds out that Mr. Radley has filled in the tree hole where Boo Radley had left them presents, or you might look at the end of Chapter 11 where Jem comes to understand Mrs. Dubose's courage. Take a few minutes and find a passage that says something to you about growing up female or male."

After a brief pause Amy asks students to break into their regular discussion groups and compare the passages they have identified. Students work for about fifteen minutes in their groups, comparing the passages they have selected and explaining what their selections show about growing up female and male. As the hour draws to a close, Amy reminds the class that their reading assignment for the next day is Chapters 25 through 27. In addition, she tells them to consider the passages discussed in their groups, to select one that tells them the most about growing up female and/or male, and to write an explanation in their journals of why it was the most telling selection.

Amy's students had spent the month of September writing papers on topics and in forms of their own choice, a strategy consistent with Amy's approach to reading, which stresses decision making on the part of the individual student. Partly as an occasion to help generate topics, and partly to "expand" the walls of the classroom to include the natural world, Amy had arranged for her students to visit Pinery Park, less than two miles from their school. The park is small but still boasts a playground, a softball field, a few trees, and a small creek. On that day the students were encouraged to find a place by themselves in the park and write impressions of the experience in their journals.

Amy arranged in advance for a school bus so they could go to the park and return within one class period. On the way to the park, Amy gave her students some guidelines: "Here's one way to approach this if you aren't sure what to write. At first, try to focus as much as possible on your senses. If you decide to take this direction, I have a challenge for you: Use *all* your senses in your descriptions. But as I've said before, at this point, just keep the pen moving as fast as you can; don't stop and correct yourself along the way." By way of encouragement, she read them a passage on free writing from Peter Elbow's *Writing Without Teachers* (New York: Oxford University Press, 1973, p. 3): "Just put down something. The easiest thing is just to put down whatever is in your mind. If you get stuck it's fine to write 'I can't think what to say, I can't think what to say' as many times as you want; or repeat the last word you wrote over and over again; or anything else. The only requirement is that you *never* stop."

Closing the book, Amy smiled and said, "Maybe this writing will be the clay for the interesting sculpture you will shape later! I hope so. At any rate, the important thing is to have fun with your writing, and to write a lot."

Alex interjected: "I used to hang out in this park a lot when I was a little kid, before we moved. We used to mess around in that little creek that runs through there. Can I write about that?"

"Of course! Write about whatever comes to your mind. A place will often be a 'trigger' for memories. It may be that you end up writing about something completely other than the park, too, but that's fine. The point is to find something that you really want to write about."

"Can we write a poem?" someone in the back asked.

"Sure!" Although Amy found it useful for everyone to focus on a particular form or topic from time to time, she generally wanted to give students as many opportunities as possible to explore for themselves. "Let the topic you choose determine the form the piece takes. Let the writing dictate the direction."

The next day, students brought drafts to class, some of them nearly finished pieces, others little more than rewritten notes. Alex brought a completed draft of a poem about four kids pretending their creek was a mighty river; Angela, upset by all the trash she had seen, had written two pages toward an essay about the city's general neglect of the environment. Demetrius had a rough outline, imagining himself as a pioneer in the area 150 years before the town was built. Maria and Susan were writing a play based on a conversation between an ant and a centipede, a play they planned to perform for Maria's sister's fourth-grade class.

Amy asked students to form groups of three to share their writing and to brainstorm their revisions. Amy moved from group to group, helping out where she could in each group, responding to particular students' requests for help. She shared her own attempt at a poem with one group and graciously took their advice. In her brief conferences with students, she was encouraging, attempting to support the direction each writer seemed to be taking, emphasizing the texts' strengths as she saw them, but primarily listening to student concerns and questions. She modeled for students her focus, at this early stage, on broader concerns such as content and organization.

Over the next few days, students shaped their writing for themselves, and Amy helped them move through various stages of revision, focusing on the editing process. Students took turns typing and revising their texts on the lone computer in Amy's classroom. She asked students to write comments on each other's papers one evening; the next evening she took all the drafts home and wrote her own response. In recent years she has been concerned about the kind of comments—or lack of them—students make on their peers' writing; as a result, she now concentrates on helping them to be both positive and constructive in critiquing the work of their fellow students.

Above all, Amy tries to celebrate her students' efforts at making meaning for themselves. Inspired by the vibrant classroom described in Nancie Atwell's *In the Middle: Writing, Reading, and Learning with Adolescents* (see Suggested Reading at the end of this chapter), Amy strives to create her own version of a reading and writing workshop in her classroom, a learning environment where individuals learn on their own as much as possible.

As they were to do several different times during the year, Amy's students desktop-published (on the school's best printer) a copy of their writings from this park project. Calling the stapled booklet "Pinery Park: Poetry, Plays and Prose," they shared copies with fellow students, with their other teachers, and with their school principal.

Analysis of the Approach

The physical arrangement of any classroom tells us something about the teacher's theories, and Amy's class is no exception. By putting her desk in the corner and making it a storage area rather than the center of classroom activity, she signals that what the students do is central to the work of the class. Specifically, the arrangement of the room says that this class gives prominence to students' responses to reading and writing. This approach to teaching English assumes that language is, among other things, a source of pleasure, that reading engenders feelings, that those feelings provide the basis for more sophisticated responses to the students' experiences of the world. Above all, this approach validates the individual student's unique, expressive capacities for learning.

Teachers who believe in the language-as-expression approach want to take the "sage off the stage" and put students at the center of the class. Such teachers recognize that students will have diverse responses to texts and that this diversity should be fostered, but that at the same time the common points of agreement should be recognized. The goal in this way of teaching is not to impart a certain set of facts but to enable students to trust their own responses; to understand why they respond as they do; to respect the responses of others; to move beyond initial engagement to more sophisticated responses such as interpretation, evaluation, and construct-perception. *Construct-perception* here means "perception that a work of art is a human construct rather than a natural phenomenon."

Notice that Amy, in the class period described above, began by asking her students how they *felt* about the portrayal of growing up in Chapter 24 of *To Kill a Mockingbird*. Amy believes that engagement through feeling should come first, but she wants her students to become more sophisticated in their responses than those early motion-picture audiences who threw their chairs at the villain on the screen. By asking her students to consider other passages and other viewpoints in the novel, Amy pushed them toward seeing the novel as a human construction rather than a natural phenomenon; this perception then provided the basis for still other kinds of response and understanding. Even though she did not say it specifically, Amy helped her students see that the text we call *To Kill a Mockingbird* results from a series of choices made by the author. She will remind her students of this later when she asks them to think about their own writing.

Once she had enabled students to perceive this novel as something constructed, Amy pushed them on to acts of interpretation. By asking them to identify and talk about specific passages that illustrated perspectives on growing up, she engaged them in discussions of meaning. Exploring Jem's encounter with Mr. Radley or Scout's difficulty with being a girl leads students to think about what the text means as well as what it says. Finally, the assignment to write in their journals about the most revealing passage invites students to evaluate, to make decisions about which one is "better."

Moving through these four kinds of response—*engagement, construct-perception, interpretation,* and *evaluation*—has a central place for teachers who take the language-as-expression approach. (See Box 6.2.) This progression assumes that each form of response has value. Engagement through feeling may be the least sophisticated kind of response, but it is no less important than evaluation. In this view, students should experience all four types of response, and a concentration on any one (such as, say, evaluation) limits students' capacity to fully appreciate their reading.

At first glance it may seem as if the language-as-expression approach applies only to the reading of texts, but it is an approach that applies equally well to speaking and writing. Indeed, this approach emphasizes the connections among reading, speaking, and writing. Sometimes Amy asks her students to explore in writing their ideas or feelings about a topic that is a theme of a book before they read the book, in order to prepare them for the reading. Both writing in response to reading and writing in preparation for reading demonstrate the connections that can be made between reading and writing. Similarly, discussion prior to reading a particular text—as well as speeches or debates based on a reading of that text—demonstrates the close connection that can be made between reading and speaking.

Writing or speaking in response to reading gives students an opportunity to express their own feelings, understandings, and judgments of texts they read. At the same time it enables them to see the relationship between their own writing and that of the authors whom they read. One goal in a writing-as-expression classroom is to help students see themselves as authors who have a great deal in common with the authors whose books they read in class.

As Amy's class demonstrates, writing supports each type of response

---

BOX 6.2
FOUR TYPES OF READER RESPONSE

• *Engagement:* The reader becomes subjectively involved with the text. Feelings, identification, and empathy are part of this response, which is evoked through such questions and statements as: Through whose eyes did you see this event? Do you like this character? Compare your feelings after reading these two selections. Has anything like this ever happened to you?

• *Construct-perception:* The reader begins to see the text as an object, as something created by another human being rather than a naturally occurring phenomenon. This response can be evoked through such questions as: How does the author convey the passing of time in this selection? Notice the statement on page 000 and the one on page 000. Does this seem like a contradiction to you? How would this selection change if it were told from another point of view?

• *Interpretation:* The reader tries to explain what the text means, and multiple interpretations are encouraged by such questions as: What do you think the title means? How could you translate that metaphor into other words? What effect does the repetition have? What do you think this passage means? What other meaning could this phrase have? Why did X do Y?

• *Evaluation:* The reader compares one text with others and assesses its impact and importance. This response is evoked by such questions as: Do you think this is a good poem/ play/novel? Which part did you like best? Why? Do you like this text more or less than the one we read last week? Why? Do you think this is a better book than the one we read last week? In what ways? Which style is more effective?

---

students make to the novel they are reading. They write about their feelings regarding a specific section, they write about their perceptions of various incidents the author has chosen to include, they write about their interpretations of Harper Lee's portrayal of growing up male and female, and they write about their evaluations of one portion of the novel. These various kinds of writing help students clarify their thinking about the book.

In addition to enriching students' understanding of the texts they read, the language-as-expression approach encourages students to view their own writing as texts worthy of others' attention. Amy's requirement that students share selections from their journals on a regular basis embodies the belief that students should read one another's writing.

A language-as-expression approach clearly puts the student's voice and perspective at the center of the classroom. Unlike the language-as-artifact approach, which privileges the professional text, this approach assumes that the individual student's reading, speaking, and writing are important. In dealing with literature, what an individual student thinks about a text is important not because it is "better" or more intelligent than a classmate's, a teacher's, or a professional critic's reading (though it may be), but because the only way for students to truly understand and appreciate what they read is to experience it in terms of their own framework of feelings, experiences, and beliefs. Their initial responses to literature enable students to become interested in and engaged with literature. This engagement then provides the foundation or point of departure from which their other kinds of response can develop.

Similarly, in a language-as-expression approach, students' own writing begins in active engagement with a subject. Teachers may provide guidelines and suggestions, but most choices about writing are left to the student. Rather than assuming that students need to learn a set of rules or to move progressively from sentences to paragraphs to fully developed essays, the language-as-expression approach assumes that students should begin by writing about what they care about. Furthermore, this approach presumes that writers do not all follow exactly the same processes, that they do not all work best in the same way. Just as individual readers bring different things to their reading of a text and take different things from it, so individual writers, both through the development of different habits and through differences in personality and perspective, behave very differently, and there is no single successful formula for expressing oneself through writing.

Teachers who follow a language-as-expression approach adopt a very different role than, say, teachers who follow the language-as-artifact approach. Putting students at the center of the class means that the teacher becomes more of a facilitator than a performer in the classroom. Rather than serving as the single authority in the class, the teacher becomes an inquirer, one who sees students as co-inquirers who are capable of exerting their own authority in the learning process.

Taking the role of a facilitator does not mean a teacher works less hard or retires to the corner of the room. It is simply a matter of working differently. Teachers in a language-as-expression classroom create a context in which students can express responses freely and effectively, they prepare students for group work by providing models and making expectations clear, and they learn to evaluate processes as well as products of student work.

Language-as-expression teachers employ different rhythms of learning and routines than do their peers who take other approaches. The pace or rhythm for the class is dictated largely by the progress and response of students rather than by a rigid plan designed to cover all the material in a given book or unit. Pauses play an important role in each

it is important to have time to digest what one has learned.

class session. They provide students time for thinking, questioning, and writing. During class discussion, pauses often occur between questions and answers. Teachers learn to wait quietly, to recognize that silence after a question doesn't mean that nothing is going on. Students who know that the teacher will not rush ahead to answer his or her own questions but will wait for students to think become much more thoughtful about what they say in class.

The routines or established procedures of a language-as-expression classroom emphasize student activity rather than teacher talk and performance. In classes following other approaches, student talk is often limited to responding to a few questions from the teacher. In a language-as-expression class, students have many more opportunities to use language. They often pose questions, give one another directions, and suggest ways of proceeding. In writing, too, different processes are assumed. A teacher who believes that knowledge about language is to be "discovered" will not prescribe rigid forms or "steps" in a given student's process of writing.

Narrative is especially important in the language-as-expression classroom, as an object of study, as a mode of learning, and as an indispensable activity in class discussions. British educator Barbara Hardy contends that "narrative . . . is not to be regarded as an aesthetic invention used by artists to control, manipulate, and order experience, but as a primary act of mind transferred to art from life. . . . For we dream in narrative, daydream in narrative, remember, anticipate, hope, despair, believe, doubt, plan, revise, criticize, construct, gossip, learn, hate, and love by narrative." In order to live, "we make up stories about ourselves and others, about the personal as well as the social past and future" (Barbara Hardy, "Narrative as a Primary Act of Mind," in Margaret Meek, Aidan Warlon, and Griselda Barton, eds., *The Cool Web* [London: Bradley Head, 1977], 14).

Thus the language-as-expression approach relies heavily on narrative as students recount their responses to the literature they read and to the writing of their peers. Narrative, of course, also relates to their own writing experiences. Often their stories may move into drama as they re-create the past so vividly that it lives again in the present. And if, as Arthur Miller contends, the key difference between narrative and drama is the difference between a past and a present tense, the class hour becomes in this approach a continuous drama, with the teacher facilitating the weaving together of the stories that students tell into an ongoing blend of narrative and drama. Narrative and its sister form, drama, come more naturally to students than do the modes of exposition and argument (which are more characteristic of the language-as-artifact classroom) and are likely to be more successful in engaging students' attention. (For Miller's remarks see "An Interview with Arthur Miller" in Stephen Dunning and Alan B. Howes, *Literature for Adolescents* [Glenview, Ill.: Scott, Foresman, 1975], p. 310. For a much fuller discussion of drama in the classroom, see James Moffett, *Teaching the Universe of Discourse* [Boston: Houghton Mifflin, 1968]).

Language Study

In a language-as-expression class, language study will be integrated with reading and writing, not treated as a separate area of study. Grammar books may be present as reference guides, but students will not do exercises in them regularly. Instead, the teacher concentrates on natural and honest expression in writing and in response to reading. Students are encouraged to develop their own "voices" rather than concern themselves with learning rules about language. Teachers following this approach assume that the students, who have been using language since before they entered kindergarten, do not need instruction in rules for usage so much as they need opportunities to develop their capacity to write and speak effectively.

How will they talk about Grammar?

One measure of effectiveness in the language-as-expression classroom is avoidance of pretentious, insincere, or flat language. Ken Macrorie (see Suggested Reading at the end of this chapter) describes this kind of language as "Engfish," a term borrowed from one of his students. He explains: "This girl had given me a name for the bloated, pretentious language I saw everywhere around me, in the students' themes, in the textbooks on writing, in the professors' and administrators' communications to each other. A feel-nothing, say-nothing language, dead like Latin, devoid of the rhythms of contemporary speech. A dialect in which words are almost never 'attached to things' as Emerson said they should be" (Ken Macrorie, *Uptaught* [New York: Hayden, 1970], 18).

Rather than encouraging Engfish, language-as-expression classes encourage the development of fresh, vivid, and honest expression, the kind of language we describe as having a recognizable "voice." Voice in writing is very difficult to define, as Peter Elbow explains (see Suggested Reading at the end of this chapter): "Writing with *real voice* has the power to make you pay attention and understand—the words go deep. I don't know the objective characteristics that distinguish writing with real voice from writing with mere voice. For me it is a matter of hearing resonance rather than being able to point to things on the page" (*Writing with Power: Techniques for Mastering the Writing Process* [New York: Oxford University Press, 1981], 299). Even though voice may be difficult to define, teachers in language-as-expression classrooms encourage students to experiment and try out various forms of language so they can find their own voices.

vocab words from literature

Language study in a language-as-expression classroom does, of course, encourage students to enlarge their vocabularies and enrich their voices, but this is accomplished through reading and writing, not through studying vocabulary lists. Issues of usage and grammar are usually treated on an individual basis rather than made objects of study for the whole class. That is, when an individual student has a problem with, say, subject-verb agreement in writing, the teacher helps that student in the context of the particular paper the student is writing but does not involve the whole class unless it is a problem in the writing of many students.

Instead of emphasizing the study of formal grammar as a means for helping students achieve control over language, the teacher exposes students to a variety of styles, encourages them to play with language and manipulate it for different purposes, and provides opportunities for them to respond to each other's texts, asking questions such as, How does the tone of this piece affect you? What words and phrases in this selection help you experience the feelings this writer is describing? Why is the major point of this selection convincing or not convincing?

A study of the different kinds of meaning that language can express will help students answer questions of this sort, since these questions get at the meaning and effect of the words writers use to express themselves. Recognizing the difference between the denotative and connotative meanings of words will help students to distinguish between honest and dishonest uses of language and also to increase their aesthetic pleasure in reading, hearing, and using language. It will help them to overcome prejudice, racism, and sexism resulting from misleading and dishonest uses of language, and it will help them to become aware of the power of metaphor, symbol, and image. To put it another way, understanding the difference between denotation and connotation can help students to see and savor the uniqueness of everything in their world through language, and to avoid the illogic and prejudice that come from losing sight of that uniqueness and creating false generalizations and oversimplified categories. A language-as-expression classroom enables students to voice their joys and fears, their speculations and ideas, thereby portraying their individuality and uniqueness while at the same time respecting the individuality and uniqueness of others.

Literature Study

In the language-as-expression classroom, literature study stresses the relationship between reader and text. Louise Rosenblatt (see Suggested Reading at the end of this chapter) explains reading as a transaction:

> There is no such thing as a generic reader or a generic literary work; there are only the potential millions of individual readers of the potential millions of individual literary works. A novel or poem or play remains merely inkspots on paper until a reader transforms them into a set of meaningful symbols. The literary work exists in the live circuit set up between reader and text: the reader infuses intellectual and emotional meanings into the pattern of verbal symbols, and those symbols channel his thoughts and feelings. Out of this complex process emerges a more or less organized imaginative experience (*Literature as Exploration* [New York: Noble, 1976], 25).

Even as she insists on the unique nature of individual experiences with literature, however, Rosenblatt emphasizes that these transactions can be complete only if the initial response is open to modification by further acquaintance with the text. Students should continue to look closely at the text and let their views change and grow in response to it.

Rosenblatt was a pioneer in what has become known as the reader-response approach to literature, and this approach has a prominent place in the language-as-expression classroom. Other theorists who have contributed to our understanding of this approach to teaching literature include David Bleich and Norman Holland. (See Suggested Reading at the end of this chapter.) Bleich talks about a reader's "perceptual style," which reveals as much about the reader as a writer's style does about a writer. Perceptual style results from affect (or general emotional response) and association (similar events in the reader's life that produced similar emotions). This perceptual style shapes the kind of transaction an individual reader has with a text, and Bleich suggests that teachers can encourage students to become aware of different perceptual styles by comparing their responses with those of their peers.

In *Poems in Persons* (New York: Norton, 1975), Norman Holland, taking a psychoanalytical approach, also emphasizes the influence of individual personality on the kinds of responses to texts that one is capable of. "The reader tries," he says, "to compose from [the work he is reading] a literary experience in his particular lifestyle . . . creat[ing] his characteristic modes of adaptation and defense from the words he is reading." To take pleasure in the work he is reading, the reader "must re-create for himself from the text rather precisely all or part of the structures by which he wards off anxiety in real life." He can then "shape for himself . . . a fantasy that gives him pleasure." But limits are placed on that fantasy by the reader's need to make sense of the text and to "arrive at an intellectual or moral 'point' in what he has read." How a student *can* respond to a text is conditioned in part by that student's lifestyle, personality, and past experience.

The theories of Rosenblatt, Bleich, and Holland all emphasize a point important to the language-as-expression classroom: Students' responses to literary texts differ, and those differences should be valued. Reading is an individual act, not a generic one, and the teacher's role is not to provide the "correct" response but to welcome the multiple readings engendered by a given text and then help students move toward richer understandings. The classroom thus becomes, as Australian educator Ian Reid (see Suggested Reading at the end of this chapter) says, a "workshop," where students and teacher alike are helping each other to work actively with texts, learning from one another, rather than a "gallery" where literary masterpieces are shown off by the "curator" (teacher) and kept safely at a distance from students' engagement. A text is conceived of not as an object but as a "semantic process by which meanings are *transacted through* the verbal material, not deposited in it."

By bringing students closer to the text in this way, the language-as-expression approach makes the literature that students read a more integral part of their lives. Robert Coles recounts conversations with one of his college students who was looking back on his high school experience: "He . . . said during our talks, that he counts among his 'friends' characters in certain novels. He denies any distinctiveness or originality in that kind of friendship: many of his high school buddies . . . 'would talk about Holden [Caulfield] as if he was one of us.' Having said that, he asked me a rhetorical question . . . : 'Why don't you guys [college professors] teach that way?' What way, I wanted to know. 'As if Holden was—I mean is—as real as you or me.' . . . He was reminding me . . . of the wonderful mimetic power a novel or story can have—its capacity to work its way well into one's thinking life, yes, but also one's reveries or idle thoughts, even one's moods and dreams" (*The Call of Stories* [Boston: Houghton Mifflin, 1989], 204).

The language-as-expression approach makes texts come alive for students as characters become friends, and only then moves on to the study of those texts as human constructions.

Writing Instruction

The language-as-expression classroom also makes writing come alive for students as they write about topics, often of their own choice, that engage their curiosity and as they experiment with a variety of techniques and forms. Rather than learning handbook rules and trying to create error-free products, students use writing to express feelings, to play with language, and to explore attitudes and ideas. They are allowed and encouraged to write about the things that really matter to them.

At the same time, they are asked to be self-critical about some of the writing they do and self-aware about all of it. The teacher might ask students to focus on a piece of writing they have done and answer some specific questions: What do you like best about this writing? What needs improvement? What alternatives might you pursue in overall organization or in particular parts of the paper? Or the teacher might ask students to select two finished papers and compare them with the drafts from which they emerged, instructing them perhaps to list two or three similarities in the revisions and two or three differences.

Students often need direct instruction in looking at their writing reflectively. Teachers can accomplish this by modeling reflective language in whole-class workshops or in individual conferences. (As Box 6.5 demonstrates, helping students develop reflective language about writing is one of several preliminaries to using portfolios.) Typical questions to help students become more reflective about their writing include: What would have happened if you had reversed the order here? What made you decide to leave this part out when you revised? What is the one thing you are saying here?

Writing and reflection on that writing thus go hand in hand in the language-as-expression classroom, and writing comes to be seen as an aid to thought and not necessarily as the production of a finished piece. Different kinds of writing may be called for as parts of the same project or assignment. *Free-writing* may well be the first step in a writing project as students engage in preliminary exploration of a topic or begin to gather raw material. In free-writing, students write without stopping for a specified period of time, constantly keeping the pencil (or the keys on the keyboard) moving, and writing whatever comes into their minds. (See Elbow in Suggested Reading at the end of this chapter.) It limbers up the "writing muscles" and can help students get over a writing block, as well as discover their own voices and what they know and think about a topic. It can also be useful during later stages of a writing project in exploring an idea or considering alternatives.

Journal writing is another kind of writing that is useful in gathering raw materials for papers and strengthening connections between writing and thinking. It can also provide the same kind of outlet for personal expression as free-writing. Students can be asked to keep journals over the course of a specified period of time, making entries about whatever they are doing or thinking; but journals can also be used in a more focused way to record reactions while reading a book or working on a specific writing project. Thus they can provide the basis for class discussion of reading or for analysis of the writing process of an individual student.

James Britton (see Suggested Reading at the end of this chapter) offers a rationale for the importance of free-writing and journal writing, describing language that is closest to the self, language that expresses feelings and doesn't worry about addressing itself to an audience, as *expressive language*. In Britton's view, expressive language provides the foundation from which other, more audience-directed kinds of language develop. Britton describes student learning as having its own organic shape: "Like a plant or a coral. As teachers we very often think of the shape of learning as though it were frost on the boughs we provide or barnacles on the bottom of our boat. A child's learning has its own organic structure. Hence, the value of writing in the expressive, which is the language close to and most revealing of that individuality"("Writing to Learn and Learning to Write," in *Prospect and Retrospect: Selected Essays by James Britton* [Portsmouth, N.H.: Boynton/Cook, 1982], 109–10).

Writing instruction in a language-as-expression class provides plenty of opportunity for students to do expressive writing, writing that may not necessarily be submitted for a grade but that enables students to find out about themselves and their own ideas. It may not even all be for the teacher's eyes, for many teachers promote greater expressive candor in students' journals by telling them they may withhold any portions they do not wish the teacher to read, merely offering proof of the number of pages completed.

BOX 6.3
I-SEARCHING

In the last four years other teachers around the country and I have been challenging students to do what we call *I-Searches*—not Re-Searches, in which the job is to search again what someone has already searched—but original searches in which persons scratch an itch they feel, one so marvelously itchy that they begin rubbing a fingertip against it and the rubbing feels so good that they dig in with a fingernail. A search to fulfill a need, not that the teacher has imagined for them, but one they feel themselves. . . .

The textbooks have told students what the principal reference guides are and how to use them; but students forget or don't understand, and then they misuse them. In their laborious dull way, textbooks imply that reference works are tools for dull people. Yet true investigators are excited, sustained in their work not by instructions but by curiosity. . . .

I search. That's the truth of any inquiry. Re-search doesn't say it, rather implies complete detachment, absolute objectivity. Time to clear the miasma and admit that the best searchers act both subjectively and objectively and write so that professionals and the public can understand their searches and profit from them. Time to get down to the basics, which are not footnotes, but curiosity, need, rigor in judging one's findings and the opinions of experts and helping others test the validity of the search.

For many decades high schools and colleges have fostered the "research paper," which has become an exercise in badly done bibliography, often an introduction to the art of plagiarism, and a triumph of meaninglessness—for both writer and reader. As a teacher I've helped bring about such inane produc-

---

Even when students do such a conventional writing assignment as a research paper (perhaps required by the curriculum guide for their school), it is likely to become what Ken Macrorie calls an "I-Search Paper," in which students choose a topic of special interest or importance to them, rely heavily on interviews and other nonprint as well as print sources, and embody the results in an account of the process they went through during their search along with the results of the search. (See Box 6.3.) This assignment allows students to choose a topic they really want to find out about and, as they write their narratives, to become more aware of the process followed by professional researchers.

An approach to research papers.

The same kind of paper, detailing the steps from free-writing or rough draft or preliminary outline or notes to more finished paper, can accompany the writing of another paper on any topic. This *process paper* helps students to become more aware of the way they write. To help students prepare for writing process papers, the teacher can take them through a *guided-imagery exercise*. These exercises ask students to close their eyes and imagine a series of places and events that the teacher describes. After the exercise is completed, students write in their journals

tions myself. Now I look forward to reading I-Search Papers because they tell stories of quests that counted for the questers and they're written in a way that catches and holds readers. . . .

Contrary to most school research papers, the I-Search comes out of a student's life and answers a need in it. The writer testifies to the subjective-objective character of the project. The paper is alive, not borrowedly inert. Writing it, many students for the first time find that writing is a way of thinking, of objectifying an act that has counted for them. As the sentences go down on the page, they become both finished statements and starting points for reflection and evaluation. The passages grow with thought. And the thought is not just about the writers' searches but also about how readers will respond to the words that report and complete them. . . .

Those of us who have asked students to write I-Search Papers have discovered that above all we must protect our students' time, so they can conduct inquiries realistically—tracking leads, finding that many don't work out, and following up when things go right. They're taking other classes besides ours, and they're committed in many ways to life outside school as well as within it. For their I-Search project they need time to telephone and write people and get answers from those who don't reply at once. They need time to organize materials and compose a story of their adventure that's alive and fascinating. To do this they need a number of days unencumbered by assignments of any kind.

—From Ken Macrorie, *The I-Search Paper* (Portsmouth, N.H.: Boynton/Cook Heinemann, 1988), p. 32.

about what they have learned. A guided-imagery exercise for a process paper could ask students to think about the place where they typically do their writing, to be aware of its colors, smells, and sounds; then they can imagine the rituals they go through to begin writing, the pencil-sharpening, cola-drinking kinds of activities; next they can focus on their tools for writing—pencil, pen, typewriter, computer; and then they can imagine themselves writing the first sentence on a clean sheet/screen and thinking about how it feels. The more that students understand about their own writing processes, the more apt they are to write with both pleasure and profit.

Writing groups also help students to look on writing as a process and can give them a realistic sense of writing for a wider audience than the somewhat artificial audience of the teacher alone. Groups may follow different procedures, but one of the most effective is the one described in Box 6.4. When groups follow established procedures and when the teacher is sensitive to their chemistry, writing groups can play a central part in students' writing by helping them develop greater awareness about their own processes of writing.

writing as an ongoing process not a finished product.

Another means of helping students to become aware of their writing processes and their progress is to have them keep *portfolios.* Long a standard practice in art, portfolios are making their way into English classes both in secondary schools and in colleges. Like the collection of paintings that demonstrates the development of themes, patterns, techniques for the artist, the English portfolio enables students and teachers to examine students' work across time and detect patterns in students' development as writers, as well as in their interests and ideas. Periodically the teacher asks students to look at their portfolios, perhaps to find a topic to write about, perhaps to write comments about selected pieces, or perhaps to track the kinds of changes they make as they revise. The teacher might say, for example, "Make a list of what each piece in your portfolio is about and then select one topic and free-write about what you still want to know." (See Box 6.5 on page 160.)

Portfolios can also provide an alternative form of evaluation, with pieces remaining ungraded until students select what they consider the best ones to be considered in final grades. The classroom Nancie Atwell describes in her book *In the Middle* (see Suggested Reading at the end of this chapter) illustrates how much students can accomplish and how the portfolio system contributes to motivation. Students begin to think of themselves as real writers rather than merely as unlucky captives carrying out an assignment. That goal is shared by all language-as-expression classrooms.

Potentials and Limitations of the Approach

Potentials

1. *It is student-centered.* This approach validates student experiences and ways of knowing. Student ownership of the learning process is given priority, and the connections between the texts and the students' lives are emphasized. Students' texts are given the same importance as professional texts, and students' interpretations of texts the same importance as teachers' interpretations. The roles of facilitator, coach, and means of support for the students are the teacher's primary roles in this approach.

2. *It celebrates individuality.* In focusing on the student rather than the teacher or the text, this approach allows for individual differences and individual needs to be taken fully into account. Attention to individual responses, daily journal writing, and small-group discussion, all associated with this approach, ensure that teachers know and understand

True

BOX 6.4
PROCEDURES FOR WRITING GROUPS

1. A whole class period should be devoted to writing-group meetings.

2. Each member of the group must bring a draft to read. The teacher can make drafts a ticket of admission to class if necessary.

3. The available time should be divided by the number of people in the group, and an equal amount of time should be allocated to each individual.

4. Each member's allocated time is divided into half for reading and half for group response.

5. Drafts are read aloud once, the author pauses long enough for group members to write their initial impressions of the draft, and then the author reads the writing a second time.

During the second reading the group members take detailed notes on their responses.

6. Group members give oral responses to the author immediately after the second reading. Each member, starting with the person to the author's right, speaks in turn, and conversation among members is avoided.

7. Oral responses are from the perspective of the audience; they do not offer advice but describe the effect the writing produced.

8. The author remains silent as the group members respond and writes down all comments for future reference.

9. Authors do not apologize for their drafts.

individual students well. Each student is viewed as a unique and valuable maker of meaning in the language-as-expression classroom.

3. *It promotes independence.* Since each individual is given the freedom to make independent choices in this approach, decision-making capacities are strengthened. The focus on self-discovery and self-identity central to this approach builds confidence and motivates students, who over time develop confidence in their own ability to read and write rather than merely feeling inferior to the authors they read or assuming that there is only one "right" answer to any question about a text.

4. *It promotes creativity.* This approach emphasizes each student's creative potential and encourages students to discover themselves and to invent their own worlds. Ezra Pound's dictum "Make it new" is the central theme of this approach. The focus is on process, not product.

5. *It values feeling.* Often neglected in other approaches, students' and teachers' emotional responses to literature and life are the starting point of this approach.

BOX 6.5
REFLECTING ON THE PORTFOLIO

Portfolio reflections make visible certain aspects of students' perceptions and purposes that are not accessible from their written products alone:

1. What the student believes she has done well in a piece of writing:

The special strength of my thesis [paper] is the way I related the question [the topic for the paper] and the answer to the book. For example, in my first paragraph I refer back to ch. 5. That is where I found my main example of my statement. (8th grader, Amy)

2. What the student values in writing:

It was wild the way I put Beowulf into modern times. (12th grader, Mileak)
[I selected] the dialogue I wrote about Karen & Stan. The reason I picked this one was because this could be a very real situation. I also liked this dialogue because if it was a real situation this is probably very close to what the conversation would be like. (9th grader, Erin)

3. The student's own goals and interests—his "agenda"—as a learner and developing writer:

Today I [read] my old work and didn't like it. I decided to rewrite my camping in the woods story. (7th grader, Michael)

4. The student's strategies and processes for writing and his or her awareness of them:

I think of what things I need in the story and then write a jot list. (12th grader, Mileak)

I really thought out and planned my composition. (12th grader, Amber)

5. What the student understands that she is learning about writing:

In the last several weeks, I believe I have become a better writer. In the beginning I worried about the plot and the ending, and now I believe I have learned there really is no need for an ending. I also now don't worry so much about the plot itself but about the character, my image of the character, and the setting. Things I really had worried about second or third and not first. (8th grader, Arin)

Reflection, then, yields information that both student and teacher use to track and direct the course of learning. With the information made available through the writing folder and portfolios, teachers are equipped to be mentors, facilitators, and co-discoverers in their students' development. . . . What we have seen so far leads us to believe that when students look back at their work and their strategies for creating it, when they describe what they see and what they value, they engage in a process of learning and form of assessment that are at the heart of portfolios. Through their portfolio reflections, students also provide information about their perceptions and their learning that teachers can put to direct use in shaping both individual and group instruction.

—From Roberta Camp, "Thinking Together About Portfolios," *The Quarterly of the National Writing Project and the Center for the Study of Writing* 12 (Spring 1990):12–13.

Limitations:

1. *It privileges feeling over thinking.* If used unskillfully, this approach can stall at the engagement stage, giving attention to students' personal feelings about texts and experiences without moving them on to the stages of construct-perception, interpretation, and evaluation.

2. *It is more individualistic than social.* With its heavy emphasis on the individual as knower, this approach can neglect the possibilities for more social, collaborative pedagogies. The possibility of viewing learning as a shared or negotiated activity is diminished in this approach, and large-group continuity may be neglected in fostering individual student ownership. As a result, this approach seems to imply less commitment to political and social change, in spite of its emphasis on an individual decision-making process. The tendency here seems to be more toward creativity than change.

3. *It privileges student texts and responses over professional texts and responses.* Because of its emphasis on student writing and responses, "classic" literary texts may be neglected. Because this approach does not emphasize biographical detail about authors or the place of texts in history, students may end up knowing little about either. In relinquishing classroom authority to the students, the language-as-expression teacher has a tendency to neglect the contributions her or his own greater experience as a reader and writer might make to the classroom.

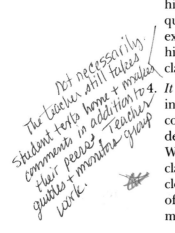

Not necessarily. The teacher still takes student texts home + makes comments in addition to their peers'. Teacher guides + monitors group work.

4. *It is time-intensive for the teacher.* Because the heart of this approach is individualized and not whole-group instruction, and because students' contributions are always unpredictable, this approach requires a good deal of planning time, effort, and flexibility on the part of the teacher. When teachers allow students' emotions and experiences to shape classroom discussions and writing, teachers will inevitably develop closer relationships with students. While this is clearly a positive effect of this approach to the classroom, teachers must be prepared to spend more time with students.

    As we try to make clear in other places in this text, adolescence is a particularly complex time of life, especially in a rapidly changing society. When teachers make themselves available to students and become acquainted with the complexities of their personal lives, the notion of "preparation for teaching" changes. Teaching may become more rewarding, but it also becomes infinitely more complicated and time-intensive. For instance, how "close" should the relationship between a teacher and student be? The tendency to view teaching as a kind of therapy is one danger of this approach.

5. *It is loosely structured.* Individual projects and small-group work are important in this approach. Often the classroom can seem chaotic and noisy; teachers, in sharing classroom authority with students and fos-

tering student talk, may have a tendency to encourage, rather than discourage, classroom noise. Teachers who employ this approach may need to educate administrators in the philosophy guiding this pedagogy. They may also need to develop a greater tolerance for noise and confusion themselves.

IMPLEMENTATION:
TEACHING A UNIT ON MYTH IN THE EIGHTH GRADE

Thematic units play an important part in the language-as-expression approach because themes centered on topics such as romance, adventure, family relationships, death, myths, or fantasy invite students to use language to express their feelings, ideas, and beliefs. These units, like those described in other chapters of this book, often unite reading, writing, language study, and media.

Desired Student Outcomes:

Understanding of myth as genre

Identification of personal characteristics typical in myths

Appreciation for diverse cultures through myths

Possible Whole-Class Activities:

Read aloud selections from a collection of Greek mythology.

Discuss the relationship between myth and belief.

Discuss the relationship between myth and fairy tale.

Discuss the qualities of major figures in myth.

Have students tell myths they know.

Read aloud selections from collections of American Indian mythology.

Discuss the relationship between myth and specific cultural groups.

Read aloud selections from a collection of creation myths.

Read aloud selections from a collection of African myths.

Watch film version(s) of myths.

Read aloud selections from a collection of Asian myths.

Read aloud versions of fairy tales.

Do a read-around of final versions of the myths written by class members.

Possible Small-Group Activities:

Discuss similarities among several myths.

Discuss differences between myths of two cultural groups.

Discuss themes common to myths.

Develop a "grammar" of myths (see Week 2 below).

Have students act out a myth.

Respond to drafts of other students' myths.

Develop criteria for evaluating class projects.

Possible Individual Activities:

Write regularly in journals.

Read, memorize, and prepare to tell a myth.

Create the representation of mythic event or character in another medium.

Write about an encounter with a mythical character.

Read assigned myths.

Write a myth or a fairy tale.

Resources:

Campbell, Joseph. *Oriental Mythology.* New York: Penguin, 1976.

Ford, D., ed. *African Worlds.* New York: Oxford University Press, 1964.

Graves, Robert. *The Greek Myths.* New York, Penguin, 1969.

Hamilton, Virginia. *In the Beginning: Creation Stories from Around the World.* New York: Harcourt, Brace, Jovanovich, 1988.

Marriott, Alice, and Carol K. Rachlin. *American Indian Mythology.* New York: Crowell, 1968.

Propp, Vladimir. *The Morphology of the Folktale.* Austin: University of Texas Press, 1958.

Tedlock, Dennis. *The Popol Vuh: The Mayan Book of the Dawn of Life and the Glories of Gods and Kings.* New York: Simon & Schuster, 1986.

Other resources include short films like "The Loon's Necklace"; feature-length films like *The Princess Bride, The Company of Wolves, The Hobbit*; and television specials or series like *The Lion, the Witch and the Wardrobe* and Joseph Campbell's series on myth.

Organization of the Unit:

Week 1

Of course, individual contributions will shape a unit such as this in the language-as-expression classroom, but one way this unit may begin is with journal writing, where students write what they already know about myths and myth making. The teacher and students should be prepared to share myths with each other. Myths can also be read aloud. Either way, it is a good idea to present the first myths orally, since myths were first transmitted this way.

As students tell myths, questions may arise about what qualifies as a myth, and it might be useful to distinguish between the more historical legend or folktale and the more didactic fable. It might be useful to agree that for the purposes of this class "myth" will include legends, folktales, fables, and fairy tales. Another issue that may arise early in the discussion is the question of belief. Myths are truth to the people who believe in them and live by them, and the teacher may use this as an opportunity to encourage sensitivity to others' beliefs.

When students have heard several myths, they can again write in their journals about their understanding of myths. The teacher might provide a focus such as "Myths are . . . " or might simply ask students to write about how a specific myth makes them feel. Students might be assigned to read and memorize a myth in order to tell it to the class. The teacher can provide the myths or require students to locate their own with the help of the school librarian. In fact, if the school library has a number of anthologies of myths, the teacher might hold class in the library one day during the first week and ask the librarian to do "book talks" about each of the anthologies.

After students have heard a number of myths, they can break into small groups to discuss the similarities they see among them. The teacher can alert them to consider such matters as common themes or issues in the myths, the relationship between reality and fantasy, or the qualities of the characters in the myths. The teacher might ask each group to elect a scribe who will report to the whole class the similarities identified by the group. Alternatively, students might list the similarities in their journals.

At some point during the first week the students should be given the opportunity to compose myths of their own or to retell a myth in terms of their own experiences. The following myths appeared in *Visions,* a literary magazine published by the students of Valley School in Flint, Michigan.

5010: VENUS

The planet of Mars had self-destructed by the year 5000. The small number of "crazy" people who had felt the end coming, as their ancestors on Earth had, escaped to the barren planet of Venus. Taking with them only their untouched fantasies of creating a peaceful haven, they hoped and dreamed of starting a new race of beautiful, fragile children, blind to hatred, bigotry and war. Peace would one day rule. . . .

In a river the color of lead emerged a baby's head. A new breed had begun. There was hope for the future on the planet of Venus. Days later many more innocent children appeared. They emerged into a simple world free from material items, provided with empty, fresh minds untouched by evil. The childen learned to communicate to each other by the tone in their eyes and the color in their movements. Their identity was distinguished by scents of special fragrances which drifted through the skies. The sweet smell of purity and freedom had been left lingering in the air by their creators.

If these children had been told of the horrible worlds that preceded them, they would have thought it only a nightmare. Their "crazy" creators had succeeded in doing what the other forgotten planets had dismissed as impossible.

If only these past worlds had a second chance to open their minds and explore their imagination to find a solution for universal peace. What wasted talent they had!

And so the new civilization of Venus lasted unchanged until the end of time.

—Dyana Cyplik
Grade 8

WHY BLOOD IS RED

Once a very long time ago, there was a famous painter named Tegdirb. Tegdirb was an excellent painter. One day Uranus (who was father of all the gods) asked Tegdirb to paint him a world of color and people. Tegdirb was very honored that Uranus wanted him to do this. He praised Uranus saying: "Oh! Uranus you are so good. You will not be sorry you picked me to paint a world for you. I will paint a large variety of colors. I will make everything so nice!" Then Tegdirb began to work on his great masterpiece, the world. Now, Tegdirb worked long and hard on the painting.

During this time, Uranus was preoccupied about other things. He was worried about his son Cronas. It turned out Uranus had a right to be worried. Later, Cronas became King of the gods by killing his father. The dying Uranus had prophesied saying: "You murder me now and steal my throne but one of your own sons will dethrone you, for crime begets crime."

So Cronas did not really pay attention to the painting. Instead he swallowed his children as they were born.

All that time Tegdirb had been working on his painting. He had painted leaves green, apples red. He used all the colors of the rainbow. He painted different people different colors. He made Indian people dark skinned. He made Chinese people have different eyes. He did not want any two people to be the same. When Tegdirb was almost done painting his picture of the world, he fell and cut himself. He began to bleed. His blood was clear but just then some red paint spilled into his blood. This turned it very dark red. He liked the new color. Then he decided all the people in the painting would have red blood. This would make things more colorful. This is how blood turned the color red.

When Tegdirb was done with the painting, he gave it to Cronas.

Cronas was very pleased. So he made up his own world in the image of the painting.

—Bridget Negri
Grade 8

One possible tangent in a myths and myth-making unit might be to focus on the similarities and differences between myths and fairy tales. For instance, the class could invite a storyteller to tell three or four versions of "Cinderella" from different cultures. (Folklorists estimate that there are over 1500 written versions of the tale from more than seventy countries.) After the class has listened to the different versions, have the students identify structural elements that are necessary for a story to qualify as a "Cinderella" story. Then encourage the students to write their own versions based on their own experiences and cultural backgrounds. The following is one version of "Cinderella."

CINDERJULIE

"And hurry up," the evil stepbrother said. "I don't have a clean cup to get some milk with!" Cinderjulie just cut up the radio louder. It was the only thing her evil stepbrother allowed to have near her while she was working. But that's only because he likes music, and even if a song came on that she liked and he didn't he changed the station anyway. Just then a commercial about a concert came on:

Tonight! June 30! 8:00. Al B. Sure! in concert at Joe Louis Arena with guests Guy and Vanessa Williams.

Cinderjulie almost screamed with joy. She had been waiting for an Al B. Sure! concert for months. She loved him more than anyone could know. She had even saved her money for just this occasion. Cinderjulie knew she would have to ask her brother if she could go so she did the dishes ten times better than she would any other time. After she finished she went up the stairs and knocked on her brother's door. He kept it tightly bolted just in case Cinderjulie wanted to destroy his Anita Baker posters for revenge, which she did. "What," he called from the inside of the room.

"I have to ask you something," Cinderjulie answered. She waited while her brother unlocked the five locks on his door and came out.

"I'm half-listening," he said.

"Oh stepbrother," she said. "The Al B. Sure! concert is tonight at 8:00 and I . . ."

"No," he interrupted.

"But I have my own money saved!"

"No."

"But I've been waiting for months."

"No."

"But it's tonight only."

"No, I have a date tonight and you have to stay with your sister," he said with a that's final look. Cinderjulie looked up in his face for just a spark of hope but nothing came. She burst into tears and ran into her sister's room as her brother closed the door.

"What's wrong?" Cinderjulie's sister asked. Cinderjulie was forced to wash dishes, clean the kitchen and bathroom, and clean her room. Cinderjulie's sister was forced to clean the living room and dining room and clean her room. Cinderjulie's stepbrother stayed on the phone.

"The Al B. Sure! concert is tonight and stepbrother won't let me go!" Cinderjulie managed between sobs.

"Hmm," Cinderjulie's sister said. "It figures. I wondered if you knew about it yet."

"You mean you knew?" Cinderjulie asked, pained that her sister hadn't told her.

"Yes, and that's why I got you this." Cinderjulie's sister went to her closet and pulled out a shin length, black and white, acid washed skirt, and an Al B. Sure! shirt that matched perfectly! Then she bent down and pulled out a purse and some black and white Nike Airs. It looked so perfect Cinderjulie had to pinch herself to make sure everything was real. She must have used the occasional money stepbrother gave them to save.

"Now look in the purse," her sister told her. Cinderjulie stuck her hand in the black purse that went with the outfit. She pulled out one rectangular piece of paper. She gasped. It was a ticket to the concert!

"Oh thank you, thank you, thank you," Cinderjulie said hugging her sister. "But how do I get to go?"

"Stepbrother has a date with one of his bow-wow girlfriends, remember?" Cinderjulie's sister said. "So when he leaves you can go, and just make sure you're back by twelve which is when he usually gets home."

"You know sometimes I think you're a genius," Cinderjulie said to her sister happily.

So at 7:00 Cinderjulie's evil stepbrother left and by 7:30 Cinderjulie was ready to go. She was the most beautiful girl in the world that night (and every night I must say).

She was a little embarrassed that she had to take the bus, but to see Al B. it was worth it, she thought. When Cinderjulie arrived it was five minutes till show time so she bought her ticket and found her seat. Suddenly the lights went out and Al came on stage and started singing his beautiful slow ballads like "Nite and Day" and "Naturally Mine." But when he started singing "Killing Me Softly" something very special happened. Al B. came offstage and started walking down the very aisle that passed right by Cinderjulie! Cinderjulie tried to stay calm. But suddenly she felt a hand gently grab her and pull her toward the stage. Cinderjulie looked up and saw Al B. Sure! singing to her. When they got on stage Al pulled her close and started dancing. Cinderjulie followed his lead oblivious to the screaming girls and hot lights. Too soon the song was over. Al B. surprised Cinderjulie again by leading her to the backstage exit.

"You can watch the show from here and we can talk afterwards," he said with a deep deep voice. Cinderjulie walked into the dressing room and sat down. There was a TV that showed Al singing another one of his songs,

"Off on Your Own." When it was Guy and Vanessa's turn to perform, Al came in and sat down. It was 10:30.

"Love your shirt," Al said, smiling. In all the posters Cinderjulie had of Al, a smile was rare. But the ones she did have were gorgeous and this was even better.

"My sister gave it to me," was all Cinderjulie managed. But after that she relaxed and she and Al had a nice long conversation. From his favorite food to his strong belief in God. Cinderjulie found out that Al was everything she thought and dreamed he would be. She looked at her watch and it was 11:55.

"Oh, Jeez," she exclaimed. "I've got to go!"

"But why?" Al asked, standing up. Cinderjulie went into a two-minute explanation of how evil her stepbrother was and how if she was gone when he got back he would get every dish out of the cabinet, smear food on it, and make her wash it. Then he would go find the dirtiest dog he could find, wash it in their tub, and make her wash it out.

With that Cinderjulie dashed out the exit. But in her haste, the purse that she bought to go with her outfit got caught on something, so Cinderjulie just pulled it off her arm and kept running. Luckily, she kept her bus fare in her pocket. When Cinderjulie got off the bus, it was 12:20 on the dot. She ran as fast as she could to her front door.

"What happened to you?" Cinderjulie's sister whispered. "I had to tell stepbrother that you went to sleep early because you were so exhausted from crying." Cinderjulie couldn't hold it back any longer.

"I met Al!" She half screamed, half whispered.

"For real?" Cinderjulie's sister asked. "You're not lying?"

"If I died right now I would have lived a full life," Cinderjulie replied. So Cinderjulie and her sister took some hot chocolate up to their rooms and Cinderjulie told her sister every single detail about her meeting with Al B. Sure!

The next morning, Cinderjulie got up, got dressed and started doing her chores. Suddenly, there was a knock at the door. "I'll get it," Cinderjulie hollered. When she opened the door there were two strange men at the door.

"Does Cinderjulie live here?" one of them asked.

"I'm Cinderjulie. Who wants to know?" Cinderjulie answered. The two men stepped away and Al walked in the room. For one split second Cinderjulie felt thankful to her stepbrother for making them keep the house clean.

"H-How did you find me?" Cinderjulie stammered, still amazed at how good Al looked. He held up the purse.

"You left this outside my dressing room, remember? " he asked. Cinderjulie nodded, remembering that she always kept emergency ID in her purse just in case. By that time, Cinderjulie's sister and stepbrother were downstairs. Cinderjulie's sister just stood and stared, muttering, "You weren't lying." But her stepbrother took a different approach.

"How dare you lie to me! Just for that you're going to do every dish in the cabinet." Cinderjulie's stepbrother grabbed Cinderjulie's arm.

"And you get out!" he said to Al. "Just because you're some dumb star doesn't mean you can come ruling my house!" Just then Al's bodyguards came in and grabbed Cinderjulie's stepbrother, gagged him and tied him up. After that, Al took Cinderjulie's hand, got on one knee, and pulled out a black velvet box.

"Will you marry me?" he asked. First, Cinderjulie looked at her stepbrother. He was struggling and grunting. Then, she looked at her sister.

"Are you out of your mind?" her sister screamed, finally out of her daze. "Don't leave him waiting. Say Yes!!!" Cinderjulie looked back at Al and smiled.

"I'd love to," she said. Her sister started jumping up and down and her stepbrother started struggling even harder.

A month later, Cinderjulie and Al B. Sure! were married, and living happily in sunny, quiet Teaneck, New Jersey. Cinderjulie's brother was doomed to wash dishes and clean the house where Cinderjulie and Al live. Cinderjulie's sister married Al's cousin, Kyle West. And just about everybody lived happily ever after.

(Julie Pointer, in *Corridors: Stories from Inner-City Detroit*, Dewey Center Community Writing Project, 1989, pp. 76–77)

Week 2

Even as the students are constructing their own myths, the process of reading myths aloud in class continues, with myths from various cultures being introduced. The teacher can introduce each myth with a brief explanation of the culture from which it came. After the class has heard and read a number of myths from different cultures, small groups can be convened to discuss differences between the myths of various cultural groups. The teacher might ask students to concentrate on the myths of two specific groups or on differences across several. Either way, the groups can report a summary of their observations to the whole class.

After students have read and/or heard about a dozen myths, the teacher can list a few main characters from each on the board. Students might select five characters from the list and write responses to these characters in their journals, and then they write a character sketch of each. A few students might volunteer to read their character sketches aloud; the teacher would check their names in the grade book. Then the whole class might discuss the qualities they find common among the various characters from myths.

Students might also write a sketch based on an imagined encounter with a character from one of the myths. This activity would also encourage students to think of possibilities for expanding their own myths. Developing a "grammar" of myths can help students understand the genre of myths more completely, and at the same time, it can enable them to see that grammar is a way of describing how language works. Drawing on the work of Vladimir Propp (see Resources), the teacher can explain that myths have a characteristic "grammar" or structural pattern. The task of the class becomes that of developing a system to describe the pattern in a way that will apply to all the myths they have read. This can be a whole-class or small-group activity. Either way, participants in the discussion will need to agree on a set of rubrics such as "main character is introduced," "conflict develops between two characters," and "conflict is resolved." The object here is not to emulate Propp's terminology but to develop the understanding that myths, too, are constructed, not naturally occurring entities.

Once students have recognized myths as human constructs, they can move on to interpretation. One way to begin this process is to consider the different ways myths have been represented in other arts. Slides of paintings representing mythic events and characters can be shown, recordings of songs can be played, and film versions can be shown. Students might write in their journals in response to these other forms, noting how they feel about these different kinds of representations. The teacher can then assign students to select a myth and represent a character or event from it in another medium. Students can make drawings or collages, make videotapes, compose songs, or create three-dimensional representations.

If students don't seem ready for this representation project, one way to prepare them is to assign each small group to act out a myth of its choice. Each student can take the role of a different character in the myth, and one class session can be devoted to watching each group's "production" of the myth. The process of translating a myth into their own language and acting it out enables students to understand the nature of myths more completely.

Students can develop criteria for evaluating these representations of mythic events and characters in small-group discussions. The teacher may want to provide some guidance by involving the whole class in a discussion of the good qualities of the paintings and/or songs presented earlier. By identifying what they like and don't like in these representations, students can move toward identifying criteria for evaluating their own representations. In either event, once the criteria have been developed, the teacher can assign small groups the task of evaluating individuals' representations, or the teacher can do the evaluation, using the students' criteria.

Week 3

The exact length of this unit will, of course, vary according to the individual teacher's schedule, but as the unit moves toward closure, students will increasingly focus on individual or group projects. They can choose one of the cultures studied in the unit and invent characters who resemble those of myths read by the class. Small groups can help students develop and revise myths into their final versions. As is true for representation of myths, students can develop the criteria by which the myths can be evaluated. The process of developing these criteria can be a useful review of the myths studied. The teacher can list each myth studied and ask students to identify what makes each a good one or one not so good as the others. These features can then be combined to create the criteria by which myths are evaluated.

An excellent way to end this unit is to do a "read-around" during one class session. This means putting copies of all the student-composed myths in the center of the room and inviting students to select one from the pile, read it, return it to the pile (perhaps after making a few comments on a piece of paper attached to the back of the myth), and select another one. Alternatively, a couple of days can be devoted to having students tell their myths to the whole class.

Evaluation:

The teacher can evaluate the myths created by the students according to the criteria developed in the small groups. The students also receive credit

For participating in the small-group activities

For reading aloud three excerpts from their journals

For creating and reading aloud a myth or a fairy tale of their own creation

IMPLEMENTATION:
TEACHING A UNIT ON WAR AND PEACE IN THE ELEVENTH GRADE

A unit on war and peace can assume a much broader definition of war than the one suggested by military history. War can be defined as conflict, which opens the way to considering conflict in individual relationships and among various groups as well as between nations. Similarly, peace can be defined not just as an absence of war but as an active force, as a love that finds ways to overcome conflict. The unit described below assumes these broader definitions.

Desired Student Outcomes:

Development of an understanding of the terms "war" and "peace" by examining a variety of representations of both

Seeing the relationship between conflict and love

Understanding the roles of women and children in war

Seeing the analogies between individual and international relationships

Appreciating the role of multiethnic understanding and international understanding in fostering peace

Possible Whole-Class Activities:

Discuss representations of war in a variety of texts.

Respond to classmates' journal entries on readings.

Read assigned texts.

Participate in training for interviews of veterans.

Respond to interviews.

Participate in guided-imagery exercise for a process paper.

Develop criteria for evaluating papers.

Participate in a debate on war as an organizing force of society. (See Leonard Lewin's essay in Resources.)

Possible Small-Group Activities:

Participate in writing groups regularly.

Discuss questions that emerge from the texts.

Prepare for a debate on war as organizing force. (See Lewin's essay in Resources.)

Prepare and present an "omitted scene." (See Week 1 below.)

Prepare for interviews.

Dramatize and act out a war narrative.

Discuss situations of conflict in personal life.

Possible Individual Activities:

Write a process paper.

Write an unsent letter.

Watch, and write a review of, a film on war.

Read and give a report on a text from the suggested list.

Write a final paper about war and peace.

Resources:

Allen, Paula G. *Studies in American Indian Literature: Critical Essays and Course Designs.* New York: Modern Language Association, 1983.

Apocalypse Now (a film based on Joseph Conrad's *The Heart of Darkness*).

Baker, Houston. *Three American Literatures: Essays in Chicano, Native American and Asian American Literature for Teachers of American Literature.* New York: Modern Language Association, 1982.

Beal, Merrill. *I Will Fight No More Forever: Chief Joseph and the Nez Perce War.* New York: Ballantine, 1989.

Bierce, Ambrose. "An Occurrence at Owl Creek Bridge" (also film version).

Burchard, Peter. *Sea Change.* New York: Farrar, Straus & Giroux, 1984 (a novel about three generations of women facing war).

Butcher, P., ed. *The Ethnic Image in Modern American Literature: 1900–1950.* Washington, D.C.: Howard University Press, 1984.

Caesura (a five-minute film dramatization of the meeting of an American and a Vietnamese soldier on a jungle battlefield, who play music together and then part, returning to the war).

Crane, Stephen. *The Red Badge of Courage.* New York: Avon, 1987 (this edition includes passages omitted from the original manuscript and letters from Crane concerning his writing).

The Deer Hunter (film).

Dickens, Charles. *A Tale of Two Cities* (any edition).

DiPietro, R. J., and E. Ifkovic, eds. *Ethnic Perspectives in American Literature: Selected Essays on the European Contribution.* New York: Modern Language Association, 1983.

Do the Right Thing (film).

Edelman, Bernard, ed. *Dear America: Letters Home from Vietnam.* New York: Norton, 1986.

84 Charlie Mopic (film).

Good Morning, Vietnam (film).

Goodwin, Jan. *Caught in the Crossfire.* New York: Dutton, 1987 (a firsthand account by a U.S. magazine editor who disguised herself as an Afghan freedom fighter and lived among the soldiers in Afghanistan for months).

Hemingway, Ernest. *A Farewell to Arms* or *For Whom the Bell Tolls* (any edition). (There are film versions of both of these.)

Herr, Michael. *Dispatches.* New York: Knopf, 1977; New York: Avon, 1980 (accounts from Vietnam).

Hurston, Zora Neal. "Sweat."

Jordan, June. *Dry Victories.* An account of how the victories of the Reconstruction became a defeat.

Jury, Mark. *The Vietnam Photo Book.* New York: Vintage, 1981.

Kennett, Lee. *The American Soldier in World War II.* New York: Scribners, 1987.

King, Martin Luther, Jr., "Loving Your Enemies."

Lauter, Paul. *Reconstructing American Literature: Courses, Syllabi, Issues.* Old Westbury, N.Y.: Feminist Press, 1983.

Lewin, Leonard. *Report from Iron Mountain, 1967.* New York: Dial Press, 1967 (contains "The Functions of War," an essay that argues that war is the principal organizing force in most societies).

Marshall, Kathryn. *In the Combat Zone: An Oral History of American Women in Vietnam, 1966-1975.* Boston: Little, Brown, 1987.

Mason, Bobbie Ann. *In Country.* New York: Harper & Row, 1985 (a novel about a young girl whose father was killed in Vietnam and about her efforts to understand her past and future).

Meltzer, Milton. *Ain't Gonna Study War No More: The Story of America's Peace Seekers.* New York: Harper & Row, 1985.

Nichols, David, ed. *Ernie's War: The Best of Ernie Pyle's World War II Dispatches.* New York: Random House, 1986.

Petry, Ann. "In the Darkness and Confusion" (a short story about the 1943 Harlem riot).

The Red Badge of Courage (film).

Ross, Lillian. *Picture.* New York: Avon Books, 1969 (an account of the making of John Houston's film version of *The Red Badge of Courage*).

Sanchez, M. E. *Contemporary Chicana Poetry: A Critical Approach to an Emerging Literature.* Berkeley: University of California Press, 1986.

Silko, Leslie Marmon. *Ceremony.* New York: Penguin, 1986 (a fictional account of an American Indian war veteran's struggle to readjust to his homeland).

Tolstoy, Leo. *War and Peace* (any edition). (There is a film version.)

Wiesel, Elie. *Night.* New York: Bantam, 1982 (account of a survivor of the Jewish holocaust of World War II).

West Side Story (film).

Organization of the Unit:

Week 1

The teacher will have decided which texts the whole class will read and which will be on the list for individual reading and reports. A text like *The Red Badge of Courage* can be good for whole-class reading because it can be understood on several levels and it raises a number of important issues. An alternative is to use a series of shorter texts—including poetry, letters, films—and reserve novel-length works for individual reading. Either way, the teacher will establish a context for the whole unit.

One way to begin is to compare different poetic representations of war. For example, one could select Rupert Brooke's "The Soldier" and Stephen Crane's "War Is Kind" and compare these to more contemporary poetic responses to war.

War Is Kind

Do not weep, maiden, for war is kind.
Because your lover threw wild hands toward the sky
And the frighted steed ran on alone,
Do not weep.
War is kind.

       Hoarse, booming drums of the regiment,
       Little souls who thirst for fight,
       These men were born to drill and die.
       The unexplained glory flies above them,
       Great is the battle god, great, and his kingdom—
       A field where a thousand corpses lie.

Do not weep, babe, for war is kind.
Because your father tumbled in the yellow trenches,

Raged at his breast, gulped and died,
Do not weep.
War is kind.

Swift blazing flag of the regiment,
Eagle with crest of red and gold,
These men were born to drill and die.
Point for them the virtue of slaughter,
Make plain to them the excellence of killing
And a field where a thousand corpses lie.

Mother whose heart hung humble as a button
On the bright splendid shroud of your son,
Do not weep.
War is kind.

—Stephen Crane

The Bloody Sire

It is not bad. Let them play.
Let the guns bark and the bombing-plane
Speak his prodigious blasphemies.
It is not bad, it is high time,
Stark violence is still the sire of all the world's values.

What but the wolf's tooth whittled so fine
The fleet limbs of the antelope?
What but fear winged the birds, and hunger
Jeweled with such eyes the great goshawk's head?
Violence has been the sire of all the world's values.

Who would remember Helen's face
Lacking the terrible halo of spears?
Who formed Christ but Herod and Caesar,
The cruel and bloody victories of Caesar?
Violence, the bloody sire of all the world's values.

Never weep, let them play,
Old violence is not too old to beget new values.

—Robinson Jeffers

The Soldier

If I should die, think only this of me:
    That there's some corner of a foreign field
That is for ever England. There shall be
    In that rich earth a richer dust concealed;
A dust whom England bore, shaped, made aware,
    Gave, once, her flowers to love, her ways to roam,
A body of England's, breathing English air,
    Washed by the rivers, blest by sons of home.

And think, this heart, all evil shed away,
    A pulse in the eternal mind, no less
Gives somewhere back the thoughts by England given;
    Her sights and sounds; dreams happy as her day;
And laughter, learnt of friends; and gentleness,
    In hearts at peace, under an English heaven.

—Rupert Brooke

War and Words

I was always embarrassed by the words sacred, glorious, and
sacrifice and the expression in vain. We had heard them,
sometimes standing in the rain almost out of earshot, so that
only the shouted words came through, and had read them, on
proclamations that were slapped up by billposters over other
proclamations, now for a long time, and I had seen nothing
sacred, and the things that were glorious had no glory and the
sacrifices were like the stockyards at Chicago if nothing was
done with the meat except to bury it. There were many words
that you could not stand to hear and finally only the names of
places had dignity. Certain numbers were the same way and
certain dates and these with the names of the places were all
you could say and have them mean anything. Abstract words
such as glory, honor, courage, or hallow were obscene beside
the concrete names of villages, the numbers of roads, the
names of rivers, the numbers of regiments and the dates.
                    —Lt. Frederick Henry in Ernest Hemingway,
                            A Farewell to Arms, Chapter 27.

Driving Through Minnesota
During the Hanoi Bombings

We drive between lakes just turning green;
Late June. The white turkeys have been moved
To new grass.
How long the seconds are in great pain!
Terror just before death,
Shoulders torn, shot
From Helicopters, the boy
Tortured with the telephone generator,
"I felt sorry for him,
And blew his head off with a shotgun."
These instants become crystals,
Particles
The grass cannot dissolve. Our own gaiety
Will end up
In Asia, and in your cup you will look down
And see
Black Starfighters.
We were the ones we intended to bomb!
Therefore we will have
To go far away
To atone
For the sufferings of the stringy-chested
And the small rice-fed ones, quivering
In the helicopter like wild animals,
Shot in the chest, taken back to be questioned.

—Robert Bly

The teacher might read these poems aloud and then circulate copies of them for the class to read again silently and write responses in their journals. The teacher could focus this response by asking students to create a dialogue between Crane and Brooke about war or could choose to leave the journal entries unstructured. Among the issues that might be considered are the differences in attitude toward war, the role of nationalism/imperialism in war, the roles assigned to women and children, and the style of each poem. Asking several students to read their journal entries will introduce other issues as well.

As the assigned class reading is begun, students might write nightly responses in their journals, and the teacher could ask a few volunteers to read aloud their responses the next day. These responses would be used to help direct class discussions. To move students to perceive the text as constructed by a human being, the teacher could ask them to identify a scene or event that is referred to but not included in the text (the "omitted scene") and write a brief account of it in their journals. This introduces the fact that authors make selections of what to include in texts. Small groups could choose one of these scenes and dramatize it for the whole class. Discussing these scenes would further enhance the students' understanding of the constructed nature of texts.

Week 2

By the second week of this unit the teacher could begin preparing students to interview a war veteran. Excerpts from collections such as Edelman's and Goodwin's (see Resources) might give students a flavor of the kinds of subjects veterans may want to discuss. Students should be cautioned, however, that some veterans may be very reluctant to discuss their war experiences and that as interviewers they should be sensitive to that fact. If it is possible, the teacher should arrange to have a veteran be interviewed by the whole class. When students see the varying accounts that emerge from the same interview, the difficulty of asking the "right" questions, and the problems connected with getting the interviewee's exact language, they will be more inclined to prepare for their own out-of-class interviews.

After they have interviewed a war veteran, students might write reports of their interviews. These reports could be read aloud in class or collected into a class publication so everyone would have an opportunity to read them. Discussing these interviews will lead into the area of interpretation because there will inevitably be differences of opinion about the same war among the veterans. This exposure to interpretation will enhance students' reading and discussion of assigned texts.

Week 3

After the interviews are under way, the class might turn to the issue of how war is perceived by the larger society. Lewin's essay on "The Functions of War" (see Resources) provides an excellent way of focusing on how war can be seen as organizing economic, political, sociological, ecological, scientific, and cultural forces in society. After they have read and written responses to this essay, students could meet in small groups to develop arguments for and against Lewin's position. The class could then participate in a debate about war's role in society. Preparing for and participating in this debate would enable students to evaluate Lewin's text.

As the assigned class reading continues, students could write an unsent letter. Like the omitted-scene exercise, this letter would provide an opportunity for students to move beyond initial responses to more complicated perceptions, because they would need to imagine issues that were not included in the text they were reading. The unsent letter should be written in the voice of one character in the text and should be addressed to another character. These letters could be revised in small writing groups.

One of the sources that might be used in focusing on the letter genre as a means of responding to war is *Dear America: Letters Home from Vietnam*:

Only the crickets
Are bold enough to speak
Suddenly they stop
The rapid respiration
Of frightened men's remains.
You think of home and wait
Mostly you just wait.
The mortar lands nearby
Ringing in your ears
Leaves you deaf
For the rest of your life
But just how long
Will that be?

—SP4 GEORGE T. COLEMAN
Assistant hotel manager, Princeton, N.J.

I killed my first "gooks" last night—about 20 of them. I spotted them about 800 meters in front of our position by using a starlight scope, and called in artillery on them. I only had to make one adjustment, and then they were blown away . . . It didn't bother me at all, because self-preservation is the name of the game over here.

—MARINE LIEUT. DESMOND T. BARRY JR.
Attorney, New York City.

Those dead Cong didn't seem like people [as] we dragged them into piles and cut their equipment off them. They felt like a pile of rags or something, can't really explain it. We shot all their wounded [the] next day. The official body count was 79 . . . Some of the Charlies were just kids, 14 or 15 years old. They must be crazy or something.

—PFC LOUIS E. WILLETT
Received mortal wounds covering a
squad retreat; posthumously awarded the
Congressional Medal of Honor.

I know that at one point, my feet about to crack open, my stomach knotted by hunger and diarrhea, my back feeling like a mirror made of nerves shattered in a million pieces by my flak jacket, pack, and extra

mortars and machine-gun ammo, my hands a mass of hamburger from
thorn-cuts and my face a mass of welts from mosquitoes, I desired greatly
to throw down everything, slump into the water of the paddy and sob.
                                    —MARINE LIEUT. VICTOR DAVID WESTPHALL
                                                        Killed during an ambush.

Reflections on the Letters

   Although not all the letters written by soldiers expressed the same
attitudes toward war, there was definitely a strong feeling one was left
with after reading them. This feeling was one of opposition toward the
war. The graphic depictions of violence, the hopelessness expressed concerning the war, and the sheer confusion over why and who they were
fighting led to this. When I read the letters the people writing them
seemed so fictional. I believe this is due to two main things. One, my lack
of knowledge concerning Vietnam, and, two, all the different forms of
media I have seen about the war have clouded my vision. For instance, in
the movie theater I have seen two main types of films on Vietnam. The
first genre is the gung-ho look at Vietnam, where the American soldiers
are untouchable. *Missing in Action* is a good example of these. The second
kind of film is the serious look at Vietnam like *Platoon,* where soldiers lose
battles, limbs, and their lives. When I read these letters I cannot help but
envision individuals from these movies. In some of these letters the
soldiers write things like "I killed my first gooks last night . . ." In others
they write poetry and grieve over lost friends. So, because of these two
extremes in both the movies and in the letters, the letters seem as fictional
as the films. Thus, I can't tell how I feel about Vietnam.

                                                        —Mary*

Students might choose to write their own letters in response.
Week 4
Early in the unit students would be told that they are responsible for
writing a paper on an issue of their choice that emerges from studying
war and peace. The teacher would explain that journals are usually the
best source of ideas for these papers. By the fourth week the teacher
would ask students to submit a paragraph-length description of the issue
they plan to address in their final papers. The teacher might respond to
these descriptions and the students can continue to work on them
throughout the remainder of the unit. The teacher should specify dates
when first drafts, revisions, and final papers are due. Regular meetings
with writing groups would help students with these papers, and the
teacher might, in addition, arrange brief individual conferences with

---

* Excerpted from *Dear America: Letters Home from Vietnam,* edited by Bernard
Edelman for the New York Vietnam Veterans Memorial Commission. Published
by W. W. Norton (1985) and Pocket Books (1986). Reprinted by permission.

students as their writing progresses. The teacher might also require a process paper to accompany this assignment.

Week 5

To expand concepts of war and peace to include interpersonal as well as international conflicts, the teacher could assign readings that emphasize ethnic and personal differences. Looking at texts such as those by Allen, Baker, Beal, Butcher, and DiPietro (see Resources) will suggest many possible readings, and class readings of texts such as those by Hurston, Jordan, King, Petry, Sanchez, Silko, and Wiesel will provide insights into cultural differences. Building and breaking boundaries between people can become the thematic focus as the unit moves toward examining issues of conflict and love.

Many of the same exercises used in the first part of the unit could be repeated using this material; it is particularly effective to set characters and issues from the first part against those from the second. In addition, since issues of conflict and love surface in students' own relationships, students could be encouraged to look at texts in terms of their own experiences. One way to introduce this would be to read the first paragraph of Dickens's *A Tale of Two Cities* (see Resources) and invite students to develop a paraphrase of "It was the best of times, it was the worst of times" and use it as an introduction to a journal entry in which they write about a time of crisis in their own lives.

Evaluation:

As was explained in the eighth-grade myth unit, students could develop the criteria by which their written products are evaluated. This process of development would strengthen their evaluative skills and at the same time help them understand that grading is not a mysterious process.

The teacher can make quantitative and qualitative evaluations of the students' work during the course of this unit. Quantitative evaluation would be based on the completion of specified assignments:

> Writing a certain number of journal entries and reading the entries aloud to the class
>
> Dramatizing an omitted scene
>
> Participating regularly in whole-class and small-group discussions
>
> Conducting an interview with a war veteran and reporting on it to the class

Qualitative evaluation would be based on the student's process paper, unsent letter, final paper, review of the film, and review of reading assignments.

Suggested Reading

ATWELL, NANCIE. *In the Middle: Writing, Reading, and Learning with Adolescents.* Portsmouth, N.H.: Boynton/Cook, 1987.

Atwell provides a detailed description of a middle school classroom where students select their own topics for writing, participate regularly in workshops, and discuss their reading in small groups. The author, a middle school teacher herself, provides many how-to explanations.

BLEICH, DAVID. *Readings and Feelings: An Introduction to Subjective Criticism.* Urbana, Ill.: NCTE, 1975.

Bleich describes a literature program that encourages students to become more aware of their individual responses to literature. This awareness enables them to see that reading, writing, and thinking about what they read can help them understand themselves better.

BRITTON, JAMES, "Writing to Learn and Learning to Write." In *Prospect and Retrospect: Selected Essays by James Britton.* Portsmouth, N.H.: Boynton/Cook, 1982, pp. 94–111.

This article introduces the key concepts of expressive, transactional, and poetic language that underlie Britton's theory of writing development. A more expanded version of this theory can be found in *The Development of Writing Abilities (11–18)* by Britton and several of his colleagues.

ELBOW, PETER. *Writing with Power: Techniques for Mastering the Writing Process.* New York: Oxford University Press, 1981.

"Power" as it is used in this book refers to voice in writing, and Elbow offers strategies, including peer feedback, revision, and free-writing, to help writers develop power. This and Elbow's earlier book, *Writing Without Teachers,* provide many exercises and strategies that can be used in a language-as-expression classroom.

HOLLAND, NORMAN. *5 Readers Reading.* New Haven, Conn.: Yale University Press, 1973.

Here Holland reports a study of the reactions of five students to William Faulkner's short story "A Rose for Emily." The meaning of the story for each student is determined by his or her "identity theme," or the organizing configuration with which an ego mediates among the forces acting on it.

———. *Poems in Persons.* New York: Norton, 1975.

Holland describes the responses of readers to a poem and elaborates his theory of response as conditioned by personality.

MACRORIE, KEN. *The I-Search Paper.* Portsmouth, N.H.: Boynton/Cook/Heinemann, 1988.

This is the revised edition of *Searching Writing,* which sets forth Macrorie's version of the research paper and involves students more actively in gathering and presenting material both from print and nonprint sources.

———. *Uptaught.* New York: Hayden, 1970.

This book describes Macrorie's attempts to get students to break out of the flat, mechanical writing he calls "Engfish." It includes strategies for peer-response groups as well as many examples of effective student writing.

NATIONAL COUNCIL OF TEACHERS OF ENGLISH. *Books for You: A Booklist for Senior High Students*, 10th ed. Urbana, Ill.: NCTE, 1988.

Published every three years, this reference book provides brief descriptions of over 1200 titles. The editors solicit teenagers' responses to the books, and divide them into over forty thematic categories such as social situations, humor and satire, animals and pets, drugs and alcohol, and fantasy.

NATIONAL COUNCIL OF TEACHERS OF ENGLISH. *Your Reading: A Booklist for Junior High and Middle School Students*, 7th ed. Urbana, Ill.: NCTE, 1988.

Published every four years, this reference book is similar to *Books for You*, except that it concentrates on books of interest to junior high/middle school students. The thematic categories appear under generic headings such as fiction, drama, poetry, and nonfiction.

REID, IAN. *The Making of Literature*. Australian Association for the Teaching of English, 1984.

Following in the tradition of Louise Rosenblatt, Reid describes classrooms where students and teachers work together to create meanings from reading.

ROSENBLATT, LOUISE. *Literature as Exploration*, 3d ed. New York: Noble, 1976.

First published in 1938, this book represents one of the earliest explorations of students' responses to their reading. Rosenblatt's transactional theory of reading has influenced many English teachers during the past six decades, and it still offers important insights for today's teachers.

7

Language as Social Construct

SARAH IS AN EXPERIENCED TEACHER in an alternative K–8 urban school in a metropolitan area where a large majority of the students are African American. The school is located in an area of the city that appears bleak and is known to be dangerous: There are gangs, violence, drugs, massive unemployment, and much poverty to contend with. Abandoned storefronts and burned-out buildings intermingle with a few gentrified restaurants and some struggling, long-standing community businesses. Many of the students in Sarah's class live in the nearby housing projects, and some of them who aren't that fortunate live with their families in the nearby homeless shelter. Some of the shelter students attend Sarah's class less frequently than her other students, but nearly all of her students would be classified by most standard measures as at-risk.

But the atmosphere in Sarah's class works against the apparent despair. Her sixth- and seventh-grade classroom is an explosion of activity. The walls are lined with students' colorful "Me" collages. There is a large poster of Martin Luther King, Jr., and a display on the environment. A sign declares, insists, WE ARE FAMILY, and another says, "A people without a history is like a tree without its roots." A map of the area is accompanied by a question: "Can you find your block on this map? Books line the walls and fill two carousels. There are literally thousands of books, including much fiction, both classics and popular novels, and nonfiction related to seemingly every subject the students might be working on. Some of her twenty-seven students are talking, some of them are laughing together, most of them are studiously involved in a variety of activities.

Sarah doesn't believe that students all have to work on the same things at the same time; she has a rather fluid concept of a teaching unit. "None of these things is ever really finished," she says, "and kids work at different paces, with different interests and ability levels. I think you have to be comfortable with that in a classroom. You can't rigidly control the pace at which people learn." She works with their various strengths and interests as much as possible and is willing to shift gears if students want to move in wholly new directions. Hers is a "whole-language" classroom (see Box 10.5) that emphasizes using language to learn about the world in which the students live. Her students this semester are being given many opportunities to work on projects that could have a direct impact on their own lives. She believes that part of empowering her students to read and write means getting them to believe they can change the world in which they live. Thus, Jerry and LaShunda are working on a report on the controversial incinerator located nearby; Eboney and Tammi are working on a fictional story about a woman from Kenya, based on their research about that country; Allen is writing a play about slavery; Tuere is writing about a recent classroom visitor, Ms. Rose Bell, director of United Neighbors, a volunteer organization based in the nearby projects; Temeco and Regina, who have themselves just finished writing about Ms. Bell, are knitting baby clothes for 961-BABY, an organization run by Ms. Bell that helps unwed mothers; Leslie and Carol, who have just finished reading Anne Frank's *The Diary of a Young Girl*, are writing their reports on the book in the form of journal entries.

Though Sarah encourages collaboration, she hopes that learning with others will eventually help her students to become independently functioning critical thinkers. One of her basic teaching principles is to allow them to have control in some significant ways over the terms of their own learning environment. "They need to be able to shape to some extent what happens in this classroom, to know that I support them and am working *with* them, that I respect them as learners," she says. "In so many aspects of their lives, students are made to feel powerless. They need to feel empowered in my classroom." Although expectations for their work are high (they have weekly conferences with Sarah to discuss their various projects), students are given wide parameters for what they can do in her class. She has students set goals for themselves and monitor their own

Sounds corny!

progress toward those goals. During lulls in other activities, she regularly asks students to negotiate goals and procedures with her.

The class as a whole (nearly all students are involved in every project, but there are exceptions) is working on various broadly conceived (and often, to some extent, interdisciplinary) projects: a writing project in science that investigates the environmental impact of the controversial incinerator located nearby, research "books" on foreign countries, a computer telecommunications project with several other schools on the Arab-Israeli conflict, a "How to Avoid World War III" project, and a "Struggle for Equal Rights" unit (described more completely below). Sarah invites parents into her classroom regularly. She also invites guests, some of them area businesspeople and volunteers from community organizations—"as long as they will work and help kids with their writing," Sarah insists. The students interview these guests and occasionally visit them in their offices or workplaces.

Sarah's classroom is not often quiet. It is rich in talk, most of it (but of course not all) on task; students share ideas in workshop groups on how to shape each other's writing, and they often disagree. Today Tuere, Tameka, and Eboney, and two other groups, are working on their I-Search papers about various countries. They are reading and responding to each other's writing, answering questions that Sarah has provided. "I think you should put in more about what they wear. I liked that part," Tuere tells Tameka about her story on Ethiopia. "I like the pictures you drew," Eboney says. Tameka thinks that she "should maybe try writing a story about a person who lives there," in addition to what she already has done. Tuere and Eboney like the idea and give her some suggestions on how she can do that. Tuere likes the idea so much she decides to try some of the suggestions in her own story. Sarah, having a writing conference with DeShawn and Shawn, overhears the talk and suggests a couple of books they can read to learn how others have done it.

Allen is working with a visiting volunteer who is talking with him about his I-Search project, the play about slavery that is to be produced by fifth graders. An in-service teacher who works in Sarah's class six hours a week is helping Ronrico get started on his project, a study of the religions of India. Most of the other students are either working on various projects alone, writing in journals or working on other writing, illustrating writing they have already done, working on the computer, or reading and taking notes. Two kids are writing notes to each other, and three others still seem to be talking with each other about last night's televised basketball game. They have projects waiting on their desks in front of them, but Sarah says they do most of their work at home, and some of the work just doesn't get done.

Sarah is hustling from person to person, group to group, paying as much attention as she can to those who need it most. The students in her class are writing for each other as well as for Sarah, and they are planning

[handwritten margin notes:] a little too idealistic

"where will these 'volunteers' come from? It is very difficult to get people to donate their most precious resource—time (even if they are interested in education.)

on publishing some of their writing (on ditto masters) to share with the principal, the district language arts coordinator, and their friends and parents. The students see a real purpose for their writing, since they will be sharing it with others who have an interest in it (and in them).

What is Sarah's perspective on language and teaching? "I hate a rigid environment," she says. "So much of teaching is lockstep, and doesn't take advantage of the strengths that kids have as learners, their ability to talk with each other, their interests. I think you grow in language when you work with others and work on things you really care about. Part of the reason for the high dropout rate in city schools is that the schoolwork they have to do has nothing to do with the world from which they come. There are real problems in the world, and I think they have to know about them and learn how they can deal with them in their own, perhaps small, way."

Analysis of the Approach

Sarah's classroom exemplifies the language-as-social-construct perspective. For her and teachers like her, teaching English means teaching reading and writing as an active, dynamic process where meaning is generated through the interaction of students, their teachers, and various texts, both spoken and written. In other words, teaching English is teaching literacy. The challenge is not to cover a specific set of texts or objectives in a specific period of time, but to engage students in activities that ask them to discover and make sense of whatever they have chosen to study. These themes have as a common denominator a concern for collective community life. As Sarah says, she wants her students to believe they can change the world they live in. Reading and writing play critical roles in her students' ability to understand, respond to, and participate in community life.

The concern for community—the classroom community and the communities in which the students live—stems from another important element of the language-as-social-construct perspective, which recognizes that schooling takes place in particular social and cultural contexts. Sarah's kids, for instance, live immersed in an urban neighborhood. Their lives are complicated by poverty, crime, drugs, and prejudice. Her language-as-social-construct classroom attempts to open up these very real issues for discussion and debate in the learning activities of students. Sarah's students will need to learn what other possibilities exist for them and what political empowerment means in the most concrete sense if they are to play a role in changing these conditions. Investigating local, national, and world issues that impinge on students' lives enriches their understanding and helps them acquire the kinds of survival skills necessary to have a voice in the political and cultural life of the community.

Teachers who adopt a language-as-social-construct perspective also assume that acquiring and improving literacy is an important step in the process of social and political empowerment, whether students live in the inner city or the suburbs.

The language-as-social-construct perspective offers a radically different view of literacy. Within this framework, literacy is a process of social engagement, where texts are seen as part of a dialogue among people with common, competing, or often opposing interests. Students must learn to negotiate and critique these positions to come to their own informed stands. As they read and write about issues, they create their own tentative versions of the world. For example, when Allen researches and then writes his own play about slavery, he is interpreting his history. He is creating a version of what slavery was, how it affected people, and how it has shaped our collective life. For Allen and the students in Sarah's class who see his play, the text adds to the ways they have understood slavery and to their understanding of their cultural heritage.

In a language-as-social-construct classroom, the opportunity to explore topics of historical or cultural interest is seen as an important way to develop the students' sense of their place in the larger community. Students' opinions and attitudes are shaped not only by the texts they encounter in school, but also by other texts encountered outside the classroom—the voices of the immediate community, of cultural affiliations, and of society in general. Teaching from a language-as-social-construct perspective invites the community into the classroom to encourage students to explore critically, through reading and writing, the issues that are important to them. This perspective emphasizes student research by drawing on community resources. Members of the community are frequently invited to class to speak with students; students read community histories and newspapers to develop their own writing projects, which then emerge from what they discover. (See Box 7.1.)

The underlying principle guiding such student-conducted research is that knowledge is created through social interaction; it is not preexisting or acquired by exposure to certain texts or information. As a result, student research is seen as generating knowledge through reading and writing activities. The primary goal of this perspective is to empower students to develop their own voices, as in the language-as-expression model (from which it draws heavily), but in a potentially more culturally critical way. With emphasis on the social ways that students learn, it also stresses the need for interaction and collaboration. This perspective rejects the notion of the individual in isolation, emphasizing the individual as a member of a complex social world. Classroom activities are designed to help make explicit the roles and relationships that constitute this world.

The language-as-social-construct perspective views language as a flexible, socially defined system through which humans negotiate meaning and understanding in their lives. It is above all social, constantly

---

BOX 7.1
COMMUNITY RESOURCES FOR READING AND WRITING PROJECTS

- Long-standing community residents.
- Local businesspeople.
- Local public libraries, which are good sources of community history.
- Government agencies, including municipal, county, and state offices. City offices often have speakers' bureaus.
- Museums: historical museums, art museums, and others.

- Local newspapers, a source of publication and of research information.
- Political and philanthropic organizations such as political parties, unions, and volunteer associations.
- Local colleges and universities.
- Local writers and artists.

---

evolving, and generative. The role of the teacher becomes that of a more experienced peer who questions and clarifies in an effort to assist the student to reach more sophisticated and novel solutions or responses. This view of language learning has been developed in the work of Soviet psychologist Lev Vygotsky. (See Suggested Reading at the end of this chapter.) According to Vygotsky, language learning occurs as children interact with the social world. Interacting at first with family and friends, children begin to use language to accomplish the rudimentary tasks of childhood such as getting attention and satisfying hunger. As the scope of the child's universe increases, language becomes an important psychological tool that helps the child solve problems and understand concepts. Thus, language learning and cognitive development are seen as integrally linked and socially grounded. Children learn through interaction with objects and other people.

In *Mind in Society*, Vygotsky described this theory of learning through the concept of the "zone of proximal development." Basically, he argues that children have an "actual developmental level" at which they have the ability to understand concepts or complete tasks without assistance. In addition, children can complete more complicated tasks with the assistance of adults or more able peers. This level Vygotsky calls the "level of potential development." Between these two levels lies the zone of proximal development, and it is here that most school learning best takes place. The teacher and/or peers, through interaction, coach a student to move beyond what he or she can currently do only with assistance toward what can be done independently.

It is important to keep in mind that learning conceived this way takes place in real social contexts. As Lev Vygotsky says in *Mind in Society* (p. 88),

"[H]uman learning presupposes a specific social nature and a process by which children grow into the intellectual life of those around them." Children growing up in different social settings learn different things and learn in different ways, depending on the home culture in which they are raised.

For example, Shirley Brice Heath documented the different kinds of language learning of students from two neighboring communities and how these different experiences shaped the students' school performance. (See Suggested Reading at the end of this chapter.) Students from Roadville, one of the communities Heath studied, came from primarily white, working-class families where telling stories of actual events, as opposed to "made-up" events, was rewarded. (In fact, fictional stories were considered "lies.") On the other hand, students in Trackton, a black, working-class community, were encouraged to fantasize and embellish stories, the more elaborate the better. These two groups of students presented very different approaches to classroom assignments because of their community language experiences, leading Heath and others to underscore the importance of cultural practices in the way students learn to become literate. Studies such as Heath's contribute to a language-as-social-construct perspective by highlighting the extensive, but culturally specific, knowledge children possess about language. This knowledge is "embedded in complex social and emotional meanings that need to be acknowledged and built upon, not ignored or dismantled" (Deborah Brandt, "Versions of Literacy," in *College English* 47 [1985], p. 135). Teaching from a language-as-social-construct point of view implies, then, that students will have the opportunity to build upon what they already know, the meanings that have come to them through their participation in a complex cultural world.

Exploring this world and learning to understand its implicit rules for discourse and social practice become the staples of language-as-social-construct classrooms. These classrooms are concerned with the processes of interaction between individuals, groups, and texts as a means for students to enlarge their repertoire of language skills, using them in activities such as I-Search papers, publishing projects, and student-conducted community research. Teachers organize their teaching around those skills or activities that will help students complete their projects. Learning to interview community members, analyze transcripts, develop stories or essays from the data collected, and work in groups become essential tasks of the classroom. These classrooms encourage conversation, and teachers incorporate ample opportunities for students to share their discoveries. Teachers who believe that language is socially constructed will yield the podium to students, also yielding authority for the direction and flow of the conversation.

It is important that classroom authority be shared in the language-as-social-construct perspective. Teachers see their classrooms as a community, a microcosm of the "real" world, where, as Jay Robinson says in *Conversations on the Written Word* (p. 108), "the ways students and teachers communicate among themselves—the sets of relations they establish among themselves—are the critical issues in language development" (See Suggested Reading at the end of this chapter). Thus, when Sarah's students share their texts and offer each other suggestions, they are learning to negotiate the world through language, discovering new possibilities for language use and new meanings for the words they use. Distinctions between reading, writing, literature, and grammar become blurred, since students read each other's texts as both readers and writers, for information and to critique. They also read literature to inform their writing, examining the craft of the writer as well as the meanings they take from the reading. In other words, students are encouraged to see themselves as authorities, taking responsibility for their points of view.

This perspective encourages a pedagogy linked to empowerment and the possibility to engage in "praxis," a term introduced by Paulo Freire. (See Suggested Reading at the end of this chapter.) According to Freire, praxis, a learner's critical reflection on the world in order to change it, occurs when individuals use language in the process of "self-expression and world-expression, of creating and re-creating, of deciding and choosing and ultimately participating in society's historical process" (Freire and Macedo, 1987). A Brazilian educator concerned with literacy, Freire believes that most education is characterized by a "banking concept" where education becomes "an act of depositing, in which students are the depositories and the teacher is depositor" (Freire, 1986). This form of education places students in a passive role and denies what Freire sees as the political nature of schooling: The schools determine who gets taught what and in what way.

So how are Freire's views relevant to the language-as-social-construct classroom? First, they acknowledge the political aspects of schooling. Second, they provide the grounds for addressing political topics in the classroom, actively engaging students in a dialogue about controversial topics. Third, they focus on empowering students' voices, claiming that all people have a vested interest in the decisions that govern their lives, and schooling ought to prepare all students to share in the decision-making processes. Finally, Freire sees critical literacy, a literacy that empowers students to affect their own social, political, and cultural circumstances, as the primary goal of schooling.

Teachers who subscribe to a language-as-social-construct perspective assemble, with their students, the ways and means of such political empowerment. Many of the projects they choose occur outside the usual boundaries of the classroom and the school. Students and teachers collectively design projects that involve students in the community and emphasize critical reflection about the learning that takes place by "doing." The projects take their shape through a collaboration among teachers, students, and the community. Students might share insights they have acquired from interviewing members of the community, detailing their positions on controversial political topics. They might start a letter-writing campaign or write a story based on another person's experiences. They might engage in such projects as recycling programs, surveying school board members on controversial topics, or testing water quality and reporting the results to the city council. In this way, notions of research and critical examination of even ordinary experience become central parts of the curriculum. ——

In order to prepare students for their own community research, teachers should introduce concepts and skills that will enable students to conduct their inquiries. (See Box 7.2.) Interviewing skills, survey and polling procedures, letter-writing conventions, the use of library resources, critical reading of both other students' work and professional literature (such as novels, magazines, and newspapers) can all be important in community research. These are generally handled as whole-group minilessons similar to those described by Nancie Atwell in *In the Middle*. (See Suggested Reading at the end of this chapter.) For example, students who are exploring the theme of working might read together selections from Studs Terkel's *Working*, listen to tapes from his interviews, and then discuss what emerge as the critical issues for his interviewees. For their own projects, some students might choose to interview adult family members, generating their own set of questions. Other students might investigate a specific career, combining interview and print sources in their research. Still others might read James Herriot's *All Creatures Great and Small* and then write a personal memoir of their own work-related experiences. Assignments like these can provide models for what kids want to do in the world, as the walls of the classroom dissolve. The teacher would combine individual and small-group activities with whole-group lessons, determined by what students needed. Throughout this process students would have conferences with both peers and teacher, receiving suggestions and comments about their work.

The class as a whole might take on a project, such as the "cross-age" teaching unit described later. These classroom projects are important to developing a sense of community in the classroom and to fostering collaboration among students. With a common goal, students share perspectives and make collective decisions about the whats and hows of the project. They have the opportunity to negotiate and reach consensus over what they will write about, how it will be organized, and even what the final product should be. The point is that students assume responsibility and authority for the nature of the projects they complete.

Whatever projects teachers and students undertake, they should be grounded in the concrete contexts of the classroom, the school, the community. They should be chosen in light of student interest and a concern for the historical and/or cultural significance they represent.

help exercises like these break the college/career tracks in high schools. OK

something can be interesting + giving it a chance.

Student interest s/b taken into consideration to some degree, but often the teacher knows that something can be interesting + must lead students into giving it a chance.

BOX 7.2
INTERVIEWING STRATEGIES

STRATEGY 1:

1. Invite three students to participate in mock interviews. Ask them to play one of three roles: the hostile interviewee, the overly talkative interviewee, the reluctant interviewee. Fellow students should not know that the interviewees are playing specific roles.

2. Divide the class into three groups, asking each group to develop questions for each interviewee.

3. Rotating from interviewee to interviewee, have each group of students conduct an interview.

4. As a class, discuss how the interviews went, addressing questions such as: What did the students notice about each interviewee? How well did the interviews go? How can the interviewer overcome difficulties and develop strategies appropriate to various kinds of interviewee personalities? Invite the interviewees to participate in the group discussion, revealing the roles they played and giving their observations of the interviews.

STRATEGY 2:

1. Invite a community member to the class for a group interview.

2. Share with the class a brief description of the person who will be interviewed.

3. Generate a list of questions on the board; let the questions reflect what the students are interested in finding out about that person.

4. As a group, evaluate and order the questions, revising, adding, deleting questions. Discuss possible follow-up questions based on the interviewee's responses.

5. Have a student recorder copy the questions for duplication for all students.

6. Have a student volunteer start the interview; allow the other students to open up the questioning according to the flow of the conversation.

7. Audiotape the interview if possible.

8. After the interview, share responses both to the content and to the process of the group interview. Have students transcribe parts of the audiotape to study the differences between talking and writing and to gather material for possible inclusion in their own writing.

9. Have students write drafts based on the interview, in forms and on topics of their own choosing.

(See Box 7.3.) They will vary from school to school, depending on the location and character of both school and community. But whether the school is rural, suburban, or urban, the surrounding community is sure to offer opportunities for study and controversial issues for research leading to discussion and action.

(handwritten margin note, left side: "that lends itself to the [zen] if there is one.")

BOX 7.3
IDEAS FOR CLASSROOM PROJECTS

1. Investigate a current community controversy. Decide, as a class, research strategies, action plans, and committees that need to be formed.

2. Select a theme or issue (for example, working, adolescence, poverty, family life, pollution). Decide, as a class, the various ways that the issue can be described or understood (for example, through media, creative writing, research). Divide into groups and develop a multimedia/multigenre presentation that can be shared with other classes.

3. Compile and publish a neighborhood history. It might include interviews with long-standing community members, family histories, neighborhood histories, descriptions of historic places or important historical events. Copies of the student publication could be distributed to other classes and/or the libraries. *Good Idea if the result is worthy.*

4. A related project might include researching the ethnic heritage of the community. Students could investigate their own ethnic backgrounds, as well as the history of immigration to the community, cultural traditions, traditional community roles. Students could concentrate on various aspects of their heritage: its history, literature, art, religion, or politics. This project would also lend itself to multimedia presentations.

5. Students could select issues or problems within the school. They could interview other students, teachers, and administrators. Then, analyzing their findings, they might make a presentation to the faculty or the school board or write a series of articles for the school newspaper.

(handwritten note: "Perhaps each year there could be a collective project that would add to a series or collection having a common theme (eg. local color). Gives students a sense of perminency of their work. Importance.")

Potentials and Limitations
of the Approach

Potentials:

(handwritten note: "Good?")

1. *It is student-centered.* This perspective takes student empowerment seriously. Students are invited to shape the curriculum as well as individual assignments. As a result, they become highly invested in their reading and writing projects. Allowing students to select some of the texts they read and offering opportunities for independent research give students greater authority over what they learn.

2. *It promotes high expectations.* Teachers adopting this perspective expect a great deal from their students. Research has shown that students perform better if their teachers have high expectations for them.

3. *It teaches critical, political, and social skills.* A language-as-social-construct perspective is aimed at developing students' critical awareness, preparing them to be active citizens in the political world. It encourages students to question what is "given," allowing them to create their own interpretations, their own knowledge. It also puts into practice a social theory of learning where collaboration and conversation hold important places.

4. *It is flexible.* The variety of classroom structures or activities is virtually limitless in a language-as-social-construct classroom. Teachers might use writing workshops, collect oral histories from the community, publish students' short story collections or I-Search papers. Students might read self-selected texts individually, in small groups, or as an entire class, depending on the purposes for the reading. In other words, student inquiry, what the students decide to investigate, drives the curriculum.

Limitations:

1. *It is unconventional.* Although practitioners of language as social construct are convinced that they teach students to become critical readers and writers, able to respond to a variety of texts with insight, teachers may not introduce students to the texts that universities and colleges expect students will have read. Many school districts adopt curricula as a matter of policy, including required texts. In times when uniformity across districts has become a prominent feature of school accountability, there may be considerable resistance to teaching methods that abandon the literature textbook in favor of research in the community.

2. *Teachers, especially new ones, may not be able to implement a community-based, experiential curriculum in the ways described in this chapter without administrative authorization.* Budgetary restrictions may make it difficult to arrange field trips, provide buses, etc.

3. *It privileges writing over reading, student texts over professional texts.* Because of the emphasis on publication projects and community-based research, much of student reading can center on students' own or other students' texts. This activity is an important part of learning to "read as a writer," but there are limits to what students can teach each other. Teachers may have to struggle to build literary texts into their teaching plans in ways that are also consistent with the language-as-social-construct perspective.

4. *It privileges the group over the individual.* With the emphasis on the class as a social group, individual problems may be neglected and individuals may feel lost.

5. *It makes unusual demands on the teacher.* The great variety of possible activities and the need to substitute more flexible arrangements for

conventional classroom structures require expenditures of the teacher's time and energy beyond those of the traditional classroom. Not all teachers would feel comfortable with this approach.

IMPLEMENTATION:
TEACHING AN EQUAL RIGHTS UNIT

Why do a unit concerning a struggle for equal rights? "One of my kids got shot last year in the projects," Sarah says. "These kids are facing problems of discrimination every day, in some way or another," she continues, in explaining how the unit came about. "I wanted them to do something on history, and some kids had suggested the civil rights movement. I liked the idea, and had done that before, but I broadened the topic to a struggle for equal rights generally, so that kids could work on different things rather than just racial ones."

Sarah began the unit with three one-hour films from the series *Eyes on the Prize* I. (Although this series has six one-hour segments, each is relatively self-contained.) Sarah sees several purposes in using the films. "As students living in and attending a school in a poverty-stricken community that suffered from the riots in the late sixties, they need to know the history of the civil rights movement; they need to take it seriously and see how they as individuals are affected by racism and how they can take part in making necessary changes in their community and in this society. In a larger sense, this has to do with how they treat others, of course, and how they respond to ideas from people they have not been acquainted with." Students are encouraged to reflect on their own lives and what they can do to help others.

Desired Student Outcomes:

Seeing connections between the classroom and the outside world, pursuing topics of individual or group interest and significance, and reflecting upon students' own lives and situations

Understanding of how the larger political/social world functions and becoming empowered to act in it

Possible Whole-Class Activities:

Arrive at suggestions of topics for study by individuals or small groups.

Explore previously acquired knowledge and attitudes.

Research topics of interest in a variety of print and nonprint sources, including films.

Discuss issues raised in research by individuals, groups, or the whole class.

Interview or listen to presentations by visitors on their experiences and their views.

Videotape interviews.

Take field trip(s) to do further research.

Collaborate with another class on one or more projects.

Possible Small-Group Activities:

Arrive at suggestions for small-group projects and their implementation through brainstorming and/or more closely focused discussion.

Discuss issues posed by research findings.

Discuss progress of project(s).

Present project(s) in extended or summary form to the whole class.

Possible Individual Activities:

Work out proposal for individual project(s).

Take notes on reading, viewing of film, or visitors' presentations.

Write in journal on previous understanding of topic.

Respond in journal to research findings.

Write an essay, short story, play, or song based on research.

Resources:

Eyes on the Prize I and II (two PBS documentaries that contain six and eight one-hour segments, respectively).

Contemporary newspapers and newsmagazines

Separate but Equal (ABC miniseries that dramatizes the background leading up to the 1954 Supreme Court desegregation decision).

Visitors from the community.

(*Note*: The books and articles listed under Resources in the cross-age teaching unit below would also be useful as resources for this unit.)

Organization of the Unit:

Weeks 1 and 2

The class watches three segments from *Eyes on the Prize,* a prize-winning PBS series on the civil rights movement. Before viewing the film, students write in their journals about their understanding of the nature of the civil rights struggle, and what they know about it. Sarah provides questions for them to answer about key figures, events, and issues to see what they know before the unit begins. Students write about and discuss these issues in the first two days of the unit. Sarah helps to ground these issues periodically in the students' own lives, and her own; for instance, she asks them if they have ever been treated with prejudice by members of another race or class; she asks them to discuss the issue of prejudice in terms of their families, neighborhood friends, their own classmates, and their own classroom.

The students are prepared for viewing each segment with background provided by Sarah about the broader historical context of what they will see depicted; students ask questions for clarification and further information before and after (and sometimes during) each segment. She asks students to take notes on the individual segments, and has them respond in their journals: first, to whatever "struck them the most profoundly—what they would remember most from the film," and, second, to her specific questions about content. Since each of the three chosen segments is a little less than one hour long, they work within one regular, uninterrupted class period comfortably. The day after each showing is spent in discussion, sometimes reading responses to the film from journals, sometimes stopping to write further responses to issues that come up. Each day following a film segment, students get into small groups to briefly discuss (and sometimes also to write) their responses to specific questions, followed by large-group discussions focused on sharing and extending what has been discussed in the small groups.

On day 8, after the third segment has been shown, students discuss the segment, and then in small- and large-group meetings, discuss what projects they might like to do in response to what they have seen. Sarah helps broaden the discussion from a focus on racial relations to a struggle for equal rights generally. She asks them about comparable struggles, and she and students together bring up such examples as the problems in China, Central America, and Eastern Europe; the conflict between light- and dark-skinned African Americans; and the issue of women's rights. On the next day the students get into groups to help each other brainstorm projects they might produce over the next three weeks. Sarah moves freely from group to group, stopping to encourage, advise, and sometimes counsel individual group members who seem most stuck. At the end of the week students have to submit a proposal to Sarah about what they might work on. Proposals for projects include literary analyses of books they will read (Leslie Marmon Silko's *Ceremony*, Anne Frank's *The Diary of a Young Girl*, Alice Walker's *The Color Purple*), a study of area migrant workers, the history of the Detroit riots of the late sixties, interviews with parents about the sixties for reports. Sarah says: "Eboney wrote a story based on the holocaust. She had seen *The Diary of Anne Frank* on television, saw connections to *Eyes on the Prize*, and asked if she could read more about that and write about it. Isn't that great!" Two other students join Eboney in her research, writing reports and journal responses. Sarah brings several copies of local newspapers to class to help students search for relevant topics, and since the imminent release of Nelson Mandela is in the news at this time, three students decide to write about that. One student writes songs (updates of late sixties protest songs, in rap form), another writes a report about Mandela, another writes a story about a black boy growing up in South Africa under apartheid. Sarah helps those who have difficulty deciding what to write about, or finding something to do, and helps find materials for those who have already made their decisions. Most of the work is done at home at first, with increasingly more class time devoted to the projects as Sarah and the students generally determine is necessary.

Weeks 3, 4, and 5

The class invites two visitors from the community to talk to the class about issues of equal rights and any other issues students might be interested in having them address. Sarah wants the visits to be potentially practical, as well, to lead to purposeful work students might be able to do in response to the visit, both in writing and in activities outside of class. For instance, they invite the editor of the local African-American newspaper, who is interviewed on a variety of topics: black-white relations, the new city incinerator, working in and writing about his community, and his philosophy of life. In order to prepare for the visit, they write down interview questions; during the interview (which they videotape) they take notes; and after the interview they discuss both the process and the content of the interview and write individual responses. Students request a student-written column in the paper for the purpose of publishing some of their writings. The students also visit the newspaper offices and conduct a follow-up interview.

Another visitor, Rose Bell, a long-time volunteer and resident in the area, is the founder and director of United Neighbors, out of which she runs a service for unwed teenage mothers called 961-BABY. Students interview this inspiring woman and write essays, stories, and poems about her; some of the students get involved in her organization, knitting much-needed simple baby clothes and blankets, making posters, carrying supplies.

During these three weeks students also read poetry by Langston Hughes, stories by Richard Wright and Leslie Marmon Silko, and essays by Martin Luther King, Jr., and Nelson Mandela. Sarah also reads aloud two stories about the struggle for equal rights written by former students, one about an act of cruelty toward a fellow student because of the clothes she wears, another a story from the perspective of one of the "Little Rock Seven" students. Students meet at least one whole hour in each week to discuss progress toward completion of the unit projects; to get into groups and share writing, discuss snags, share ideas; and to give Sarah an opportunity to meet individually with as many students as possible. She also asks students to write letters to her about their progress and invites them to hand in what they are doing at any time for comments.

Weeks 6 and 7

Originally, less than six weeks was planned for the project, but it spills over into a longer period of time. During this time students are asked to give a presentation of their projects—to read or tell briefly about what they have accomplished. Most of the students give presentations during this two-week period. Two other, quite obviously unplanned incidents occur, however, to give even more significance to the issues of the struggle for equal rights. Sarah explains:

> The point of "The Struggle for Equal Rights" unit is to make a link to the world of the projects (or whatever neighborhood the students live in) and a link to the world beyond too. And then, it was just days after we had watched the film on the Jonesville Nine [from *Eyes on the Prize*], when two things happened. Allen came to school very upset; on a visit to a white suburb, he had been called racist epithets while walking down the street. "I felt just like one of those kids from Jonesville," he said in class. We discussed it, and, of course, it was very powerful. Some of the students wanted to respond somehow, and the class wrote a letter to the Chamber of Commerce. We got a letter of apology, which isn't much, maybe, but it was empowering in some respects for the kids. And they got behind Allen in a truly wonderful way.

At about the same time, Nelson Mandela is released from prison, and the African-American Museum schedules a Freedom March down one of the main downtown avenues on that day. Students chant, with older marchers, "Free South Africa!" and sing "We Shall Overcome" as their mothers and fathers did before them. Students are seeing themselves as a necessary link in a history of social reform, and they write enthusiastically about the experience in their journals.

"Once you start to see learning in more social ways, you begin to rethink boundaries," Sarah says. "You begin to ask, 'What is the classroom? What is English?' But then, it's important to see this: I definitely think of education as a source for change, much needed change. If you want things to stay the same, and some people definitely do, then isolate kids; make them do vocabulary lists, spelling tests, grammar drills; make them shut up and feel stupid. But then you definitely disempower them."

Sarah develops another important social link to this unit, weeks later, with a suburban working class community-college composition class taught by her friend Larry. Almost all of the students in the college class are white. The two classes exchange a series of letters and share writing they are doing with their individual pen pals. Sarah and Larry are "teacher-researching" this exciting cross-age (and cross-cultural) writing project, planning to share their results with others. Sarah has developed curriculum in such a way that it makes the most of the relationship between classroom study and the worlds the students inhabit; she is flexible enough to take advantage of all relevant circumstances that make that learning as meaningful as possible.

Evaluation:

Sarah evaluates some of her students' work quantitatively, some of it qualitatively. She checks off whether they have done the interview questions, the journal entries, the letters reporting their progress, and the oral descriptions of projects to the class. She assigns grades to some of the journal entries and to the projects. In the case of collaborative projects she asks each student to describe and evaluate his or her part in the project.

IMPLEMENTATION:
A CROSS-AGE TEACHING UNIT IN HIGH SCHOOL

Dorothy and Bob, two high school teachers at a large suburban high school in a middle-class community, are interested in having their students learn firsthand the meaning of schooling, learning, and teaching. Both teachers have tenth-grade classes in American Literature that are taught thematically. The year-long plan focuses on the question, Who am I?; each marking period is devoted to exploring the students' lives in various contexts—family, school, and community. Dorothy and Bob enjoy collaborating on their project, though they say that either one of them could have done it alone.

Dorothy and Bob ask their students to participate in a cross-age teaching project where students become, on a periodic basis, the teachers of first, second, or third graders at a local elementary school. Having collaborated before, Dorothy and Bob use a common preparation period to plan activities they will carry out in their own classrooms. In addition, the teachers want their students to become teacher-researchers by keeping field notes of their experiences and writing case studies of their elementary students.

The high school students develop their own lesson plans, review and evaluate children's reading texts, and consult with the elementary school teachers in order to prepare for their sessions. After each session, the students write process notes, detailing their interactions with their elementary students. These notes provide the raw data from which students create their own case studies and reflect upon what they learn about teaching and learning. The students also examine what it means to read, why reading is important in a person's life, and what helps a person become a better reader. These activities take place while the students are reading Toni Morrison's *The Bluest Eye* (New York: Pocket Books, 1970). To draw connections between the reading and the teaching project, the students examine Morrison's use of elementary primers to introduce various chapters of *The Bluest Eye,* the disparity between the world of the primer and the world of the characters, and the implications of this disparity in the characters' lives.

Classroom activities are structured around a set schedule: three days working on the cross-age teaching project, two days reading and discussing *The Bluest Eye.*

Desired Student Outcomes:

Experience in analysis—both literary and empirical—through examination of texts and events

Skill in using observable data as a source of evidence

Understanding of literacy and its relationship to various individuals

Understanding of the ways texts create worlds: the elementary primer, the novel, individual experiences

Understanding of the relationships between people of different classes or ethnic heritages as portrayed in *The Bluest Eye*

Relation of the characters' experiences to the students' own experiences

Broadened awareness of other cultural groups and socioeconomic classes

Possible Whole-Class Activities

Participate in discussions about *The Bluest Eye.*

Develop and evaluate teaching strategies.

Participate in field trips to elementary school.

Read and discuss excerpts from professional case studies.

Respond to questions comparing *The Bluest Eye* and Maya Angelou's *I Know Why the Caged Bird Sings.*

Possible Small-Group Activities:

Participate in discussion groups about *The Bluest Eye.*

Participate in discussion groups on teaching.

Participate in peer review of case studies.

Possible Individual Activities:

Read *The Bluest Eye.*

Write journal responses to *The Bluest Eye.*

Make field notes from teaching experiences.

Draft and revise a case study and submit it to elementary
   school teachers.

Develop lesson plans (this can also be done in small groups).

Review children's storybooks.

Resources:

Atwell, Nancie. *In the Middle: Writing, Reading, and Learning with Adolescents.* Portsmouth, N.H.: Boynton/Cook Heinemann, 1987.

Branscombe, Amanda. "I Gave My Classroom Away." In Dixie Goswami
   and Peter R. Stillwell, eds., *Reclaiming the Classroom: Teacher Research as
   an Agency for Change.* Portsmouth, N.H.: Boynton/Cook Heinemann,
   1987.

Cooper, Marilyn, and Michael Holzman. *Writing as Social Action.*
   Portsmouth, N.H.: Boynton/Cook, 1989.

Garrison, Roger. "Graduation Before Graduation: Social Involvement
   and English." *English Journal* 79 (1990): 60–3.

Heath, Shirley Brice. *Ways with Words: Language, Life, and Work in Communities and Schools.* New York: Cambridge University Press, 1983. (See
   especially section on becoming a language ethnographer.)

Medway, Peter. "Language with Consequences: Worldly Engagement for
   Critical Inquiry." *English Education* 22 (1990): 147–64.

Robinson, Jay L. *Conversations on the Written Word: Essays in Language and
   Literacy.* Portsmouth, N.H.: Boynton/Cook Heinemann, 1990. (See
   especially, Chapter 11, "The Politics of Literacy," written with Patricia
   L. Stock.)

Organization of the Unit:

Week 1

The cross-age teaching project is organized around two important pedagogical beliefs: (1) learning occurs through experience shaped by reflection and conversation and (2) learning is most meaningful when it is
grounded in real contexts, allowing students to draw their own conclusions in collaboration with their teachers and their peers. The unit begins
with an introduction to the marking-period theme: Who am I in school?
The students then watch a videotape of the students at Adams Elementary, a school many of the high school students had attended themselves

and that still enrolls their relatives and other children living in their neighborhood. The classroom discussion centers on what the students saw in the videotape, what the elementary students were doing, and why they might be engaged in such activity. For example, they watch the first graders learning to physically manipulate pens and pencils to form letters, tracing shapes for practice. The teachers also distribute pictures and letters of introduction sent along with the videotape as another way of getting acquainted with the children the high schoolers will be teaching.

The first visit to Adams is a "get-acquainted" meeting. In preparation for the visit, the high school students write in their journals about what they want to learn about their prospective pupils and how they might use observation as well as conversation to gain insight into their learners. During the visit, the elementary students meet their new "teachers" and spend an hour talking, reading, drawing, and playing classroom games.

The following day the high school students share stories, write reactions to the visit, and talk about what they need to prepare for their first teaching assignment. The students actively participate in the construction of guidelines for planning. In doing so, they draw upon their own experiences in school. Their sense of instructional planning mirrors the educational plans that have been an ongoing part of their own schooling. Their preparation is based on such questions as: What are we going to teach? How will we teach it? What books or materials will we use?

As this planning goes on, the students begin the reading of *The Bluest Eye*. This text is shaped by a complicated narrative style that Dorothy and Bob know will be difficult for many of their students, so they begin the book by introducing two of its features: (1) the use of primer text at the beginning of the book and at the start of several chapters and (2) the use of multiple narrative voices. On the first day, students are divided into small groups and are asked to read the opening two pages, as follows:

> Here is the house. It is green and white. It has a red door. It is very pretty. Here is the family. Mother, Father, Dick, and Jane live in the green-and-white house. They are happy. See Jane. She has a red dress. She wants to play. Who will play with Jane? See the cat. It goes meow-meow. Come and play. Come play with Jane. The kitten will not play. See Mother. Mother is very nice. Mother, will you play with Jane? Mother laughs. Laugh, Mother, laugh. See Father. He is big and strong. Father, will you play with Jane? Father is smiling. Smile, Father, smile. See the dog. Bowwow goes the dog. Do you want to play with Jane? See the dog run. Run, dog, run. Look, look. Here comes a friend. The friend will play with Jane. They will play a good game. Play, Jane, play.

Here is the house. It is green and white. It has a red door. It is very pretty. Here is the family. Mother, Father, Dick, and Jane live in the green-and-white house. They are happy. See Jane. She has a red dress. She wants to play. Who will play with Jane? See the cat. It goes meow-meow. Come and play. Come play with Jane. The kitten will not play. See Mother. Mother is very nice. Mother, will you play with Jane? Mother laughs. Laugh, Mother, laugh. See Father. He is big and strong. Father, will you play with Jane? Father is smiling. Smile, Father, smile. See the dog. Bowwow goes the dog. Do you want to play with Jane? See the dog run. Run, dog, run. Look, look. Here comes a friend. The friend will play with Jane. They will play a good game. Play, Jane, play.

Hereisthehouseitisgreenandwhiteithasareddooritisveryprettyhereisthefa milymotherfatherdickandjaneliveinthegreenandwhitehousetheyareveryh appyseejaneshehasareddressshewantstoplaywhowillplaywithjaneseethecat itgoesmeowmeowcomeandplaywithjanethekittenwillnotplaywithjaneseem othermotherisverynicemotherwillyouplaywithjanemotherlaughslaughmo therlaughseefatherheisbigandstrongfatherwillyouplaywithjanefatherissm ilingsmilefathersmileseethedogbowwowgoesthedogdoyouwanttoplaywithj aneseethedogrunrundogrunlooklookherecomesafriendthefriendwillplay withjanetheywillplayagoodgameplayjaneplay

(Toni Morrison, *The Bluest Eye* [New York: Pocket Books, 1970], pp. 7–8 Copyright © 1970. Reprinted by permission of Toni Morrison).

In each group they discuss the opening by answering these questions:

1. Does this text look familiar? Where do you think it comes from?

2. What happens to the text as you get farther down the page? What effect does this have?

3. Why do you think the author opens the book this way? What do you think it might mean?

Next, each group is given a copy of a children's primer. They work together to answer these questions:

1. What are these primers like? What kinds of stories do they contain? Who are the characters?

2. What is life like in these books?

3. After looking at the primers and answering these questions, do you have any more ideas about what Morrison might be doing by starting her book this way?

Students then list their responses on the blackboard and the whole class discusses them, focusing on any responses that seem to be very different or controversial.

On the second day, the students are asked to think of a childhood experience, one that is particularly memorable. It might be a funny or embarrassing moment, something sad, but something that stood out for them. To help students get started, the teachers share a story from their own childhood. Students write and share their stories, reading from their journals. Then students are asked to pick one of the people in their stories and rewrite a section of it from that person's perspective.

Finally, the students note the ways the type style changes in various sections of *The Bluest Eye*. The teachers point out that each time the type changes, a different narrator is telling the story. It might be a character or it might be an omniscient narrator, but students should pay attention to who the narrator is in each section. They also begin reading the first section of the book.

Week 2

The elementary students and the Adams school librarian contribute children's books for a classroom library that the high school students will use to develop their lessons. To select books appropriate for the students they will be teaching, the high school students read and evaluate these books. Each student reviews at least two books, completing an index card with the following information: title, author, illustrator, story summary, appropriate grade level (in the student's estimation), interest level (Would a child like the book?), and suggestions for teaching. At the same time, students make initial decisions about the books they might use and the lesson they will teach on the basis of their reading and their meeting with the elementary students.

Students develop their own lesson plans, describing what they intend to teach the elementary students and what activities they will use. To help in their planning, they watch the videotape made during their "get-acquainted" visit, considering the following points:

1. You are planning a twenty-minute lesson.
2. You are the teacher.
3. What goal do you have for this session?
4. What activities would help achieve that goal?

The students then prepare their lessons, checking with the teachers, seeking advice from peers, making flashcards or whatever they need for their lesson. During one of the days this week, the high school librarian visits the classroom to provide tips on storytelling, since many of the first graders are just beginning to read. She shares tips on developing character voices, reading with inflection, and practicing the story before teaching it.

After students have begun the first section of *The Bluest Eye*, Dorothy and Bob ask them to go back to page 9, where Morrison provides a kind of preamble to the text, and to respond in their journals to the following questions:

1. What strikes you about this opening?
2. What do you think will happen in this book?
3. What do you think the last line means?

After a discussion about the introduction to the story, students share their responses to Claudia and Frieda and these characters' family life. An important part of the discussion centers on places in the text that students find troubling or don't understand and details they think are significant in some way.

Week 3

The Adams students travel to Bentley High for their first student-taught reading lessons. This is an opportunity for the younger students to experience the high school, and meeting there minimizes administrative concerns such as the need for substitutes and students' absences from other classes. Pairs of first graders work with each high school student in classrooms open during that period and in the library, generally completing lessons with enough time left over to take short tours of the school and to visit the restrooms at least once. The following day, the high school students begin documenting their experiences for a teacher-research project they will complete after subsequent visits. First, the students generate what are called "process notes," describing in detail the events of the previous day. Second, they are asked to analyze these events, addressing the following questions in a journal entry:

1. What did you learn about teaching?
2. Did your meeting match your expectations? Why or why not?
3. What could you do to improve your lesson?

The students' responses to these questions focus the classroom discussion toward issues of teaching and learning. Some students find themselves frustrated by their initial attempts to teach, others find it exhilarating. In other words, these students learn something about themselves as well as about the elementary students they are teaching. The students talk at great length about what they learned from their first visit that could help them with subsequent lessons. The student/teachers note, for example, that they must plan enough activities for their pupils and that it is important to gauge the elementary students' reading ability: Some lessons are too hard, others are too easy for their students. They realize, too, that some aspects of the high school environment are not particularly appropriate for 6- and 7-year-olds. The desks are too big and the floors are uncarpeted—eliminating the use of the floors for teaching (a favorite place for elementary school children). They brainstorm ways to overcome these disadvantages.

The second visit from the Adams students proceeds in much the same way as the first visit, although the students' growing experience in teaching reduces the amount of classroom time they need to prepare. The elementary teachers also provide the high school students with information about the instructional concerns they have for each of the students, which helps them shape their lessons.

Class discussion of *The Bluest Eye* this week focuses on the Breedloves and Pecola. Students reflect on the reasons the Breedloves think they are ugly, why others agree, what it would be like growing up in this family, and how the students might react to such a life.

Week 4

The third visit takes place at the elementary school. In the event that lessons are finished early, the elementary classrooms have toys, crayons, and construction paper for the student/teachers to use.

After teaching their second lessons, the high school students again generate process notes. This time, students are instructed to pay close attention to their interactions with their elementary students, recording conversations and their students' responses to activities. Dorothy and Bob also ask the high school students to reflect on reading and what it means to be a reader by responding to the following questions in a journal entry:

1. How do you define reading?
2. How would you describe yourself as a reader?
3. How can people become better readers?
4. Why is reading important? In other words, why should people want to become better readers?

In the discussion of these journal responses, Dorothy and Bob encourage students to begin describing their elementary students as readers, using their observations to develop their own tentative case studies much as teachers do formally or informally in the course of their teaching. The students begin drafting their own case studies in their journals as a free-write, based on the classroom discussion and their personal observations.

Discussion of *The Bluest Eye* includes a review of two sequences that involve Pecola and other children in the neighborhood: the events surrounding Maureen and Junior (pages 52–66 and pages 70–76, respectively). Students write and talk about Pecola's attraction to these children; the ways they are different from Pecola, Frieda, and Claudia; and what motives Maureen and Junior may have. Responses to each question are compared by listing them on the board. To help establish a connection between the two incidents, students discuss the similarities between Maureen and Junior and are asked to generalize about different groups of people, the worlds they live in, the disparities between these worlds and what effect they have on people. Throughout this discussion, students are encouraged to draw upon their own experiences to make sense of the relationships among the characters in the book.

Week 5

Students have begun preliminary drafts of their case studies without any real models. Dorothy and Bob are interested in seeing what the students come up with on their own. Then, to help students revise their initial drafts, the teachers distribute excerpts from professional case studies of readers. They ask the students to read these passages as writers, taking note of the ways the authors weave together observation and analysis to create portraits of students. As the discussion progresses, the high school students make comparisons between the professional texts and their own emerging case studies. Most of the week is spent on revision; the students work alone, with the teacher, or with peers to shape their texts. The students also use their beginning analyses to shape the final lessons they will teach.

The week's discussion of *The Bluest Eye* focuses on Pauline Breedlove. The students have read her section of the narrative and are asked to analyze her character, based on the observations they have made in their reading. They are prompted with the following questions:

1. What was Pauline like growing up?
2. What did she become? What do you think caused her dramatic change? What do you think about her as an adult?
3. What is her relationship with her children? Her husband?

Students are encouraged to draw on specific parts of the text to explain their responses.

Weeks 6 and 7

To prepare for the next session with the Adams students, the tenth graders use their case studies to develop their lesson plans. Sharing with each other their descriptions of their pupils, the high school students are asked to consider what they think their students need to learn; how they might shape their lessons, taking into account the characteristics of the child as a learner; and what kind of activities would best motivate those specific learners. The students again prepare lessons and teach them.

After this final teaching session, students complete their process notes, detailing what has transpired during their lessons and describing the interaction between the pairs of learners and teachers. They are then asked to assess their students' progress by reflecting upon the following questions:

1. What changes do you see in your students as readers/learners?
2. What reading or writing skills do they possess that you had not observed before?
3. What do these students still need to learn to become better readers or writers?

On the basis of their responses, students again revise their initial case studies. This phase of the writing process includes both teacher and peer review.

When Dorothy and Bob discussed their students' initial drafts, they noticed that students had generally not provided enough in the way of introduction to their cases. They decide the next day to give a minilesson in introductions to help students with their writing. They have the students generate a list on the board of things the reader might want or need to know when he or she begins reading. They also ask the students to specify kinds of information that might be especially useful in the case studies. Then students spend the rest of the hour drafting or revising an introduction to their texts.

During the rest of the writing days, texts are read to eliminate ambiguities and unwarranted generalizations. When the students complete their revisions, Dorothy and Bob mail the case studies to the elementary teachers who are collaborating with them. Writing for a "real" audience of teachers is an essential part of this project. It also gives credence to the high school students as teachers, since by sharing their insights they teach the cooperating elementary teachers about students in their classrooms.

During these last two weeks on *The Bluest Eye,* Dorothy and Bob focus on encouraging critical, independent reading skills by asking students to take part in planning the discussion. At the beginning of the hour, students are given ten minutes to write in their journals a list of topics they would like to discuss. If they have not already done so, they are to complete the last few pages of the text for homework; thus the discussion topics address events in the last section of the book and the book as a whole. Some of the items the students suggest are:

• The role of Soaphead Church
• Pecola's rape, the death of her child, and her exile from the community
• Claudia's and Frieda's response to Pecola's life
• The close of the book (Pecola's dialogue with herself) and Pecola's madness

- The significance of blue eyes
- The ways in which the poor are treated and the effects of poverty

The students had previously read Maya Angelou's *I Know Why the Caged Bird Sings,* and the final class discussion centers on similarities and differences between Maya and Pecola, especially in terms of such topics as freedom and survival. Both texts address issues of poverty, displacement, rape, and personal empowerment. They also describe responses to school, community, and peers. As such they provide an opportunity for students to explore the circumstances that allow some to overcome personal tragedy while others cannot.

Evaluation:

Students are evaluated on all phases of the unit: journal entries for both *The Bluest Eye* and the teaching project, lesson plans, children's book reviews, and case studies. For the case studies, the major writing project of the marking period, students receive grades for their drafts, the substance of their revisions, and the substance of their comments as peer editors.

Suggested Reading

APPLE, MICHAEL. *Education and Power.* London: Routledge, 1982.

Apple's concern here is with a broad—and radical—view of schooling in terms of unequal power relations; the book includes some suggestions for ways to address some of these inequities.

ARONOWITZ, STANLEY, and HENRY A. GIROUX. *Education Under Siege: The Radical, Liberal and Conservative Debate over Schooling.* South Hadley, Mass.: Bergin and Garvey, 1985.

This text addresses the crisis in education from a neo-Marxist position. It argues for teacher empowerment, calling upon teachers to become "transformative intellectuals," who understand the political nature of schooling and see schools as sites for social change.

ATWELL, NANCIE. *In the Middle: Writing, Reading and Learning with Adolescents.* Portsmouth, N.H.: Heinemann, 1987.

Atwell, in this award-winning book, describes the way she used a workshop approach to reading and writing in her seventh-grade classroom.

BERGER, PETER L., and THOMAS LUCKMANN. *The Social Construction of Reality: A Treatise in the Sociology of Knowledge.* New York: Doubleday, 1966.

Two sociologists outline a theory of social knowing, challenge the traditional educational paradigm, and promote an alternative.

BIRD, LOIS BRIDGES, ed. *Becoming a Whole Language School: The Fair Oaks Story.* Katonah, N.Y.: Richard Owen, 1989.

Essays written by teachers, parents, and administrators describe the way one school, like Sarah's school, embraced a "whole-language" approach to learning.

BRANDT, DEBORAH. "Versions of Literacy," *College English*, 47 (1985):128–38.

In this review article, Brandt argues that recent research on literacy demonstrates that what counts as literate behavior is a socially constructed cultural norm, varying from community to community. This research implies that teachers at any level be sensitive to the forms that literacy can take in the classroom.

BRYANT, TIM, ed. *Focus on Collaborative Learning.* Urbana, Ill.: NCTE, 1988.

This book illustrates several different classroom approaches to learning, with an emphasis on students working together.

CREMIN, LAWRENCE. *The Transformation of the School: Progressivism in American Education.* New York: Knopf, 1961.

This book give a history of twentieth-century progressive education.

DEWEY, JOHN. *Democracy and Education.* New York: Collier, 1916.

———. *Experience and Education.* New York: Collier, 1938.

Two central texts for understanding a social perspective on teaching and learning, these books are written by the man many regard as the father of the approach.

FREIRE, PAULO. *Pedagogy of the Oppressed.* New York: Continuum, 1986.

The Brazilian educational reformer speaks against "the banking education" fostered in most classrooms and shows how his liberatory education focuses on praxis, reflective change for social action.

FREIRE, PAULO, and DONALDO MACEDO. *Literacy: Reading, the Word and the World.* South Hadley, Mass.: Bergin and Garvey, 1987.

This collection of essays examines applications of Freire's liberatory pedagogy in various settings, including the United States.

GIROUX, HENRY A. *Teachers as Intellectuals: Toward a Critical Pedagogy of Learning.* South Hadley, Mass.: Bergin and Garvey, 1988.

A progressive educator, Giroux calls for teachers to be—and get their students to be—critical intellectuals, questioning the way knowledge gets constructed in schools and society.

GOODMAN, KEN. *What's Whole in Whole Language?* Portsmouth, N.H.: Heinemann, 1986.

This book is a guide to a whole-language approach to learning for students and teachers.

GOSWAMI, DIXIE, and PETER R. STILLMAN, eds. *Reclaiming the Classroom: Teacher Research as an Agency for Change.* Portsmouth N.H.: Boynton/Cook Heinemann, 1987.

This book is written by teachers who have researched their own classroom practices.

HEATH, SHIRLEY BRICE. *Ways with Words.* New York: Cambridge University Press, 1983.

A study of the way two different struggling communities—one white, one black—differently prepare their children for the demands of schooling, the book examines the ways language use is rooted in particular social and cultural contexts.

HIDALGO, NITZA M., CEASAR L. McDOWELL, and EMILIE V. SIDDLE, eds. "Facing Racism in Education," a special issue of *Harvard Educational Review*, 1990.

This is a collection of essays by writers in a variety of fields.

MOHR, MARIAN. *Teachers Teaching Writing: Snake Hill to Spring Bank* (videotape). Urbana, Ill.: NCTE, 1984.

Mohr's Fairfax County, Virginia, students write a book based on interviews with area community members.

ROBINSON, JAY. *Conversations on the Written Word: Essays on Language and Literacy.* Portsmouth, N.H.: Boynton/Cook Heinemann, 1990.

A collection of essays centered on the metaphor "literacy as conversation," Robinson's book describes both theoretical models and practical applications of the teaching of literacy, where literacy is conceived as socially grounded action.

VYGOTSKY, LEV. *Mind in Society: The Development of Higher Psychological Processes.* Edited by Michael Cole, Vera John-Steiner, Sylvia Scribner, and Ellen Souberman. Cambridge, Mass.: Harvard University Press, 1978.

This text continues Vygotsky's examination of psychological development toward higher thought processes. It reshapes the developmental theories of Piaget by incorporating sociohistorical influences in the development of individual thought and language.

Thought and Language. Cambridge, Mass.: M.I.T. Press, 1978.

Soviet psychologist Vygotsky challenges some previous learning theories, asserting that learners are primarily social and not individual.

WIGGINTON, ELIOT. *Foxfire*, vol. I–X. Landover Hills, Md.: Anchor Books, 1972–89.

Wigginton's English classes publish books about their Rabun Gap, Georgia, community; the books are based on oral history interviews.

8

Exploring and Evaluating the Approaches

What I have finally settled on as a metaphor for teaching is being a pitcher for a baseball team. The pitcher is the most important player on the team. Most of the time, the focus of the game is on him. When the pitcher's in top form, the team usually wins; when the pitcher is off, it's hard for the team to win. . . . In a classroom, the teacher has to be in top form. He or she is the focus. The teacher controls the tempo of discussion just as a good pitcher controls the tempo of a game. . . . While a pitcher is the most important player on the team, he is not alone. Victory or defeat does not depend exclusively on him. . . . The main point I want to make . . . is that in my view being a teacher is being part of a group (playing the same game) while at the same time also having the most responsibility.

—Andrew

Swimming in the ocean is as powerful an experience for me as teaching and my feelings about teaching. The first parallel I notice between them is the fear each elicits. For a long time I was fearful of venturing past the shallow waters—fearing that I was not strong or able enough to traverse the crashing waves. There was also a (not quite) hidden fear that the ocean would swallow me; that was part of its power and mystery. Similarly, I worry if I am knowledgeable or creative enough to be a teacher. Will the students swallow me whole and spit me back out? The undertow, a flow of water beneath and in a direction opposite to the surface current, calls to mind the currents in a classroom, lying just beneath direct observation: students' home life, previous educational experience and relationships with each other, currents that have little or nothing to do with school. . . .

Yet, swimming beyond the crashing waves there is a calmness, and I can see life—both fish and plant—beneath the surface. Only then can I appreciate the wonders and beauty of the sea. I feel it is crucial to see students in the classroom as individuals with varying skills and needs, and my role as teacher is less frightening from this perspective. Isabel, for whom English is a second language, may need one-to-one tutoring to facilitate her experience. Thomas, an "advanced" student, may benefit from tutoring Isabel, experiencing the satisfaction of helping a fellow student and gaining a deeper appreciation for the English language. . . .

When I emerge from the water, I am renewed, different than I was before. Trusting that I have the strength, I find the ocean a powerful force, and I can use that power both to travel and be transformed.

—Joan

The teacher can be seen as a fire-builder. The students are the wood, and the fire, or process of burning, is the process of learning. The fire-builder begins by arranging the wood in the best possible way for burning. . . . He knows about wood, and about other necessary factors in the burning process, like air and heat. But he can't be too sure about the wood he's dealing with, and must be flexible and ready to experiment. . . . So the fire-builder arranges, then provides the spark to start the fire. . . . It only really gets going when all the pieces "come together" to produce one big fire. This is the cooperative, interactive action of the students. . . . All too often, fire is produced by a fire-builder using lighter fluid. There's a big flame and it seems as though there is a good fire. But it is mainly the fluid burning, and the wood is only barely affected before the fire burns out. This is similar to the common type of "learning" that takes place when students memorize things and can regurgitate them on tests. The information doesn't really affect them, doesn't change them. It is very superficial and short-term, like the lighter fluid fire.

—Ken

I will explore one metaphor that I find appealing. That is, teacher as movie director, students as all the other set people necessary to make a movie, including everyone from set designers to makeup artists to producers to stars. One big reason I like this metaphor is because ultimately the director is behind the scenes. He or she works with everyone on the set, and yet allows them center stage. It is the picture that is most important in the end. . . . For a teacher this means encouraging the perspective that learning is the goal, and the class works toward that goal together. . . . Another reason this metaphor appealed to me is that on a movie set, there are probably hundreds of people who all have very different talents and objectives. A good director respects the variety of talents as she or he knows that each has something valuable to contribute to the picture. . . . Likewise, a teacher must recognize and respect the diversity of talent in his or her classes. Each student may need to learn in a different way, or may make different contributions to the class. . . . Teachers should not force a makeup artist to be a set designer, or a behind the scenes producer to be a leading lady. They need to learn over time what feels comfortable for their students and what unique things each student may have to contribute.

—Ruth

IN CHAPTER 3 we invited you to think of your own metaphor(s) for teaching English. The four metaphors that you have just read resulted from a similar assignment in an English Methods class. At first glance, these metaphors seem to point to similar things about teaching: the sense that the teacher should control or arrange his or her classroom; the assertion that the students are also at the center of the classroom in important ways and that, in the last analysis, the success or failure of the learning process depends upon them; the feeling that cooperation, teamwork, interaction, mutual respect between teacher and students are crucial classroom elements.

Within these broad similarities, however, there are important differences in the degree of ownership that students are encouraged or allowed to assert over their own learning, the kind of responsibility the teacher assumes for what students learn, the kind of interaction between students and teachers. The teacher as pitcher is much more the center of things than the teacher as fire-builder who sparks the blaze, which really gets going, however, only "when all the pieces 'come together' to produce one big fire." The teacher as movie director has to bring together people of widely varying talents and abilities in an enterprise that is truly cooperative and new each time, while the pitcher is playing in a game with well-established rules that all of the team must follow. Teaching as swimming in the ocean emphasizes the feeling that the teacher is much less in control than in any of the other metaphors.

In other words, these metaphors enabled future teachers to think about the various roles that a teacher and a student might play and the different shapes that a classroom might take. Other students in the same methods class explored such metaphors as the teacher as tour guide, as cab driver, as farmer sowing seed (à la Christ's parable of the sower in Luke 8:5–8), as salesman, as drug pusher (getting his students hooked on his subject), as gardener, as orchestra conductor, as coach, as construction site overseer. Still others worked out metaphors for the classroom as a symphony orchestra, as a cruise to a faraway place, as a powerful thunderstorm that gives a new perspective to familiar sights. How do all these metaphors compare with the one(s) that you worked out? Did your metaphor(s) help you compare and evaluate the four different approaches you read about in Chapters 4 through 7?

Philosopher Frithjof Bergmann gives metaphors for different kinds of teaching that catch some of the most important differences among three of our four approaches. (See Box 8.1.) His metaphors reflect different ways for teachers to regard the student: Does the teacher see the student as an individual who must learn in sequences? Does the teacher enhance and build on knowledge and skills that the student already has or does the teacher try to substitute "better," more sophisticated knowledge and skills? Bergmann's metaphor of the juggler catches the essence of the language-as-development approach with its emphasis on sequences in building skills. The teacher, or juggler's assistant, must try to determine the point at which the student juggler is ready for each new learning task. Bergmann's Prussian garden catches some of the practices found in the language-as-artifact approach, though not all teachers using this approach would necessarily clear the land so drastically. His Japanese gardener and the language-as-expression teacher are similar, bringing out the best that is inherent in the land or the student by building on what is already there. One might add another metaphor: A band of acrobats making a giant pyramid, each member building upon the other, might accurately catch the essence of the language-as-social-construct approach, relying as it does on individual contributions to a group endeavor.

Examining the Differences

Bergmann's metaphors, those of Andrew's, Joan's, Ken's, and Ruth's class, and your own (as well, of course, as those of your classmates) should have helped you develop a feel for some of the major differences between approaches to the teaching of English. Now let us look more closely at those differences from three sets of perspectives, with an eye toward the relationship of each to theories of language learning: (1) the focus of the

---

BOX 8.1
FREEDOM AND EDUCATION

One way of thinking about teaching would go like this: imagine an accomplished juggler. He had talent to begin with, but through practice he has now reached a point where he is able to keep six dinner plates up in the air. With his face strained in concentration, his quickly moving hands toss up disk after disk as they descend. Someone else stands next to him with still more plates, ready to hand him the seventh, and after that perhaps the eighth. If it is done at the wrong moment, either before the juggler's skill is far enough advanced, or clumsily, off by a split second, the result will be that with a crash all of the plates fall to the ground. The new plate has to be offered at exactly the right time and in precisely the right manner for it to be included and to stay aloft together with the others.

It is good to think of the student not as idle or passive, but to imagine that his mind is as skilled and as engaged with its own problems as is that juggler's. To thrust a new piece of knowledge on him is not obviously an improvement, is not guaranteed to make him better. In fact, the wrong addition will bring everything that he could so far do to a collapse. Early on in teaching, one must come to the recognition that only some very few out of the ideas one has to offer will be of real use to the student, that the most important and most demanding part of teaching concerns this process of assimilation, the creation of the unlikely circumstance which allows a student to incorporate one more idea into his own thinking.

There is a second, similar analogy: perhaps the most crucial difference in teaching is not adequately captured by the opposition between the "authori-

---

classroom, the role of the teacher, and the emphasis on particular elements of the subject of English; (2) the look, feel, and processes of the classroom; and (3) the appropriateness of each approach for a particular kind of student.

The Difference in Focus

In the language-as-artifact approach the teacher and the text are the central points of focus in the classroom, and the teacher's role is seen as that of guide through the intricacies of the text and the processes of reading and writing. In the language-as-social-construct approach the teacher is also a guide, facilitating interaction between students and between students and the larger community; but the focus is on the process by which the students construct knowledge, in contrast to the teacher-centered language-as-artifact approach. Each approach tends to emphasize a different role for students, the first, a skill in reading and analyzing texts, the second, a sense of power to change one's world. Both of these

tarian" and the "permissive." Perhaps it would be better to think in terms of a comparison between two ways of gardening. One could be called the "Prussian" method of growing something. It first flattens the terrain with a bulldozer. Nothing is left standing, the ground is leveled and laid out in geometric squares. Then one sprays the earth with various weed-killers to make sure that nothing unexpected sprouts, and only after that does one cut straight furrows, neat like rows of chairs, in which one then plants turnips.

The other way of gardening has been perfected by the Japanese. Typically, they start from the trees and shrubs and stones that are already there, and in a very delicate and careful process prune and trim and rearrange till the surprising beauty of an ordinary moss, or of a root curling through it, has been clari-

fied. Of course, new plants and rocks are added, but the whole evolves with a great care for the previous arrangement.

That difference, applied to education, shows in sharper outlines where the real oppositions lie. The main objection to what is usually labeled the "authoritarian" may be its eradication of the natural predispositions of the mind, or of the whole person—the pretense that the mind is a *tabula rasa*, or worse, the making sure that it becomes one. And so, too, for the advocates of freedom. The talk about not interfering and not exercising influence (not "molding" students) conveys the absurdity of a mere abstention and misrepresents what they really mean, which is expressed far better by the image of that other way of gardening, which sees itself as a ministration, as an enhancement, of that which is already there.

—From *On Being Free* by Frithjof Bergmann, pp. 120–1. © 1977 by University of Notre Dame Press. Reprinted by permission of the publisher.

approaches emphasize the classroom group, while the language-as-development and language-as-expression approaches tend to be more concerned with each individual's growth and development, the former, through attention to the stages of learning and psychological development, the latter, through attention to the responses and personal needs of individual students.

Each approach requires a different kind of planning. The language-as-artifact teacher will first analyze texts, guiding students through the process of close reading; the language-as-development teacher will need to determine what learning task is suited to each student at that student's particular stage of development; the language-as-expression teacher will need to find ways to stimulate and facilitate each individual student's search for personal empowerment; and the language-as-social-construct teacher will need to facilitate group interaction and social empowerment by guiding students in their choice and pursuit of activities. Thus "artifact" and "development" teachers will be more apt to plan activities for students; "expression" and "social-construct" teachers will be more apt to try to find ways to stimulate students to plan their own activities.

The Difference in Feel

Each of these classrooms will have a different look and feel about them. "Artifact" and "development" classrooms tend to be more obviously structured than those of the other two approaches, though there is apt to be a greater variety of individual activity in the "development" than in the "artifact" classroom. Looser structures, dictated by student responses and student needs, are more characteristic of the "expression" and "social-construct" approaches, and the classrooms themselves will probably seem more open, with individuals or small groups often going off in different directions. Teachers in both of these types of classrooms, however, need to devise strategies for helping students to use their increased freedom wisely.

The Difference for the Student

There are as many different kinds of learners as there are students (although we can identify certain patterns of learning). This means that no approach is ideal for every student and that some approaches are more effective for certain kinds of students than for others. Students may be highly motivated or not motivated at all, they may be skeptical or trusting of teachers and school, they may be oriented toward oral or visual or writing skills, they may be eager to learn or resigned to school or rebellious toward school.

The language-as-expression approach is apt to work best with students who feel comfortable exploring themselves and their feelings, although this approach may also help develop more interest in English studies in rebellious or seemingly unmotivated students. The language-as-social-construct approach is apt to capitalize on students' interests in discovering knowledge together; it motivates students to see reading and writing not just as school subjects but as an important part of their learning process. The language-as-artifact approach will most likely appeal to students who prefer a more structured and more teacher-directed classroom atmosphere, although these students should also be encouraged to direct some of their own learning. The language-as-development approach—in theory at least—is designed to work with any and every student by recognizing the student's particular stage of development and hence discovering what the next step should be for that student. Each approach, if taught effectively, may have something to offer all students, but each approach has its particular potentials and limitations.

The Difference for the Teacher

Whether an individual teacher can use a particular approach with maximum effectiveness will depend in part on the outcomes a teacher has selected as important, in part on the context and character of a particular group of students, and in part on the teacher's distinctive temperament. But—most important—teachers also change over time in their theoretical or philosophical orientation toward teaching and hence in the approaches that suit them best. It may be instructive here to consider two teachers who have changed their teaching styles over the years to accommodate new theoretical orientations, arrived at through experience in the classroom.

Cathy, starting out with a language-as-artifact orientation, has changed her role during the seventeen years of her teaching career. She realized that students can and should play a much more active part in their learning processes than she previously allowed and that she, in turn, could be more effective as "a facilitator instead of a lecturer or a performer." She has incorporated elements of the "expression" approach into her teaching practice and now helps her students achieve greater ownership of their learning. (See Box 8.2.)

Roger, in contrast, started out seven years ago by trying to give his students complete ownership without helping them discover how to design and conduct their own learning projects. He came to realize that "most kids needed more structure" than he was providing, and that his students needed, not a friend, but a "wiser adult who would listen to them and support them, and guide them." He now thinks of "each kid's individual needs," as the "development" or "expression" teacher might. He has learned to respect his students and is trying to earn their respect in return. He has modified his initial procedures (which were almost a caricature of the "expression" approach) so that he now can capitalize on the potentials of the language-as-expression approach with much greater effectiveness. (See Box 8.3.)

The Approaches in Action

The potentials and limitations of each approach can perhaps be even more clearly highlighted by looking at how different approaches might use the same texts. The use of a text, how it is read and why it is read in a particular class, is one of the important ways to distinguish between these approaches. First, we consider Mark Twain's *The Adventures of Huckleberry Finn,* a text commonly taught in high school English courses. Then, we examine a nonfiction selection, Margaret Mead's *Blackberry Winter,* less

BOX 8.2
CATHY

When I started out I was very, very traditional. I didn't have anything to go on but what the other teachers were doing in my school. I borrowed handouts, quizzes, tests, sometimes whole units from them just to survive. I was told to be tough and I was, too! The old thing about not smiling until Thanksgiving? Boy, that was me. I was so structured, but I think that was good because it helped me get over my nervousness.

But I also believed that was the only way to teach. I prepared lectures on *Huckleberry Finn* and left five minutes at the end of the hour for discussion, and wondered why my kids didn't want to talk! I even lectured on writing. . . . One year I even handed out the notes I wanted my kids to memorize for a survey of English literature. I taught, the students regurgitated. . . . Though I was worried about teaching, I felt confident about the stuff I was teaching (deeper inside I wasn't so sure).

When I think of it, though, I wasn't giving kids enough credit to think for themselves. I still do most of the talking in most of my classes, but I've learned how to use groups more effectively, and I pride myself now on finding ways to get kids to talk to each other during discussions and not just answer my questions. That is a big change for me. Part of it is just that I see that kids have a natural ability to talk and share with each other. . . . Part of it is that I am less uptight about my agenda. I think that kids are smart, and I try more to connect things with their lives. I'm not just pouring things into their ears. . . .

I suppose teaching at first was a little like a first date with me in class. I was excited, but also so afraid I might fail that I had to make sure every space was filled, preplanned. Now I'm more comfortable with the silences, or more comfortable, at least, to let my students fill those silences with their words. Oh, it takes so much pressure off you to be more of a facilitator instead of a lecturer or a performer. It's just as much work, but I feel I'm a better teacher.

commonly taught in junior highs and high schools. Our concern here is with general principles, not with variations that might result from differences in grade level. We have also deliberately chosen different genres, a novel and an autobiography, hoping that you will be able to extrapolate from these examples how the various approaches might be applied to any genre—drama, poetry, short stories, even visual media such as films.

. . . in Teaching *Huck Finn*

In making *Huck Finn* a part of the curriculum, all teachers, regardless of approach, would be concerned with its various themes: Twain's indictment of slavery, the brotherhood that develops between Huck and Jim,

---

BOX 8.3
ROGER

I was wild at first. Oh my God, all I wanted to do was make friends with the kids. I so much wanted them to like me! In my first year, I went to a party some kids had invited me to. . . . I thought I was trying to be cool. Of course, I was only four or five years older than these kids, so it didn't seem so strange to me. But one of the guys' mothers barged into the party, and let me know she disapproved of my being there. Of course, I knew immediately that I had made a mistake, and I never did anything like that again.

But I did make other, similar mistakes those first two years. I let everybody get away with murder; it was chaos in my classroom. I had no rules. I was—I thought—everybody's favorite teacher. I was fun and funny, and I was involved in lots of extracurricular activities, but I know now I wasn't really respected. I was filled with lots of progressive ideas: I thought I would have them call me by my first name, no straight rows, no fixed deadlines. I was really into freedom for all kids, and no fixed assignments or due dates, but I found that most kids needed more structure. And they didn't need me to be their friend, exactly, but to be an-

other, wiser adult who would listen to them and support them, and guide them to some extent.

I still am a performer; I entertain. I'm exhausted at the end of the day. I think it is hard work to keep close to the kids' sense of humor, and to keep up on what they're interested in so you can connect what you are studying in the classroom to the students' lives. Kids are wonderful, if you listen to them and show them you respect them. I like to think of each kid's individual needs. I pride myself on building a relationship with each of my 130 kids, and you can do it, even in some small way. But you have to give them reason to respect you, too. I try more to help them develop as writers, and as thinkers; that's the important thing to me now.

I think it has to be a balance between giving kids too much structure and not too much. I still have wild days, when everything seems to be out of control, and I have to make sure the door is shut because of the noise—most of the noise is productive; they're learning—but I am more in control of the noise these days.

Huck's search for a father, the struggle between society and individuals. Teachers would also want to ensure that students could distinguish between Huck, the narrator, and Twain, the author. The uses of dialect and Twain's careful attention to it might also be examined by students in any classroom. Classroom discussions would certainly take up the novel's ending, dealing with the cruelty with which Jim is treated. Finally, most teachers would want to explore the significance of the fact that Twain's book was published in 1884, nearly twenty years after the Civil War. They might ask students why Twain would want to write about an issue that had, technically, been resolved. Beyond the major thematic issues, each of the approaches would use the text, or teach it, very differently.

The language-as-artifact approach, the one most of us likely experienced in our own high school years, would remain closely tied to such issues because of its emphasis on close reading. For example, students would be expected to discuss or write about Huck's struggle with his conscience for not turning Jim in as a runaway slave. Huck believes that he will go to "everlasting fire" for his failure to disclose Jim's whereabouts and reminds himself that if he had gone to Sunday School, he would have learned to act differently. However, his friendship with Jim wins out and he says, "All right, then, I'll go to hell," as he tears up the letter that reveals Jim's location. The language-as-artifact teacher would be concerned that students see how the text reveals the contradictions in a society that professes religious ideals but also condones slavery. Students would also be asked to discuss the various people whom Jim and Huck meet in their adventure, stressing what social ills each episode represents, as well as the relationship between the novel's ending and the rest of the text, both tonally and thematically. The close examination of the text itself—the themes, metaphors, and symbols—would be central to the study of *Huck Finn*.

In language-as-development classrooms, students might be introduced to the historical contexts of slavery, and the abolitionist movement that worked to end it, in order to develop students' prior knowledge. Students might discuss the parallels between each of the episodes, much as in the language-as-artifact classroom, but maps or diagrams would be used to help them discover the patterns in each encounter. They might draw their own maps of the Mississippi River to chart Huck and Jim's travels, locating each of the groups the two meet. Such activities would facilitate reading comprehension by helping students focus on the pattern of events. The teacher might also have the students predict the ending of the novel, asking them not to read beyond the point where Huck pretends he is Tom Sawyer at the Phelps farm. After reading the actual ending, the students and teacher could compare the differences between the novel and the students' texts, discussing the various choices writers make in crafting an ending. In order to discover how each character contributes to the novel's themes, students could also develop biographies of characters, describing their personalities, positions on slavery, and their attitudes toward Huck. The point of reading the novel would be to encourage students to develop more sophisticated reading skills—analyzing character, analyzing structure, and inferring themes from the book's events.

The concern for students' responses to the text would occupy the language-as-expression teacher. What is the nature of Huck's dilemma over Jim's runaway status? Have the students themselves been caught between what they were taught and what they believed was right? How did they respond? What is Huck's relationship to Pap and how might students cope with such a father? Is Jim, though a slave, freer than Huck? Does Huck, in spite of his condemnation of the Dauphin and the Duke, also have a kind of sneaking admiration for them? What do students think of the way Huck defers to Tom? The language-as-expression teacher might also have the students write their own adventures, pretending they have run away from home and describing who they meet along the way. Another writing assignment could have the students rewrite the ending, imitating Huck's voice, but making the final scenes more satisfying. Reading the novel would provide the springboard for students' own creative interpretation and for opportunities to express their own solutions to dilemmas similar to Huck's.

In the language-as-social-construct classroom, *Huck Finn* might be used in a thematic unit about individuals' struggles for freedom; in fact, the novel would be specifically chosen because it addressed these issues. Teachers using this perspective might be especially concerned about the distance between the historical period of the novel and its publication date, because they would want to explore the enduring concern with freedom and individual rights. Reading the novel might be connected to reading selections from *Narrative of the Life of Frederick Douglass, an American Slave*, or Harriet Jacobs's *Incidents in the Life of a Slave Girl*, or even Kate Chopin's *The Awakening* because of its concern for women's independence. Students might research a group of people who have had to win their rights or freedoms. (See the middle school unit on equal rights in Chapter 7.) The teacher might suggest that students draw upon their own ethnic, national, or political heritages, exploring the histories of their ancestors—for example, the Armenian struggle for national rights in the Soviet Union, the women's movement, the holocaust, or the labor movement. Students might read literature relevant to the specific topics they choose, using library resources. They might also write stories of their own, imagining the characters and their dilemmas. Of note in reading *Huck Finn* might be the closing scene where Huck "lights out" again, seeing that act as a prognosis for change in political or social systems. Whatever elements were emphasized would depend to a great extent on the unit's theme and students' interests. In language-as-social-construct classrooms, these factors—unit theme and student interest—would define what was read and for what purposes.

. . . in Teaching
Blackberry Winter

The same sorts of differences between approaches can be illustrated with selections from Margaret Mead's autobiography, *Blackberry Winter*. Teachers of all approaches would choose such a text as an example of the genre. They might, however, introduce students to different chapters of the text for different purposes. For example, the language-as-artifact teacher might choose the prologue, an essay in which Mead describes her purposes for writing the autobiography and her sense of the relationship between generations. Mead's use of extended metaphor, the autobiography as film editing, the ways we fit imperfectly into our own generations, and the debt we owe to our parents and grandparents for shaping our lives might generally form the analysis in this type of classroom. After examining Mead's rhetorical style, students might be assigned a personal essay in which they develop a metaphor for their own lives or an analysis of the opening quote from which the title is drawn and its relationship to the prologue. Imitating the craft of professional writers is another way that this approach centers attention on the text as artifact.

Similarly, the language-as-expression approach might use the two metaphors, autobiography as film editing and blackberry winter, to encourage students to develop their own metaphors. Teachers using this approach might also choose a different chapter, perhaps the one entitled "On Being a Granddaughter." Because this approach considers the connection between the student and the text a highly personal one, students could read this chapter and then write their own descriptions of their relationships with a parent or grandparent. Students might be encouraged to portray both the person and the relationship through a narrative of events. They might be asked to respond to questions such as: What have you learned from this person? How would you describe this person's character? In what ways has this person been important in shaping your personality? The writing assignments in this classroom would emphasize the exploration of self in response to the autobiography of another.

If students in a language-as-social-construct classroom are exploring their experiences in school, they might read Chapter 7, "In and Out of School," in conjunction with the opening of Dickens's *Hard Times*. Both passages describe school experiences, but with very different perspectives on schooling. These passages might be used to discuss students' views of schooling and generate stories that reflect students' experiences. Mead's example of a progressive education, mostly at home, contrasts dramatically with Dickens's stern but satirical portrait of a nineteenth-century classroom, and the teacher might encourage creative responses. As in the language-as-expression classroom, students would have opportunities to connect their reading of *Blackberry Winter* to their own experiences, using passages read to help them imagine their own stories. The language-as-social-construct approach might take an issue like schooling beyond personal response, though, examining the political and social dimensions as well.

An essential part of the language-as-development approach consists of teaching students reading-comprehension strategies. Any chapter a teacher using this approach chose would emphasize ways of constructing and organizing meaning from the text. For example, Chapter 8 ("College: DePauw") describes Mead's first college experience. The opening paragraphs provide in general what Mead and her parents expected from her college education. She then compares her experiences and expectations with her brother's and sisters' concerns and discusses her disappointment with DePauw. The language-as-development teacher might use this chapter as a way of honing students' comparative skills. The teacher might introduce the structure of the chapter, asking students to "read for" certain information: How was Mead's orientation different from that of her siblings? What did she expect to learn at college? Why was she disappointed at DePauw? These activities are central to the approach because they provide students with direct instruction in the kinds of strategies accomplished readers use. In order to help students grasp the important elements of the chapter, the teacher might also query students about their knowledge of college life, explaining those elements for which students have little background knowledge.

Differing Perspectives on Literacy

What our consideration here, and in the four preceding chapters, should have made clear is that each approach has something of value for students. The goal of each approach, in the broadest sense, is to produce "literate" or "educated" students, even though each approach would define these terms somewhat differently. As these approaches demonstrate, the notion of literacy, its definitions, and its uses are far from settled questions; the concept has changed throughout the course of history according to philosophical or theoretical dispositions. For example, we noted in Chapter 1 that during the early history of our country, people were considered literate if they were able to sign their names. This definition is certainly no longer adequate in our technological society, nor are the functional definitions based on minimum "standards" such as the ability to read and write simple directions or to fill out employment application forms. Instead, we are coming to see the need for multiple literacies that go beyond basic reading, writing, and speaking skills. Educational philosopher Maxine Greene puts it this way: "Education for freedom must clearly focus on the range of human intelligences, the multiple languages and symbol systems available for ordering experience and making sense of the lived world" (*The Dialectic of Freedom* [New York: Teachers College Press, 1988], 125).

We have seen "cultural literacy" as one of the goals of the language-as-artifact approach. Historically, this term referred to a knowledge of cultural traditions to be found in a canon of accepted literary works, those works most often included in secondary school anthologies. The idea of such a canon has come increasingly under fire, however, since it included the works of mainly "dead white males," and today other literary traditions, particularly those of minority, women, contemporary, and experimental writers, are finding a place in English classrooms. As we will discuss later in this chapter, definitions of literacy based solely on the printed text are also coming under scrutiny, since so much of our information comes to us in visual or auditory forms.

The importance of a revised canon rests not only on the need to include neglected writers. Recent language research has revealed the various ways in which communities of people share and use language. These language groups have systematic patterns that may or may not conform to an arbitrary, and not uncontroversial, definition of "standard English." Language use, dialect patterns, and the ways of thinking associated with language are shaped by many factors: geography, class, gender, and ethnicity. For example, in a landmark study of community language, *Ways with Words,* Shirley Brice Heath describes the language practices of two adjacent North Carolina communities, Roadville and Trackton, and the influence these practices have on children in school. (See Suggested Reading at the end of this chapter.)

Though both Roadville and Trackton are working class communities, the parents of the respective towns introduce their children to different ways of using language. In Roadville, a predominantly white neighborhood, children learn early that language represents the "truth" of things; fantasy and make-believe are systematically discouraged. Following directions, "doing things right," and hard work engender roles and worldviews that may clash with teaching strategies that ask students to explore alternatives or make creative responses. In Trackton, on the other hand, children are, in part, assessed by their abilities to embellish stories, adapt their language to different contexts, and interpret meanings depending on various situations. Verbal performances in this predominantly African-American community play important roles in the interactional patterns between adults and children. To teachers, perhaps unfamiliar with ritual insults and verbal games, these performances may be misinterpreted as disrespectful or inappropriate in classroom situations.

What implications do these two examples have for teachers of English? How might language practice influence students' performance in reading, writing, and speaking? The language students learn at home will shape the nature of the responses they make to teachers' assignments. Roadville children, for example, might find writing fiction at odds with their understanding that people must tell the truth, the actual events in their chronological order. Trackton students might find summarizing a difficult task. Teachers need to be sensitive to the values implicit in students' language, helping them expand their repertoire of language uses without alienating them from their communities. Teachers can build upon the strengths of students' home language, too, if they recognize them. Just as each student brings specific talents, each student also brings his or her own version of literacy to the classroom, one that can contribute unique insights to discussions and written texts.

The variety of language use is another argument for the inclusion of many types of writing in the English classroom. The traditional canon with its overwhelming representation of white male authors leaves little opportunity for students to see their own language reflected in the texts they read. As indicated in Chapter 1, the demographic changes in the American population make it unlikely that students in any given classroom will all come from the same ethnic groups or social classes. If English teachers are to develop in their students a lifelong interest in literacy, they will also need to reach beyond the canon for their class reading lists. Teachers in "expression" and "social-construct" classes may find this easier to do, but teachers in other classrooms also need to take advantage of the literacy skills students bring to their classrooms. In our multicultural society, cultural literacy is coming to mean an acquaintance with and appreciation of more than one cultural tradition.

Technological advances in our society have suggested the need to view literacy as more than an encounter with printed texts. As Walter Ong says, "Our understanding of the differences between orality and literacy developed only in the electronic age, not earlier. Contrasts between electronic media and print have sensitized us to the earlier contrast between writing and orality. The electronic age is also an age of 'secondary orality,' the orality of telephones, radio, and television, which depends on writing and print for its existence" (*Orality and Literacy: The Technologizing of the Word* [London: Methuen, 1982], 3). Television and motion pictures depend even more crucially for their existence upon seeing, and the need for visual literacy is highlighted by the important ways in which these media affect the lives of teachers and students alike. (See Foster in Suggested Reading.) Many teachers used to regard movies—and especially TV—as cultural enemies from which students should be weaned so that they could read and appreciate literary "classics" instead. Other teachers used films merely as "babysitters" for their classes—easy ways to fill a class period when they were tired or were planning what a substitute might do. Now teachers are coming to realize that television is a powerful influence in our lives, neither wholly for good nor wholly for ill, and that both television and motion pictures have come of age as art forms. The importance of television in politics and national affairs means that citizens need to understand that medium in order to participate intelligently in the political process. Further, the cultural tradition that is being shaped by television and motion pictures is becoming an important part of our heritage.

Instruction in "seeing" visual texts can help students to spot dishonest or propagandistic uses of visual "language," just as instruction in verbal language can help them spot dishonest and propagandistic uses of words. "Seeing" a visual text means putting oneself in the position of both the camera and the editor and assessing point of view—both literal and figurative—much as one would with a written or oral text, though this may be harder to do with (seemingly objective) visual texts than with written ones. The process calls for close observation as well as for the use of imagination, skills that students need to develop for the sake of their writing and speaking as well as their looking. Seeing a short film like the classic *The Red Balloon*, for example, can provide an opportunity to discuss the functions of narrative and the differences between telling a story in words and telling it in pictures. Comparing John Steinbeck's *The Grapes of Wrath* with the film version can illustrate different thematic emphases for the same situation.

Experience with visual texts can also help students to visualize written texts. Writing a movie or TV script for a poem or a scene from a novel can help students to look more closely at the written text and to express their feelings about it. Visual texts can also serve as a stimulus for writing and discussion. Finally, there are now many excellent films that are adaptations of novels and short stories, while others present useful background for particular writers or literary periods or movements. (See "Books, Films, and Culture: Reading in the Classroom," in Suggested Reading at the end of this chapter.)

Also stemming from technological advances in our society, computer literacy has come into focus in many schools. Computer instruction may even play a part in the English classroom; word-processing skills may be especially useful in a classroom that focuses on the process—and not merely the products—of writing. Computers can make it easier for students to make revisions; in fact, research seems to indicate that students more readily make such changes when they have access to computers. The concept of a "draft" has shifted dramatically as students working on computers take the opportunity to revise their works in progress. In addition, most word-processing programs are equipped with "spell-checking" accessories and grammatical guides, which can be used as teaching tools. As with the advent of the calculator in mathematics, such programs have implications for the nature of literacy instruction in English.

Some school districts—particularly those located near major research universities—have also in recent years been able to take advantage of electronic mail facilities. Through them, students can converse with a wide variety of other people—fellow students or those in neighboring schools, university students, local businesspeople, and other members of the community. While computer conferences are not yet widely available in school districts, they do point to the future. It is not hard to imagine teachers and students conducting extended discussion about their work via computer or writing responses in electronic journals. As with any other teaching technique, there are limits to what computers can do: The composing process on a computer may not work equally well for every student; a computer conference may enable more students to participate in a discussion but at the same time may lessen some of the immediacy and the excitement of give-and-take in a classroom.

Each teacher must make choices about what kinds of literacy to emphasize, and these choices will depend upon the context of a particular class, a particular school, a particular community, and a particular student. Sylvia Scribner, who has studied different kinds of literacy and the relationship between learning in school and learning outside of school, puts it this way:

> Recognition of the multiple meanings and varieties of literacy . . . argues for a diversity of educational approaches, informal and community-based as well as formal and school-based. As ethnographic research and practical experience demonstrate, effective literacy programs are those that are responsive to perceived needs, whether for functional skills, social power, or self-improvement. . . . Individual objectives may be highly specific. . . . The road to maximal literacy may begin for some through the feeder routes of a wide variety of specific literacies ("Literacy in Three Metaphors," in Eugene Kintgen, Barry Kroll, and Mike Rose, eds., *Perspectives on Literacy* [Carbondale: Southern Illinois: University Press, 1988], 81).

Scribner's view of multiple literacies encourages many approaches and many types of classrooms. However, the form a teacher's class takes will, in the end, be determined by the goals set for students, the theory of language adopted, and the learning it fosters.

Teaching specific literacies to specific students is both a daunting and a rewarding task, with the final goal, as we pointed out in Chapter 3, of helping students to achieve some control over their education, though the amount and kind of control will depend on which of the four approaches is emphasized in the classroom. One must be prepared to sometimes fail, because teaching literacy is a task for which the teacher cannot always know the best strategy and that, we cannot emphasize too strongly, the teacher cannot accomplish without the help of the students. But we learn from failures—sometimes more than from successes—and seeming failures may not be failures at all. As Robert Fulghum says, "Discontent and ferment are signs the fires of education are burning well. In education, look for trouble. If you can't find any, make some." (See Box 8.4.) We hope this book will help you to do just that, whichever approach(es) you decide will work best for you and your classroom.

[handwritten margin notes at top: "Give tools to acquire knowledge Not just information. Language as Development."]

BOX 8.4
A PERSONAL LITANY

I kept a journal during the years I taught. And in time I boiled my experience down into some one-line statements that became a personal litany to be said when school began and when school was not going well . . . :

Learning is taking place at all times in all circumstances for every person.

There are as many ways to learn something as there are people.

There is no one way to learn anything—learn how you learn—help the student do likewise.

There is nothing everyone must know.

All I have to do is accept the consequences of what I do not know.

There is no one way to be human.

Imagination is more important than information.

The quality of education depends more on what's going on at home than in the school. And more on what is going on in the student than what is going on in the teacher.

In learning, don't ask for food; ask for farming lessons. In teaching, vice versa.

If nobody learns as much as the teacher, then turn students into teachers.

Every student has something important to teach the teacher.

Discontent and ferment are signs the fires of education are burning well.

In education, look for trouble. If you can't find any, make some.

[handwritten margin note: "would be nice to believe. But is Mind shut off to learning?"]

[handwritten note: "All Learning grows out of tension & conflict."]

—From Robert Fulghum, "A Bag of Possibles and Other Matters of the Mind," *Newsweek: Special Issue: How to Teach Our Kids* (September 1990): 92.

[handwritten note: "Classrooms are too comfortable, not enough to keep mind alive."]

Suggested Reading

BAILEY, RICHARD W., and ROBIN MELANIE FORSHEIM, eds. *Literacy for Life: The Demand for Reading and Writing.* New York: Modern Language Association, 1983.

This provocative collection of essays provides a variety of perspectives on what literacy is and what its implications are both for the classroom and for society at large.

BERGMANN, FRITHJOF. "Freedom and Education." *On Being Free.* South Bend, Ind.: University of Notre Dame Press, 1977.

This book presents a stimulating philosophical discussion of the place of freedom in education.

"Books, Films, and Culture: Reading in the Classroom." *English Journal.* (1991): 82–7.

This article presents an annotated bibliography of films that teachers recommend for classroom use. In the brief introduction, ideas for "reading" films as an art form are discussed.

BRUNER, JEROME. *The Process of Education.* Cambridge, Mass.: Harvard University Press, 1960.

Bruner shows that basic concepts of science and the humanities can be grasped intuitively at a very early age. He argues that curricula should be designed to foster such abilities and to build on them in increasingly formal ways as education progresses.

DOUGLASS, FREDERICK. *Narrative of the Life of Frederick Douglass, an American Slave* (edited by Benjamin Quarles). Cambridge, Mass.: Harvard University Press, 1960.

This autobiography documents Douglass's life as a slave in Maryland, the cruelty with which slaves were treated, and his escape to freedom.

ELBOW, PETER. *Embracing Contraries: Exploration in Teaching and Learning.* New York: Oxford University Press, 1986.

Elbow explores the way that teachers must be both "directors" and "facilitators" at different times in the learning process.

FOSTER, HAROLD M. *The New Literacy.* Urbana, Ill.: NCTE, 1979.

This book is a useful exploration of the importance of visual literacy and the uses of film in the English classroom.

GREENE, MAXINE. *The Dialectic of Freedom.* New York: Teachers College Press, 1988.

Greene, an educational philosopher, argues that freedom must be achieved through continuing resistance to the forces that limit and oppress; she explores the relationship between freedom and imagination, with an emphasis on the role of the arts in educating the imagination.

HEATH, SHIRLEY BRICE. *Ways with Words: Language, Life, and Work in Communities and Schools.* New York: Cambridge University Press, 1983.

An anthropologist, Heath spent ten years studying the language of two communities in the Piedmont area of North Carolina. She also worked with teachers and administrators enrolled in graduate courses who studied language communities as a way to improve the educational experiences of the students they served.

HIRSCH, E. D. *Cultural Literacy: What Every American Needs to Know.* Boston: Houghton Mifflin, 1987.

Hirsch, consistent with a language-as-artifact approach to learning, asserts the need for teachers to provide background cultural knowledge for students. The book includes an appendix that lists the basics of such knowledge.

JACOBS, HARRIET. *Incidents in the Life of a Slave Girl* (Maria Child and Jean Fagan Yellin, eds.). Cambridge, Mass.: Harvard University Press, 1987.

Another slave narrative, this autobiography describes Jacobs' path to freedom, including her seven-year confinement in an attic where she hid from her owner, and her efforts to secure the freedom of her children.

KINTGEN, EUGENE, BARRY M. KROLL, and MIKE ROSE, eds. *Perspectives on Literacy.* Carbondale: Southern Illinois University Press, 1988.

The editors have put together a comprehensive collection of essays on the nature and practice of literacy from a variety of writers' perspectives.

MEAD, MARGARET. *Blackberry Winter*. New York: Morrow, 1972.

Mead describes her family life, her anthropological adventures, and her views on the world.

ONG, WALTER J. *Orality and Literacy: The Technologizing of the Word*. London: Methuen, 1982.

Ong explores the differences and the relationships between orality and writing, pointing out the effects of each upon larger social and cultural issues.

SCRIBNER, SYLVIA. "Literacy in Three Metaphors." In Kintgen, Kroll, and Rose (see above), pp. 71–81.

In her essay, Scribner develops a broad definition of literacy in terms of human needs and purposes, asserting that different kinds of literacy provide functional skills, social power, or self-esteem.

SELFE, CYNTHIA L., DAWN RODRIGUES, and WILLIAM R. OATES, eds. *Computers in English and the Language Arts*. Urbana, Ill.: NCTE, 1989.

This is a useful collection of essays that provides different perspectives on the various uses of computers in English.

9

Evaluation

Grades are like a paycheck. You do this work and you get this grade for your work. People just go to get paid. It's a tool we use, overuse maybe, for motivation. For you [students] to do your best.

—Mary

In grading, if teachers are fair, they are motivating their students. I feel, however, much of the time teachers grade more on personal opinion than on actual student results. Personal opinion is important, say, if a student shows much effort. If however, teachers grade you according to how well you kiss up to them, grading loses its real value. . . . Students may be "graded" or judged by an unfair teacher, and because this judgment is taken so seriously, a student's future may actually be altered by one misjudgment.

—Jennifer

Ever since middle school, grades have been an extremely important factor in [my] education. Not so much important to me but for my parents. In my house I was expected to get As and if I didn't I would be grounded or punished in some way.

—Jessica

All throughout my school career I have strived for the highest grade I could possibly achieve [an A]. Because I spent my time concentrating on my grades, I forgot to learn as much as possible. Before every test I would memorize what I needed for an A. The problem with that was that I couldn't remember it afterwards. Therefore, I didn't learn.

—Greg

What you learn, or have to learn, is how to play the game. We talk a lot about taking grades out of high school, but there's not a college or a job where you're not evaluated by your performance. . . . I really grade on personal growth. If I have a kid who writes really well at the beginning who doesn't take any risks or doesn't make any strides, I can't give that student an A all the time. . . . I'm interested in the ways you [students] think, think your way through a problem. That's what I want to give credit for—your best effort thinking critically about some topic. . . . I don't care if someone remembers the name of the head pig in Animal Farm. *I don't remember it, but I remember the concept of power from the book. That's what I want my kids to remember.*

—Kathie

I remember the fights that used to break out between students over grades. Friendships would end because of them. It was a game, who could outdo who.

—Richard

In my experience grades have always proved to be a motivating factor. Throughout high school it was an academic competition just like any other competition, including sports. . . . I think sometimes it's a shame that so much importance is put on grades but how else are we to measure and reward those who work hard as opposed to those who don't?

—Carrie

Grades are very important to me. If I have worked hard at something, I would like a good grade to tell me that I did well. I don't think that grades should just check if you got the answers correct, I think that they should measure how much you have improved. Improvement is rarely measured in the classroom. Most teachers just want the right answer.

—Dawn

I hope the grade that I give students, that they earn, is a reflection of their effort and what they have learned in the class. Sometimes, though, it's how they have gotten around, how they have manipulated the teacher. That's what I've found out from students who've come back to talk to me. . . . I can't explain always why one paper is an A and another isn't. It's too subjective. It's how I respond to it, knowing the student and the assignment. . . . I hate grades.

—Gail

Grading . . . hinders the progress of writing. I recently received a paper back . . . in which I got a B+. The only comments I received on the paper were a few "Goods" written next to paragraphs. If it was so good, why did I not receive the A? I, in turn, learn nothing that will help me do better on my next paper.

—Jonathan

Many times people just say things because they know that that will get them a good grade. If grades weren't involved, then the students would be more apt to say what they feel rather than saying something to please the teacher. . . . I would rather just get comments upon good and bad points.

—Aaron

In a math or science class I can tell how well I am doing by a grade because you are either right or wrong. But in an English class the grading is very subjective. I might think that I wrote a great paper and get a B on it without really any indication by the grader of why it wasn't an A paper. Other times I know that I could do a lot better on a paper if I wanted to and when I hand it in I get an A on it. These grades mean very little to me because I know when I deserve a good grade and when I don't. Plus different teachers will grade the same paper in different ways so I could give the same paper to two teachers and get an A and a C on it.

—Dana

The way we create grades and the manner in which they are used go so against my philosophy that I feel a great deal of guilt for participating in the process at all. As I see it, and have experienced it, grading functions primarily as a means of pigeonholing and classifying students rather than as any kind of educational tool—or any kind of desirable carrot to dangle in front of students. . . . The problem . . . is that a letter on a piece of paper is such a limited representation of an individual's "performance" in a class. . . . Unfortunately, I think that too often grades are the only means of affirmation teachers offer their students. This being the case, the majority of students, those who are not being affirmed with As, are fairly consistently having their worth questioned . . . . How is it that our evaluative tools exclude so much of the richness that students possess?

—Matt

I had a teacher last year who put the names of kids who got As and Bs on the board. The kids who didn't get As, who got Cs, really felt bad about it. They were kind of mad, too. . . . For me, there's too much emphasis put on grades. I've seen good students cheat to get them.

—Michael

It is very discouraging to me to get a poor grade when I've worked hard. . . . The work I do is for myself, but the grades I achieve reflect upon me, and if I receive poor grades I feel dumb, and if I receive good marks I feel smarter and continue to get good marks.

—Jeni

Throughout my life, the grades that I have received in school have not changed me much. I always accepted my grades with little pride or remorse because what I learned was much more important to me than what some underpaid and overworked teacher thought. . . . Knowledge will give you everything, grades give you little.

—John

(Remarks of teachers appear in italics, remarks of students in standard type. The students are all twelfth graders, except Michael, who is an eleventh grader.)

WOVEN THROUGH THE REMARKS of these students and teachers regarding grading are several themes: an intense competitiveness among grade-seekers, the inevitable subjectivity of grading, the tension between measuring growth and measuring ability, the inability to capture complex performances with a letter grade. Students and teachers alike seem distinctly uncomfortable or dissatisfied with the way grading systems function. Clearly, the students don't feel that grades are always fair or helpful. The teachers seem divided on the question of fairness. While Mary and Kathie seem to assume that it is possible to be fair, Gail and Matt question whether grades can ever do justice to students.

What is judged and rewarded in English classrooms obviously varies from teacher to teacher. Kathie says she grades on "personal growth" and rewards critical thinking; Gail grades her students on both "effort" and "what they have learned in class." Matt feels that grades cannot give a fair or complete evaluation of "performance" and that inevitably students read grades as judgments of personal worth rather than of performance. The students like John (who seems unaffected by grades) are the exception rather than the rule. Students also report widely divergent beliefs about what "counts" in grading. Carrie has faith that hard work is rewarded, but Jennifer thinks teachers may also "grade you according to how well you kiss up to them" rather than on the effort you put into your work. Dawn believes that grades should reflect hard work and improvement, although she feels that "most teachers just want the right answer." Students and teachers, bound by a belief in objectivity, may sometimes overvalue a knowledge of the "facts" associated with "right answers," neglecting the greater significance of an understanding of the contexts into which those facts may be fitted. (See Box 9.1.)

For teachers the most important issue about the grading system seems to be how to balance judgments of quality against assessments of effort and improvement. For students, the most important issue seems to be that they see grades as judgments of themselves rather than of their work alone; students generally feel that "effort" and "improvement" should have first priority in the grading process.

Standardized tests and college entrance examinations, given in order to compare students, school districts, states, and nations, exert tremendous influence over curricula and grading policies in individual classrooms and schools. In their desire to measure performance "objectively," politicians, community leaders, parents, principals, and teachers often trust shallow, easy-to-score measures designed to address a narrow band of student skills. They sometimes lose sight of a central purpose of schooling—to create independent learners and citizens capable of detailed, accurate self-assessment.

While educators can't remain blind to the fact that grades and test scores are often used for dubious social purposes, they should understand that schools, teachers, and students should be accountable to their communities. Though some school districts are moving away from traditional means of evaluation, most places still require letter grades. Teachers need to realize they have a responsibility to develop classroom grading systems that foster, not hinder, student growth and learning. Even more critically, they must find ways to "read" individual students' levels of understanding and growth as readers, as writers, as participants in activities, as listeners, as learners in order to set goals and adjust their own methods.

The Purposes of Evaluation

Broadly speaking, evaluation in schools serves two rather different purposes: *instruction* and *management*. *Formative*, or *diagnostic*, *evaluation* figures prominently in instructional evaluation during most stages of the learning process. Formative evaluation can tell a teacher "where the students are" and thus aid in the planning of a day, a unit, or a semester by suggesting the kind and level of instruction that is appropriate for an individual or a class. The kinds of responses an athletic coach makes during practice are analogous to formative evaluation. The teacher-coach

---

BOX 9.1
BULL VERSUS COW

The phenomenon of bull, in all the honor and opprobrium with which it is regarded by students and faculty, says something, I think, about our theories of knowledge. So too, the grades which we assign on examinations communicate to students what these theories may be. . . .

It is a curious fact that there is no academic slang for the presentation of evidence of diligence alone. . . . I must beg the reader's pardon, and, for reasons almost too obvious to bear, suggest "cow." . . .

When the pure concepts are translated into verbs, their complexities become apparent in the assumptions and purposes of the students as they write:

To cow (v. *intrans.*) or the act of cowing:
   To list data . . . without awareness of, or comment upon, the contexts, frames of reference, or points of observation which determine the origins, nature, and meaning of the data. . . . To write on the as-

sumption that "a fact is a fact." To present evidence of hard work as a substitute for understanding, without any intent to deceive.

To bull (v. *intrans.*) or the act of bulling:
   To discourse upon the contexts, frames of reference and points of observation which would determine the origin, nature, and meaning of data if one had any. To present evidence of an understanding of form in the hope that the reader may be deceived into supposing a familiarity with content. . . .

If a liberal education should teach students "how to think," not only in their own fields but in fields outside their own . . . then bulling, even in its purest form, . . . [is] more important . . . than the collecting of "facts that are facts" which schoolboys learn to do. Here then, good bull appears not as ignorance at all but as an aspect of knowledge. . . . The student who merely cows robs himself, without knowing it, of his education.

—From William G. Perry, Jr., "Examsmanship and the Liberal Arts: A Study in Educational Epistemology," in *Examining in Harvard College: A Collection of Essays by Members of the Harvard Faculty,* Harvard University Press. Reprinted by permission.

makes suggestions on drafts, offers strategies for reading, provides alternative ways of looking at a problem, gives progress reports, and generally tries to help students improve their performances. Comments from peers in writing groups or class discussions, as well as peer editing, may also serve the instructional function.

Summative evaluation, employed mainly for management purposes, is concerned with issues such as accountability, standards, and placement and is likely to serve broad social purposes rather than personal growth. Evaluation that is made after a task or series of related tasks is completed can be described as summative and usually serves management purposes.

Summative evaluation pronounces a final judgment, often in the form of a grade. The kinds of responses a referee makes during a game are analogous to summative evaluation. The teacher-referee writes an A or a C at the bottom of the paper (usually accompanied by a comment that can also serve both formative and summative purposes), recommends the student for advanced English, or puts a grade on the report card. Expectations for teacher accountability come from other teachers, the school administration, parents, and the larger community. All of these constituencies expect teachers to provide convincing demonstrations of teaching and learning, and evaluation plays a central role in these demonstrations. Evidence such as grades, test scores, portfolio assessments, and students' acceptance into colleges contributes to the teacher's demonstration of accountability.

One of the complicated things about evaluation is trying to keep the roles of coach and referee separate. It's easy to start acting like a referee when work is still in progress. The teacher who does this is likely to make the mistake of marking spelling errors in a journal entry about reading or expecting mechanical perfection in a draft for a paper. One way to keep the two roles straight is to make conscious choices about the timing of different kinds of evaluation. Teachers vary in choosing the point during an assignment—or a semester—when they switch from formative to summative evaluation. Some teachers, especially those who employ portfolios, may use only formative evaluation until very near the end of the marking period or semester.

Evaluation, whether for instruction or for management, involves comparisons. If the purpose is for management, students' performances are likely to be compared, on the basis of a task they have completed or a stage they have reached, with the performances of other students—in a class, in a school, in a school district, in a state, in a nation. Although there are inequities and disadvantages in comparisons, since all students may not fit easily into the same mold or pigeonhole, as Matt so fervently points out, social institutions often demand comparisons, if only to preserve their own hierarchical structures.

Instructional purposes also suggest comparisons, not of individuals with other students, but rather of students' potential with their performances or of the strategies they have used with alternative strategies that might have led to different results. As Michael says, the students with Cs "felt bad" and "were kind of mad" when their performances were publicly compared with those of other students; one can surmise that any motivation from the comparison was likely to be negative. However, students can be actively—and profitably—involved in evaluation for instructional purposes through self-analysis, peer evaluation, and discussion, comparing strategies and specific aspects of performance when the focus is growth, not "final judgment."

Assessing Growth in the English Classroom

English teachers have special concerns when developing classroom evaluation systems. English is widely perceived as a much more "subjective" area than science or math. (However, Dana's view that "you are either right or wrong" in those other subject areas does not by any means do justice to their complexity.) It is indeed true, as Dana says, that two English teachers might grade the same paper very differently, one giving it an A and one a C. However, the experience of groups of teachers who grade papers together suggests that, after orientation and group discussion about the criteria to be applied, the members of the group can be expected to grade the same paper within the range of one full letter grade, not two. Together, members of an English department or a district language arts committee can negotiate criteria for student writing, and grading policies may flow from that conversation. The total context for the paper in a given classroom is also important: What is its purpose? How does it fit with previous performance or previous assignments? How does it compare with other papers in the group?

Part of the attraction of English teaching as a career lies in the fact that English is not an exact science, but a multidimensional discipline that allows both students and teachers to express personality and personal views. English itself, as currently construed, is extremely complex, involving reading, response to texts in talk and writing, collaboration, research, and commitment. All of those dimensions must be considered when a teacher creates systems for evaluation and for grading. Up to now we have been looking at evaluation in much too narrow a context, focusing mainly on the grading system. Yet evaluation can also mean responding to student work, diagnosing student skills, gathering information to compare large groups of students, counting pieces of student work, inviting students to participate in analyzing their own performances, or a number of other activities, none of which involves grading directly. Students should be helped to see evaluation as a human concern in many different contexts, both academic and nonacademic, and grading as only one of many kinds of evaluation.

Encouraging Self-Evaluation

As the students quoted at the beginning of this chapter suggest, evaluation is a natural human activity that people engage in automatically. "I know when I deserve a good grade and when I don't," Dana says.

Accurate self-evaluation is invaluable outside the classroom as well as inside. Any worthwhile educational program attempts to develop these self-assessment skills along with other abilities.

During the process of learning itself, students should be urged to ask themselves questions that involve constant evaluation: Do I understand the paragraph I have just read? If not, what do I still need to figure out and how can I go about it? Can I find a better way to sum things up in the concluding paragraph of the paper I am writing? Will a reader understand what I'm trying to say? In this story I'm reading, what connection do I see between the ending, which disturbs me, and the preceding part of the story? Why did the ending bother me?

Questions like these that involve the student in reflecting on the task at hand should be supplemented, of course, with comments and questions from the teacher and student peers in class discussion, writing groups, conferences, and the like. When the teacher looks at a draft and suggests changes, it can help students learn how to revise and/or edit their writing more effectively. When the teacher invites students to select the best piece of writing from their portfolios (see Box 9.9 and Chapter 6) so it can be graded, they learn critical thinking skills. When peers in a writing group say, "I didn't understand what you were saying in this paragraph" or "I especially liked the description here at the beginning—the details you chose made me see what was happening" or (in a class discussion) "I don't see what's wrong with . . . ," students begin to develop a useful sense of audience.

Finally, end-of-task evaluation is most useful when, along with teacher response, it involves the student's thoughtful consideration of certain questions: Exactly what have I managed to do? How does this fit with what I did last week or last month when . . .? What else might I have done? What might I still need to do? When self-evaluation is emphasized in all stages of instruction, students become more independent readers, writers, and speakers.

Strategies for Evaluation

Within the broad boundaries we have been sketching, many evaluative strategies are used in different contexts for specific purposes. Although evaluation can be seen as a continuous process, it seems particularly crucial at the beginning of a school year or semester, when teachers are trying to understand who their students are as learners and as people. Thoughtful evaluation can aid teachers in choosing materials or methods appropriate for individual students or entire classes. Most of the following strategies may be used for either formative or summative purposes.

However, some strategies may be more appealing than others, depending on a teacher's theory of language learning.

Oral Reading

Ask each student to read a couple of paragraphs aloud from a class text. (Teachers can schedule these individual readings when the rest of the class is working on writing or meeting in small groups.) To be sure, reading aloud is a slightly different task than reading silently, and students may trip over a few words, but considerable halting and/or misreading can indicate that the student may need to learn new reading strategies to deal with the material.

Miscue Analysis

Ask students to read aloud into a tape recorder. By analyzing the errors made, you can determine something about the level and kind of reading difficulties and abilities. For example, if the text is "the scent of the flowers" and the student reads "the smell of the flowers," the teacher can assume that the student comprehends the text and has simply misspoken. On the other hand, if the student reads "the scene of the flowers" or "the send of the flowers," the teacher can assume that the student has not comprehended the text. (See Box 9.2.) Miscue analysis provides a more in-depth look at reading than simple oral reading does. (See Goodman in Suggested Reading at the end of this chapter.)

Writing Sample

Request that your students compose several pieces, preferably written for different audiences and purposes under differing time constraints. Make it clear that you want students to introduce themselves and that you don't plan to grade what they write. Writing samples can provide considerable information about the writing skills and backgrounds students bring to the class. By reading these initial samples, you can also get to know your students more quickly.

Error Analysis of Writing Sample

If you wish to analyze students' writing abilities in detail and isolate problems or difficulties they may have, you can do an error analysis for each student. First, read and note all the errors in the paper and then divide the errors into types such as spelling, punctuation, syntax, capitalization, and so on. Within each of these categories you can divide further so that you determine whether a given student's spelling errors, for example, center on endings, medial vowels, or phonetic spelling. (See Box 9.3.) Error analysis can guide your decisions about what to emphasize in later instruction, either with individuals or with the whole class.

BOX 9.2
PROCEDURES FOR MISCUE ANALYSIS

1. *An appropriate selection for the pupil is made.* This is a story or other reading selection which is somewhat difficult for the pupil. He reads the entire story, so it must not be longer than he can handle at a single sitting. It must be long enough to generate 25 or more miscues (50 or more in the case of research studies). More than one selection may need to be tried to find one that is appropriate. The selection should have the continuity of meaning that unified stories or articles provide.

2. *The material is prepared for taping.* The pupil reads directly from the book. The teacher or researcher needs to have a worksheet on which the story is retyped, preserving the lines of the story exactly as they are in the book. Each line on the worksheet is numbered with page and line of the story, so that miscues may be identified as to where they occur.

3. *The reader is audiotaped and the code sheet is marked.* The reader is asked to read the story. Before he begins, light conversation puts him at ease. He is told that he will not be graded for his reading and that he will be asked to retell the story after he has read.

   He is also told that no help will be given while he is reading. He is encouraged to do the best he can to handle any problems. He can use any strategies he knows, he can guess or skip a word and go on.

   As he reads, the teacher or researcher follows, marking the mis-

cues on the typescript. Too much happens for everything to be noted as it occurs, so the entire reading, including retelling, is tape-recorded. Later the tape is replayed to complete the marking of the miscues on the worksheet. The worksheet becomes a permanent record of the session. It becomes the basis for the miscue analysis.

4. *The subject retells the story.* After he has read, the subject is asked to retell the story without interruption. Following the unaided retelling, the reader is asked open-ended questions to probe areas he omitted in his retelling. These questions do not use any specific information which the reader has not himself reported. The teacher or researcher does not steer the reader to conclusions. The reader's mispronunciations are retained in the questioning. A comprehension rating is based on an analysis of the retelling.

5. *The miscues are coded according to the analytic procedure used* ("Taxonomy," *Reading Miscue Inventory,* or other).

6. *The patterns of miscues are studied.* Because miscue analysis gets at the process and goes beyond the superficial, it produces information that can become the basis of specific instruction. If the reader shows insufficient concern for meaning, the teacher can devote attention to building this concern. If a specific problem occurs, such as confusion of *wh* and *th* words (with, that; when, then; where, there), strategy lessons can be de-

signed to help the reader cope with the problem.

In noting such a problem the teacher can carefully find its limits. The reader does not interchange other words starting with *w* or *t*. He does not mix words like *whistle* and *thistle*. Only these function words are confused. In this way the teacher can design a lesson which will help the reader use meaning and grammatical structure to detect when he has made a miscue of this type. The instruction will help the reader correct when he makes the miscue, and in the process such miscues will begin to disappear as the reader makes better predictions.

The ability to use the information gained from miscue analysis in working with learners is . . . dependent on the teacher's moving to a view of reading and reading instruction consistent with views of reading as a meaning-getting, language process.

—From Ken Goodman, *Miscue Analysis* (Urbana, Ill.: NCTE, 1979), pp. 7–8.

Reading/Writing Autobiography

Ask students to write a history of their experiences with reading and/or writing. (Some examples are given in Chapter 3.) These reading/writing autobiographies should include descriptions of what the students have read and written both in school and outside school, as well as discussions of their characteristic processes of reading and/or writing. (Directions for the assignment could be based on some of the questions given in Boxes 3.2 and 3.4.) Like the writing sample described above, reading/writing autobiographies can provide information about a student's reading and writing abilities through the writing itself, as well as through the student's self-analysis. The inevitable clues about students' attitudes, problems, and strengths provided in these texts can make the task of individualizing instruction less formidable.

Systematic Observation

Watch students in the actual process of reading, writing, or discussing. Behaviors such as forming words with one's mouth while reading silently, rubbing fists against one's eyes, or putting one's head on the desk are often clues to understanding a student's reading problems. During writing, if a student has trouble forming words with a pencil, pauses frequently, or sighs, these behaviors can signal writing difficulties. In a class discussion, one student's noticeable silence, unrelated responses, or constant volunteering may signal problems in listening or communicating. Records of systematic observation can be kept in teacher logs or on forms designed for records of student portfolios. This method of keeping track of student performance is gaining legitimacy among educators.

BOX 9.3
ERROR ANALYSIS

The following passage was written by a "basic writer"; each number designates an error. The analysis of the passage that follows it was written by Mina Shaughnessy.

The majority of the student[1] alway[2] major in some kinds of field[3] that will help them in the near future Some of them end up working in factory[4] because of their education. Sometime[5] I say to myself that it really don't[6] matter whether you go to college or not because people with college degree[7] can't even get a good job. Some countrie[8] or manufacture[9] will not hired[10] them because they feel that they will only work for two month[11] and then leaves[12] and they[13] company maybe just lose money.

Of the eighty-nine words in this passage, thirteen (14.6 per cent) are wrong. This is a discouraging number of erroneous forms. Yet a closer look reveals that ten of these errors reflect difficulties with the one letter s (1, 2, 3, 4, 5, 7, 8, 9, 11, 12). Two are common verb-form errors (6, 10), at least one of which the student could easily learn to correct (*will not hired*). And the final error (13) is the use of juxtaposition to indicate possession. In other words, three basic problems are reflected in this passage, all of them common to large numbers of writers who err not for want of intelligence or care but because of opposing language habits and analogical thinking. The student who learned to make these errors reveals, through them, all the linguistic sophistication he needs to correct them.

—From Mina Shaughnessy, *Errors and Expectations* (New York: Oxford University Press, 1977), p. 29.

Essay Exams

Tests in English classes often consist, in part or entirely, of essay questions. These questions, usually composed by the teacher, ask students to pull ideas together, make a comparison, argue a position, or describe a relationship. Essay tests can ask for student writing of varying lengths, ranging from a short paragraph to a full-length essay. The simplest form of the essay exam is introduced by words such as "discuss" or "explain" or "compare." Alternative forms of essay exams offer a quotation to evaluate, two contrasting viewpoints or judgments to choose between, or a hypothetical situation to resolve. (What would happen if Character X in Book A were put in the situation of Character Y in Book B?)

Teachers can develop creative essay exams that give students an opportunity to learn and have fun even as they are demonstrating their learning. "The Diseased Book Blurb" in Box 9.4 is a good example. A test based on this blurb could include both short-answer and essay questions.

BOX 9.4
THE DISEASED BOOK BLURB

Imagine that you are an editor for a publishing house and you have asked your assistant to prepare some blurbs for the jackets of books you are publishing. Your assistant is apt to be commercially minded—he has read too many Harlequin romances—and you sometimes wonder how carefully he has read a book. You feel that the blurbs should be as honest and accurate as possible and should not leave out significant details, nor mislead or distort. As a result, you have an obvious problem with the blurb your assistant has created for *Huck Finn:*

> Come along on a spine-tingling adventure as Huck and his Negro slave Jim sail up the Mississippi River to escape from Huck's cruel stepmother, who wishes to

make a gentleman out of him at all costs. Watch them battle snakes, storms, and floods as they encounter and conquer nature's awesome power. Meet the Duke and the Dauphin, the vacationing members of British royalty who befriend Huck and Jim and help them to escape from the clutches of the slave dealers. Agonize with Huck as he makes his painful choice to remain on the river for the rest of his life rather than return to "civilization." Share Jim's final tragedy as he is caught and sent back to a life of slavery, separated from his wife and children.

Write a memo to your assistant, pointing out his errors in fact and interpretation. Or rewrite the blurb yourself to give a more accurate account of the book.

Students might, for example, begin by listing all the factual errors in the blurb, then write the longer essay suggested.

Short-Answer Tests

By asking students true-false, matching, fill-in-the-blank, and identification questions, you may temporarily relieve yourself of the "burden" of reading student papers, but short-answer tests are of very limited value. They can tell you something about whether students "are doing the reading" (though they are far from infallible even for this purpose). Their major disadvantages include their emphasis upon facts rather than interpretation or assimilation of information, their failure to ask students to do any sustained writing, and the possibility that students can repeat memorized information without really understanding it. Short-answer tests tend to encourage answer-centered rather than problem-centered behavior from students. (See Box 9.5.)

Standardized Tests

Standardized tests like the California Achievement Test, the Scholastic Aptitude Test (SAT), the Test of Standard Written English (TSWE), and

---

BOX 9.5
PROBLEM-CENTEREDNESS VERSUS ANSWER-CENTEREDNESS

Kids in school seem to use a fairly consistent strategy. Even the good students use it much of the time; the bad students use it all the time; and everyone uses it when they feel under pressure. One way of describing this strategy is to say that it is answer-centered rather than problem-centered. The difference can best be seen by comparing the way in which the two kinds of people deal with a problem.

The problem-centered person sees a problem as a statement about a situation, from which something has been left out. In other words, there is in this situation a relationship or consequence that has not been stated and that must be found. He attacks the problem by thinking about the situation, by trying to create it whole in his mind. When he sees it whole, he knows which part has been left out, and the answer comes almost by itself. . . . Finding it is like finding a missing piece in a jigsaw puzzle. If you look at the empty space in the puzzle, you know the shape of the piece that must fill it.

But most children in school are answer-centered rather than problem-centered. They see a problem as a kind of announcement that, far off in some mysterious Answerland, there is an answer, which they are supposed to go out and find. . . . [They] sally forth into Answerland in a kind of treasure hunt for the answer. For them, the problem is an answer-getting recipe, a set of hints or clues telling them what to do, like instructions for finding buried pirate treasure—go to the big oak, walk a hundred paces in line with the top of the church steeple, etc. . . .

[E]ven those teachers who are not themselves answer-centered will probably not see, as for many years I did not, the distinction between problem-centeredness and answer-centeredness, far less understand its importance. Thus their ways of teaching children, and, above all, the sheer volume of work they give them, will force the children into answer-directed strategies, if only because there isn't time for anything else. I have noticed many times that when the workload of the class is light, kids are willing to do some thinking, to take some time to figure things out; when the workload is heavy, the "I-don't-get-it" begins to sound, the thinking stops, they expect us to show them everything.

—From John Holt, *How Children Fail* (New York: Dell, 1964), pp. 88–90.

various state-developed assessments of reading or writing are designed by individuals distant from your classroom in order to compare large populations of students. Standardized tests are often used to admit students to schools, to place them in various classes, or to give school districts evidence of their students' performances in comparison with student performance in other districts. Although standardized scores may occasionally provide useful information for teachers, the teacher-developed measures discussed above will likely prove far more useful. Teachers should beware of "teaching to the test" for such tests as the SAT, which tends to dilute learning and narrow options, since the test rather than student needs becomes the dominant factor. Teachers should be aware, however, that administrators, parents, and the public at large are likely to pay attention to students' performances on standardized tests.

Coaching Student Reading

Reading, including the reading of literature, should not merely be assessed and assigned, it should be taught, even at the secondary level. If our goal is to help students become enthusiastic, thoughtful, independent readers, we must give them opportunities to select their own reading material. They also need chances to read, to reflect on their own processes and understandings, and to compare them with those of experienced readers. When teachers take the time to become familiar with young adult literature, and with their own students, they can serve as effective reading "coaches," recommending texts and discussing them informally with students.

Along with encouraging students to read independently, teachers should also coach students through classwide reading selections. By anticipating problem passages and modeling successful reading strategies to deal with such problems, teachers can provide students with transferable skills. Students should be encouraged to find ways to monitor their own comprehension and interest levels, and to consciously employ reading strategies in dealing with materials outside the English classroom as well.

Teachers should reflect on classroom routines concerning reading to make sure those routines don't interfere with the desired goal. For instance, teachers who assign two chapters of a novel a night and follow with a pop quiz over textual details the next day may be conveying the idea that reading "ahead" is inappropriate and that the reason we read novels is to "learn" them. Similarly, teachers who say they want students to read but don't provide time for reading may be conveying the message that reading is not as important as other classroom activities.

Coaching Student Writing

Creating Writing Assignments

The writing assignments teachers give as well as their responses to student writing have a profound influence on the ways students write. If students know that a teacher will grade on the basis of the number of surface errors rather than the ideas expressed, they will tend to write empty, "safe," mechanically correct papers. If they have been given overly detailed instructions for the format of a paper, they will probably be more concerned with form than with ideas. If they know a paper is going to be graded as a finished product rather than treated as a work in progress, they may also tend to be more concerned with form than with ideas. If they know their writing will be read by peers in a writing group, they will keep that audience in mind as they write. If they know that a paper won't necessarily be graded, but will be added to a portfolio for later polishing, they will be more inclined to take risks, experiment with new styles and try out new ideas—to write, in other words, for themselves rather than for a grade.

Although teachers often choose to make writing assignments for students, it may be more valuable to teach students how to discover their own topics. After all, most novelists, poets, dramatists, and literary critics freely choose their own subjects. Free-writes, journal entries, and informal responses may contain the seeds of terrific writing ideas. A good writing idea draws passionate commitment from writers, the kind of commitment that can sustain the writer through many revisions. At first glance, it may seem easier to let students choose their topics, but it generally requires that the teacher have personal experience with topic selection and idea development and revision—that the teacher be a practicing writer.

Sometimes it may seem appropriate to assign topics to students. After all, journalists, advertising copywriters, screenplay authors, and businesspeople are frequently required to write in response to specific requests. However, creating good writing assignments takes considerable time, because the written (or spoken) prompt can shape students' responses so dramatically. Among the questions teachers ask themselves in creating effective writing assignments, these are perhaps the most important: Is the topic likely to interest and engage the students? Do the students have enough background to write on this topic? Will they learn something worthwhile from doing this assignment? Are the criteria for evaluation defensible and clear to the students? Are the specifications as to audience, purpose, and format clear?

Setting Criteria for Student Writing

Through class discussion, students themselves may develop the criteria for judging the results of any writing assignment, thus engaging simultaneously in formative and summative evaluation. Before the start of a writing project or assignment, students and teacher can work together with a model of the kind of writing to be done (a short story, a sketch, an essay setting forth an argument) and determine the qualities that make a good paper of this kind. These qualities become the criteria for evaluation, and students keep them in mind as they write. When the writing is finished, the teacher can distribute copies to small groups (usually giving the papers written by members of one group to another group) and instruct students to have each paper read by several other students. Students need practice responding to one another's writing; such talk and written feedback help them get a better sense of what good writing and thinking is. It also helps them learn what it means to be thoughtful, tactful, and cooperative, affective skills necessary to many academic endeavors.

Some teachers actually teach students how to grade one another's work. Individual students assign a grade to a peer-written text based on the criteria developed by the class; only in cases of serious disagreement between the grades given by peers or in cases where the author contests the grades would the teacher intervene. The grades assigned by the students would be the ones recorded in the grade book. Students can be excellent judges of one another's work. They typically expect more than the teacher might, and (except for occasional cases where they may become involved in conflicts about grades or fail to take their evaluative role seriously) their grades are extremely fair.

Involving students in assessing one another's work demystifies the evaluation process at the same time that it fosters the development of critical thinking skills as students develop their capacity to judge quality in writing. Another benefit of this procedure, of course, is that it reduces the burden of paper grading of the teacher. A disadvantage is that grading, rather than response, can end up seeming most important.

Responding to Student Writing

In handling papers, most teachers would agree that, though they may need to make a summative evaluation (give grades) for the sake of a gradebook, formative evaluation (comments, either in talk or in writing) is much more crucial if students are to grow and improve. That burden of response is considerable for English teachers; however, wise use of teacher-student conferencing and peer conferencing can diminish the need for endless written comments.

Written comments are most effective when the paper is still in process—extensive comments accompanied by a final grade may not get read, and certainly won't do much good if further revision is not allowed. Practice pieces, journal entries, and beginnings of a piece probably don't require written comments, unless the student obviously needs direction. Writing comments on (or grading) every single piece of writing students do is inefficient and foolhardy. After all, experienced writers do not want or need evaluation on every word they've ever written—in fact, constant scrutiny can cause a writer to block.

Sometimes teachers increase the comment-writing burden needlessly by writing overly long comments to students, or virtually rewriting papers. These teachers doubtless think they are giving helpful formative evaluation, but a comment that tries to say everything that might be said about a paper often lacks focus and isn't as helpful for formative purposes as a shorter, more selective, and more sharply focused one. Comments should not do all the students' thinking for them but should rather suggest things for them to think about for themselves. Comments that are too long are also likely to give students the idea they have failed, especially if the teacher has drowned their original texts in a sea of red ink, which erodes students' confidence in their writing. At the other extreme, the paper that is returned with only a grade and no comment creates even worse problems. It fails to give the student any help in doing the next writing task (as Jonathan noted at the outset of this chapter) and is likely to result in a great deal of frustration and decreased motivation. For formative purposes, comments are most effective when they give students encouragement and help them to focus on a manageable area in which they can improve and grow as writers.

Comments will vary, however, depending on the teacher's judgment about what a student needs to hear at that particular point and also the kind of classroom the teacher has created. Box 9.6 shows two responses to a student paper as they might be made by two hypothetical teachers, one from a language-as-artifact classroom (Box 9.6a), one from a language-as-expression classroom (Box 9.6b). Both comments balance praise with suggestions for ways the paper could be improved. Both call attention to ideas, not just to structural or mechanical matters. Both teachers have singled out some of the same things for comment. The language-as-artifact teacher, however, concentrates more heavily on the text itself (both Hawthorne's and the student's) and on suggestions for making the paper an error-free product; the language-as-expression teacher puts more emphasis on the student's response to Hawthorne's text and on getting this student to think further about some of the issues in the paper.

Comments, as those of the language-as-expression teacher in Box 9.6 illustrate, often direct students to consider alternatives or make revisions. The meaning of the term "revision" can vary all the way from a mere cosmetic tidying up of surface errors to a thorough rethinking of a topic, although the latter is obviously a much more significant process, the former only a minor adjustment of a product. Students benefit from considering alternatives and working with them, though it is not safe to assume that revisions will always be wholly for the better. Sometimes in making changes a student may leave the paper stronger in some ways but weaker in others. The teacher can help to avoid this problem by being sure to make positive comments about strengths.

Box 9.7 presents an excerpt from a student paper and a revision of it. The revision cleans up some surface errors and improves the sentence

---

BOX 9.6a
"ARTIFACT" TEACHER'S RESPONSE TO STUDENT WRITING

<u>The Scarlet Letter</u>

While reading <u>The Scarlet Letter</u> by Nathaniel Hawthorne,

wrong word one has to frequently remind oneself of the fact that this

story took place over two hundred years ago, ~~so~~ *since* many of the

problems and hardships experienced by Hester Prynne are also

faced by many women in today's so called "liberated" world.

Hester Prynne lived in a very strict society ~~world~~ ruled

by the Puritan beliefs and moral standards. Because of these

standards and expectations, Hester experienced many hardships

Hester has a husband — her sin is adultery when her neighbors found out that she was with X child and yet

had no husband. The Puritans believed in living the word of

God by reading the *B* bible and living the lives he would want   *cap*

them to live. To the Puritans, this did not include single

motherhood or adultery and would therefore have to be punished

severely.

although

In Hester's case, this punishment was certainly light

sp compared to death, it *a* effected her entire life. She was

forced to wear a scarlet "A" on her clothing so ~~so~~ that people

who met her would know how terrible a person she really was.

Is it the wearing or what she has done? The wearing of the letter causes Hester and her child to be

shunned from the society and to be looked down upon and talked

about by everyone.

Do you need to qualify this? Although Hester experienced a punishment that <u>more than</u>

<u>likely</u> wouldn't happen today, many of the feelings and

situations she experienced are also experienced by many ~~people~~

single mothers in today's society. Although many people say

they are more open minded about these ~~families~~ one parent

families, most people still look down upon single mothers.

(SP) Today's society makes no effort to try to make it easier for

these women to work and raise their families on (thier) own.

(continued on p. 256)

BOX 9.6b
"EXPRESSION" TEACHER'S RESPONSE TO STUDENT WRITING

<u>The Scarlet Letter</u>

While reading <u>The Scarlet Letter</u> by Nathaniel Hawthorne,
one has to frequently remind oneself of the fact that this
story took place over two hundred years ago, (or) many of the
problems and hardships experienced by Hester Prynne are also
faced by many women in today's so called "liberated" world.

Hester Prynne lived in a very strict society ~~world~~ ruled
by the Puritan beliefs and moral standards. Because of these
standards and expectations, Hester experienced many hardships
when her neighbors found out that she was with a child and yet
had no husband. The Puritans believed in living the word of
God by reading the (bible) and living the lives he would want
them to live. To the Puritans, this did not include single
motherhood or adultery and would therefore have to be punished
severely.

In Hester's case, this punishment was certainly light
compared to death, ^but^ it (effected) her entire life. She was
forced to wear a scarlet "A" on her clothing so so that people
who met her would know how terrible a person she really was.
The wearing of the letter causes Hester and her child to be
shunned from the society and to be looked down upon and talked
about by everyone.

Although Hester experienced a punishment that more than
likely wouldn't happen today, many of the feelings and
situations she experienced are also experienced by many ~~people~~
single mothers in today's society. Although many people say
they are more open minded about these ~~families~~ one parent
families, most people still look down upon single mothers.
Today's society makes no effort to try to make it easier for
these women to work and raise their families on (thier) own.

Can you see what the problems are with the words I've circled?

(continued on p. 257)

Today society still circulates around the nuclear family, which of course consists of a father and a mother. Social and economic hardships are still faced by single mothers in today's society, and it certainly does not look like it will change. Hester had to sew other people's clothing in order to make money. This was tedious work which paid very little, yet it was all that she was able to do. She had to be able to look after her daughter and make enough to keep them both alive. This is also a problem faced by women today, finding work that enables then to work and look after their children too.

Opportunities for all women were limited then.

typo

punct. Although many people in todays society clain to be more liberal and accepting of lifestyles that go against the norm,

sp. lthere are many simularities between the Puritan sodiety of

punct. the 18th Century and todays more liberated world. Although the Puritan ideas and beliefs no longer rule the society,

no cap

punct. people in todays world still seem to live by many of these ideas and expect everyone else to live the same way. Even though people clain that we have changed over the years, one tends to question exactly how much after reading <u>The Scarlet Letter.</u>

Your paper is well organized, moving from Hester and her situation to our present-day treatment of single mothers, and you have managed to support the points you make pretty well, although one or two quotes from the text itself of The Scarlet Letter would have given even better support. You might try reading your paper aloud to be sure that your style always sounds natural. Please revise this and turn it back in next Thursday.

Today society still circulates around the nuclear family,
which of course consists of a father and a mother. Social and
economic hardships are still faced by single mothers in
today's society, and it certainly does not look like it will
change. Hester had to sew other people's clothing in order to
make money. This was tedious work which paid very little, yet
it was all that she was able to do. She had to be able to
look after her daughter and make enough to keep them both
alive. This is also a problem faced by women today, finding
work that enables then to work and look after their children
too.

Although many people in todays society clain to be more
liberal and accepting of lifestyles that go against the norm,
lthere are many simularities between the Puritan Society of
the 18th Century and todays more liberated world. Although
the Puritan ideas and beliefs no longer rule the society,
people in todays world still seem to live by many of these
ideas and expect everyone else to live the same way. Even
though people clain that we have changed over the years, one
tends to question exactly how much after reading The Scarlet
Letter. *I like the comparisons you've made between Hester and today's single mothers, although Hester, you must remember, did have a husband - her "sin" was adultery. Doesn't that complicate the situation a bit since she has violated a vow to Chillingworth, not just a social or religious code? I would also like to know more explicitly how you feel about Hester and her society: Is there any justification for what she does? Is her society right to condemn her? And how would Hawthorne answer those questions? Did you consider any of these matters in your reading journal? In your revision, due next Thursday, you might want to deal with some of these questions. P.S You might try reading your paper out loud to discover one or two places where your sentences could be made to sound more natural. Some of them don't really sound like you.*

BOX 9.7
WHEN REVISION IS REGRESSION

MY PHILOSOPHY ON LIFE
My philosophy on how a persons life should be ran is that their parents should start them off when they are a kid. The parents should have them around a positive enviroment. When the kid gets, old enough to talk and listen to you then you can see what he/she wants to be a doctor, a teacher, or an atlehic etc . . . by giving him/her toys or things that would lead the child in that field of work that the child would like to enter. Then when they get older they can make the decisions of what field to enter Now, when it comes time for this decision to be made you will be ready to pick the one which you to pursue.

MY PHILOSOPHY ON
LIFE (REVISED)
When I am to young and not old enough to know what I want to be I would want my parents to start me off in a direction what they think that I would want to go in. Next, when I get old enough to what life is about I can pursue my goals that I agree with. I will do what ever it takes to achieve my goals and the thing that I have to remember is to never give up. Always strieve to be the best, second best never counts, if you start to settle for second best then you might start to settle for third, then fourth etc. If And if you pay the price now it will be easier on you in your future life.

---

structure, but unfortunately loses the force and concreteness of the original, substituting lifeless generalizations. In writing there is always likely to be a tension between the demands of correctness and effective rhetorical strategies, on the one hand, and the need for expressive honesty on the other. The idea that parents may help a child to form interests through the toys they provide—an interesting idea—is replaced by the uninteresting cliches about striving to be the best and achieving goals. What comments might the teacher have made to produce this response? What kinds of comments might have produced a better response?

Comments or feedback on drafts, either by the teacher or by students in a writing group (as discussed in Chapter 6) are an especially useful kind of formative evaluation because they are interactive and responsive to a writer's questions. Peter Elbow distinguishes between two kinds of feedback: *criterion-based* and *reader-based*. (See Box 9.8.) Criterion-based is the kind of feedback that teachers are likely to give either for summative or formative purposes, while reader-based feedback is likely to come best from writing groups where several readers provide a richer blend of response than the teacher alone can provide as a single audience member. Students are uniquely qualified to give reader-based feedback, and the recent success of writing groups in many classrooms attests to that fact. Student writers develop a keener sense of audience, are motivated to

BOX 9.8
CRITERION-BASED AND READER-BASED FEEDBACK

Criterion-based feedback helps you find out how your writing measures up to certain criteria—in this case to those criteria most often used in judging expository or nonfiction writing. To get criterion-based feedback you ask readers four broad, fundamental questions:

1. What is the quality of the content of the writing: the ideas, the perceptions, the point of view?
2. How well is the writing organized?
3. How effective is the language?
4. Are there mistakes or inappropriate choices in usage?

But because these questions are so broad, you usually get better feedback if you ask much more specific questions such as these: Is the basic idea a good one? Is it supported with logical reasoning or valid argument? Are there too many abstractions and too few examples or concrete details? Is the whole thing unified rather than pulling in two or three conflicting directions? Are the sentences clear and readable? . . .

Reader-based feedback, on the other hand, instead of telling you how your writing measures up to preestablished criteria, tells you what your writing does to particular readers. To get reader-based feedback you ask readers three broad fundamental questions:

1. What was happening to you, moment by moment, as you were reading the piece of writing?
2. Summarize the writing: give your understanding of what it says or what happened in it.
3. Make up some images for the writing and the transaction it creates with you.

Here too you usually get better feedback by helping your reader out with more specific questions like these: Now that you have finished reading just the first one or two paragraphs or stanzas, are you an interested, cooperative reader or are you bored or resistant in some way? Point to the places where you had the most trouble and describe what kind of trouble it was for you. Summarize your understanding of the whole piece. What mood or voice do you hear in the words? What kind of people does the writer seem to be talking to: people in the know? nincompoops? interested amateurs? How is the writer giving it to you: willingly? slyly? grudgingly? hitting you over the head with it? . . . Criterion-based feedback, then, tells you how your writing measures up, reader-based feedback tells you what it does to readers.

—From *Writing with Power: Techniques for Mastering the Writing Process* by Peter Elbow. Copyright © 1981 by Oxford University Press, Inc. Reprinted by permission.

revise more extensively, and develop a more sophisticated understanding of the processes of writing than do students not participating in writing groups.

Grading Student Writing

In arriving at the grade for summative purposes, the teacher may use either holistic evaluation or analytical evaluation, both based on a set of criteria.

Holistic evaluation judges a piece of writing as a whole and gives it a grade that represents an overall impression, usually in comparison with other papers in a group. The teacher has given some preliminary thought, of course, to what qualities in general will constitute a successful paper. Then these judgments are modified by a knowledge of the students and comparisons within the group as a whole on the basis of actual performance on this particular assignment. (Gail, one of the teachers whose comments on grading are given at the outset of this chapter, appears to grade holistically.)

Analytical evaluation, in contrast, may employ any given number of criteria, but these criteria will be spelled out. They may even be assigned percentages—25 percent for structure, 10 percent for mechanics, 40 percent for ideas, and so on. (Note that judgments for some of these individual criteria must be made holistically—the worth of an idea cannot be judged in the same way that spelling errors are counted.) The criteria for analytical evaluation may be arrived at through decisions about what things are most important in good writing or what things the teacher wishes to concentrate on for a particular assignment.

When there is something rather specific that students should learn from doing an assignment—how to use details effectively, for example, or how to support an argument—teachers are likely to use the meeting of the conditions of the assignment as one criterion for evaluation. In other cases, a teacher may look on the assignment merely as a stimulus and judge the results on their own terms. If the teacher uses fulfillment of the conditions of the assignment as a criterion, it is especially important that the assignment be well constructed, clear, and worth doing.

Coaching Student Discussion

Part of the success of writing groups is due to the fact that they involve the give-and-take of oral interaction. Class discussion of writing or reading, of course, provides the same opportunity. Through talk, students learn.

Students frequently ask, "Does class discussion count?" Teachers who value active participation will answer that it does count and may well include discussion as a percentage of the final grade. Even more important than this summative function, however, is the vital role class discussion plays in formative evaluation. By listening carefully to what students say in class you can tell a great deal about what they know and how they think, and hence develop more effective instructional strategies. If, for example, students resort to giving plot summaries when asked questions about the theme of a story or novel, you know that they need to be taught more about how fiction works. Similarly, if comments about a peer's writing in a writing group or a whole-class writing workshop stay at a high level of generality—"It flows really well" or "I think it's great"—you know they need to develop a greater understanding of the processes of writing.

A common problem with seeing class discussion as formative evaluation is that a few students can dominate classroom conversation. One way to ensure that all students learn to participate in class discussions and have an opportunity to do so is to give each student five tokens (or slips of paper or poker chips) at the beginning of class. Each time students speak they must hand in a token, and after they have handed in all five they cannot say anything more. This exercise usually demonstrates to students that a few people do most of the talking, and the limitations imposed by the tokens force them to redistribute the discussion.

Another reason for trying to keep class discussions from being the province of a few students is so that all members of the class can become better listeners. When class discussion works well, students begin to direct their comments to one another rather than to the teacher, and in the process of exchanging ideas they learn to evaluate one another's ideas.

Classroom discussion may function best when students are placed in small discussion groups, where many more students have the opportunity to respond.

Some Sensible Grading Systems

If students have gotten used to the process of evaluation and self-evaluation in many different contexts over the course of the semester, final grades become less of an issue, even though they are important for management purposes. Evaluation during the semester may have included the giving of *interim grades* at one or more times. Tentative grades reduce students' anxiety by giving them a general idea of "how they're doing," enabling them to take steps toward improving, and lessening the chance of any shock from an unexpected final grade. The process of averaging the semester's individual grades—probably after weighting different components differently so as to reflect their relative importance—may be largely an exercise in mathematics. Determining which pieces of work will enter into the final grade and how much each will count will depend on what the teacher has established earlier in the semester, but it may also depend on other somewhat more formalized procedures.

In the meantime, the teacher may have used *quantity grades* to keep track of whether students are doing the work, simply noting on a sheet for each student when work has been completed and/or recording a certain number of points for each assignment, which may then be taken into account in final grades. The rationale for delaying summative evaluation is that it stops the process in a given project: once students receive a grade they assume they have "finished" that piece of work. Other teachers prefer to introduce summative evaluation earlier. The argument for this position is that grades tell students where they stand, thus providing the necessary confidence for them to continue to succeed or the incentive to improve.

A teacher's philosophy or theory of language determines to some extent the approach to evaluation. Teachers who subscribe to the language-as-artifact approach tend to provide summative evaluation sooner than do teachers who subscribe to the other three approaches, since the language-as-artifact approach emphasizes the text, leading teachers to be more interested in finished products than works in progress. In contrast, the emphasis on expressive language in the language-as-expression approach, the concern with fostering student growth in the language-as-development approach, and the focus on group work in the language-as-social-construct approach all lead teachers to postpone summative evaluation longer.

Two methods, contract grading and portfolio assessment, are particularly effective in supporting student risk-taking and growth and in reducing conflicts between teachers and students. In *contract grading*, the teacher and each individual student sign a contract at the beginning of the term after agreeing on the work to be accomplished and on some measures of quality. A contract might specify a different minimum number of assignments for a C, a B, and an A, and also describe some standards for the work. (For example, to receive an A, students agree that final drafts will demonstrate factually supported thinking, effective patterns of organization, and careful editing.) At the end of the term teacher and student discuss how well the contract has been met and agree on a grade.

In *portfolio evaluation* students are asked to review the folders that contain all the writing—ungraded—that they have done for the term, including notes, drafts, and free-writes. They then select a specified number of pieces of writing for the teacher to consider in arriving at the course grade. Teachers may elect to grade the student's writing process by considering drafts and revisions, or they may simply grade on the basis of the final papers selected by the student. In a class involving other work besides writing, the grade on the portfolio would then be averaged with grades on other components of the course. Teachers who choose to employ portfolio assessment make sure that students receive plenty of formative feedback through conferences, writing groups, and teacher comments. (See Box 9.9.)

Since students play an active role in final assessments of their own work as they select pieces to submit for evaluation, they develop a sense of ownership of their writing. The teacher can reinforce this ownership by asking students to respond to some pointed questions: Why did you select this piece of writing? What did you learn from writing this? If you were to do another revision, what would you do? A major advantage of both contract and portfolio grading is that they enable students to participate in the process of summative as well as formative evaluation.

Evaluation and Public Relations

Parents may evaluate both the school and their own children's progress (or lack thereof) on the basis of the grades they bring home. And parents may well be inconsistent in their attitudes: While they want the school to maintain standards so that the achievements of their children will not be discounted by college admissions officers or future employers, they may also want their children to receive the grades they need to ensure their futures, whether those grades are fully deserved or not. "Couldn't you give Johnny an A− instead of a B+? He needs it to get into college." Some parents may even feel the school has an obligation to bring their children up to a certain standard of performance. Parents may also tend to judge the quality of the school and the progress of their children by the standard they know best—what it was like when *they* went to school.

All this means that teachers need to help parents understand the significance of the grades their children receive. Teachers, parents, and students alike must keep in mind the limitations of letter grades in conveying the complexities of student performance. This is tricky business, since grades and standardized test scores may well be used to predict future success in college or in a profession. However, such predictions are not infallible, and in talks with parents, teachers should be wary indeed about stereotyping students on the basis of grades. They should also help parents understand that grades are designed only to be a measure of certain aspects of performance, not of intrinsic worth. Grades cannot measure many of the most valuable things that students get from the academic side of their education—the feeling of engagement with a novel when a character becomes a "friend," the recognition that not all poetry is necessarily "dumb" but that a poem about baseball or friendship can give both insight and pleasure, the realization that something they've written has connected with the thinking of a fellow student, the sense of confi-

BOX 9.9
DEVELOPING A MODEL FOR PORTFOLIOS

For at least two years, a small group of teachers in Arts PROPEL has been trying out various activities and guidelines designed to help students toward the creation of portfolios. This strand of teacher experimentation has been supplemented with researchers' interviews of individual students to discover how students look at their work, what they value in writing, and what options and alternatives they see for revisions or for future writing. . . . We can get a sense of how portfolio thinking evolves . . . if we look . . . at teacher conversation. . . . [The teachers] have already begun to identify the kinds of learning they want students to derive from portfolios, and to think about how the desire for this learning might be translated into the features of the portfolios. They have also decided that they would like students themselves to select the pieces of writing from their folders that will go into the portfolios. But they are still grappling with the difficult problem of encouraging students to include pieces of writing that do not in themselves show students to best advantage—pieces that show how students have struggled with writing and learned from their struggles.

Kathy: My students will put in a piece that they're not pleased with, if they get a chance to comment on it. They feel they have control over the piece if they can say why they're not satisfied with it.

Jerry: If we want more than "best" pieces, maybe we need to ask that all the pieces in a portfolio be accompanied by students' reflections on them. If students can indicate what they see in the pieces, they can feel they have some control over how the pieces will be seen by others. And looking back at their writing—successful and unsuccessful—helps students to see it as a related, continuous process. Maybe reflection is what's most important in the portfolio.

Dan W: But each piece of writing is important, too. I think each piece should have written reflection attached—maybe just a couple of comments— and go into a folder. Then the kid could select later the pieces that go into the portfolio.

Jerry: That's good. Through the reflections, then, kids could be doing assessment all the time, thinking about and evaluating their own work. Sometimes it would be assessment of an individual piece. Sometimes it would be of a body of work in the folder or of pieces in the portfolio.

Kathy: What's most critical—whether we're talking about folders or portfolios—is that students read and use and learn from what's in them.

Jerry: I think we all agree. What's important on a day-to-day basis is kids' use of folders and eventually portfolios, and what they do with them, including how they talk about them. The experience of making portfolios becomes the basis for students' learning about their writing and about themselves as writers.

The teachers start with what they want students to learn. They want students to become aware of the ways in which they have developed as writers, not only in their "best" pieces but also in the ones that they do not regard as entirely successful. That means teachers want students to take some risks in their selections for the portfolio and are aware that, even with teacher support, students might not be willing to take such risks unless they are provided with an appropriate context and rationale.

The attempt to resolve this dilemma leads the teachers to think about the portfolio's contents and then to a process they think students might profitably use to generate them. An important part of that process involves students in looking back at their work; the result of that looking back, the written reflection, becomes a basis for students' learning and their assuming control over the contents of the portfolio and eventually over the course of their learning. And since students' own evaluations of their work are essential to learning, they become part of the process of generating portfolios.

The line of reasoning just described follows quite naturally in the teachers' conversation from their attempts to solve the problem of having students include "more than 'best' pieces." It also has far-reaching implications for our views of assessment. Through the reflective activities involved in generating the portfolios, the assessment of writing becomes an ongoing process in which teachers help their students to look at their own and other students' work, to evaluate their own efforts and learn from the efforts of others. The written reflection in the portfolios enables students to engage in self-assessment and to use what they learn from it as the basis for a dialogue with their teachers and with other students. As Jerry says, "Maybe reflection is what's most important in portfolios."

—From Roberta Camp, "Thinking Together About Portfolios," in *The Quarterly of the National Writing Project and the Center for the Study of Writing* 12 (Spring 1990): 13–14.

dence from the teacher's approval of their grasp of a difficult idea. Standards and grades are concerned with the supposedly measurable aspects of performance. They cannot always reflect less tangible gains in understanding, pleasure, and confidence.

Whatever standards the teacher establishes should be open and openly discussed, not hidden and mysterious. Both students and their parents have a right to know what basis the teacher has adopted for judging, and the wise teacher will take the initiative in explaining the basis for judgment rather than merely waiting for complaints and then mounting a defense. (See Box 9.10.)

Teachers can maintain contact with parents in at least three ways: (1) through "Parents' Nights" and other occasions when parents are invited to visit the school; (2) through individual conferences, scheduled at the request of either teacher or parent; and (3) through letters, often explaining unusual class policies or activities. A letter, for example, might explain a particular grading policy such as a contract system or make clear specific teacher expectations for a major assignment like an I-Search paper. (See Chapter 6.) In thinking about relationships with parents, try to put yourself in the parents' place and ask yourself the question: What would I expect from a teacher of my children?

The General Principles of Evaluation

Certain broad general principles apply to all kinds of evaluation, whether formative or summative:

1. *Any act of evaluation by student or teacher should be seen as part of a larger, ongoing process of evaluation that continues during a term, a school career, a lifetime.* Students need to see evaluation as an inseparable part of the learning process, in which self-evaluation plays an important role. Teachers need to see evaluation as a tool of instruction, not merely the burdensome duty of determining something to write in a gradebook.

2. *Evaluation should be concerned with material significant enough to deserve evaluation.* Tests are no place to play Trivial Pursuit, nor should student papers be an invitation to exhaust the teacher's supply of red ink. (Incidentally, why not use green, which has fewer negative connotations?) Testing the student's ability to recall insignificant facts is not a good means for achieving "standards" nor differentiating among students, since such standards are clearly false ones, demanding only rote memory and not promoting true learning.

3. *Evaluation should concentrate more on what students know than on what they don't know.* Building from strengths promotes learning more effectively than concentrating mainly on weaknesses. In tests give students choices and give them adequate time to demonstrate what they know. Respect individual styles of reading, writing, and learning and try to help students improve these, rather than arbitrarily imposing alien styles on the students.

BOX 9.10
CONFERENCES WITH PARENTS

1. Be honest about your perception of a student's progress, but also admit that your perception may be incomplete and invite and respect the parents' perspectives. What do they see as their child's chief problems with English?

2. Be clear about what grades can and cannot measure. Avoid any implication that they can measure a student's overall worth.

3. Explain what you feel are the most important facts and skills for a student to learn. Do not be defensive, but assert that, although other teachers might stress other things,

these seem important to you for the reasons you state. In other words, explain your goals for your students and the relationship of those goals to your grading system.

4. Invite suggestions from parents about ways in which they might help students to progress more rapidly, but do not hesitate to dissuade them from trying to help in inappropriate ways.

5. Give parents the patience, the courtesy, the respect, the straightforwardness, and the attention you would expect if you were in their place.

---

4. *Evaluation should serve an instructional purpose if possible, even when its main purpose may be summative.* Conferences with students, where summative evaluations are explained to them, can stimulate self-evaluation and help the students to grow and improve. Students should be encouraged to think of the purpose of evaluative procedures as not just to arrive at the "right" or "wrong" answer. Students should be led to be more problem-centered, less answer-centered. (Recall John Holt's remarks in Box 9.9.)

5. *Evaluation should help both student and teacher to succeed.* Any evaluation of the students in a class is also in part an evaluation of the teacher's performance in that class. If half the class is failing, chances are the teacher has also failed in important ways. The processes of diagnosis discussed above help teachers to succeed with their students; the kinds of formative evaluation we have been discussing help students to succeed.

6. *The method and the strategies for evaluation should be consistent with the teacher's overall approach in a class.* While many of the evaluative strategies we have discussed would be appropriate for any, or at least more than one, of the four approaches we have discussed, some of them would not be appropriate for some classrooms. Portfolios, for example, could be used in any classroom (though they are less likely to

be used in the "artifact" classroom), but a true-false test would probably seem out of place in an "expression" or a "social-construct" classroom. As you determine what the major thrust of your classroom strategy will be, think about what kinds of evaluation, both formative and summative, will best contribute to achieving your goals.

Suggested Reading

ATWELL, NANCIE. *In the Middle: Writing, Reading, and Learning with Adolescents.* Portsmouth, N.H.: Boynton/Cook, 1987.

Atwell gives a detailed description of a middle school classroom where students select their own topics for writing, participate regularly in workshops, and discuss their reading in small groups. The author, a middle school teacher herself, provides many how-to explanations.

BURNHAM, CHARLES. "Portfolio Evaluation: Room to Breathe and Grow." In Charles Bridges (ed.), *Training the Teacher of College Composition.* Urbana, Ill.: NCTE, 1986.

This book describes a portfolio system used in a freshman writing course where students submit portfolios if they want a grade over a C and have the option of revising anything in the portfolio before they submit it.

CAMP, ROBERTA. "Thinking Together About Portfolios." *The Quarterly of the National Writing Project* 12 (Spring 1990): 8–13.

This article explains that portfolio evaluation emerged in response to changes in the teaching of writing and illustrates how conversations among teachers help to create definitions of portfolios.

COOPER, CHARLES, and LEE ODELL. *Evaluating Writing: Describing, Measuring, Judging.* Urbana, Ill.: NCTE, 1977.

This book presents a summary of techniques for evaluating writing, including holistic, primary trait, and syntactic structures. Most techniques work best for large-scale evaluation, but some can be modified for classroom use. A chapter on peer evaluation is especially helpful for teachers.

ELBOW, PETER, and PAT BELANOFF. "Portfolios as a Substitute for Proficiency Examinations." *College Composition and Communication* 37 (1986): 336–7.

This piece explains how writing portfolios have replaced proficiency exams for students in the freshman writing course. Students cannot receive a passing grade in the required 101 course unless their portfolios have been judged acceptable by their teachers and another who doesn't know them.

GOODMAN, KENNETH, ed. *Miscue Analysis: Applications to Reading Instruction.* Urbana, Ill.: NCTE, 1973.

This volume provides teachers with descriptions of miscue analysis, the kinds of information it yields, and its applications for the classroom.

GOODMAN, KENNETH, YETTA GOODMAN, and WENDY HOOD, eds. *The Whole Language Evaluation Book.* Portsmouth, N.H.: Heinemann, 1989.

This text argues through example that classroom-based evaluation methods must be consistent with a teacher's philosophy of language. Authored by classroom teachers, several chapters address evaluation at the secondary level.

HARP, BILL, ed. *Assessment & Evaluation in Whole Language Programs.* Norwood, Mass.: Christopher Gordon, 1991.

This book addresses pragmatic concerns of practitioners who have chosen to base evaluations on observation, portfolios, and self-assessment. Several chapters discuss secondary classroom approaches.

HOWARD, KATHRYN. "Making the Writing Portfolio Real." *The Quarterly of the National Writing Project* 12 (Spring 1990): 4–7.

The teacher-author explains how she introduced portfolios in her classroom. Stages include modeling oral and written reflection, beginning the portfolio, updating the portfolio, and finalizing the portfolio.

MURPHY, SANDRA, and MARY ANN SMITH. "Talking About Portfolios." *The Quarterly of the National Writing Project* 12, (Spring 1990): 1–3.

This article considers questions about portfolios: what should be included, what can be done with portfolios, and how the portfolio program can be revised.

SHAUGHNESSY, MINA. *Errors and Expectations.* New York: Oxford, 1977.

The author argues that expectations English teachers bring to student writing shape their reactions to errors and urges that teachers regard errors as demonstrations of misunderstanding, not as indicators of students' lack of intelligence.

WOLF, DENNIE PALMER. "Portfolio Assessment: Sampling Student Work." *Educational Leadership* (April 1989): 35–9.

This article argues that students learn to assess their own progress as learners by using portfolios, and teachers gain new views of their accomplishments as instructors.

10

The Social Dimensions of Schooling

"THE TEACHER ON ONE END of a log and the student on the other end," the proverbial definition of the ideal educational situation, is as attractive to most teachers today as it was when James A. Garfield, twentieth president of the United States, proposed it more than a hundred years ago. But today there are a lot more people on the log who come between teacher and student; some of them facilitate the learning process, others seem to hinder it, frustrating the interchange between students and teachers. No teacher can afford to ignore the complexity of today's school environment and the part that parents, colleagues, administrators, school board members, and members of the community play in shaping it. And teachers can also use parents and members of the community as valuable resources for their classrooms.

Each of these groups has its own ideas about what's wrong with the schools and how to improve them. A sampling of some of the titles of the last forty years suggests how desperate many have thought the plight of the schools to be: *Crisis in Education* (1949), *Educational Wastelands* (1953), *Crisis in the Classroom* (1970), *A Nation at Risk* (1983), *The Underachieving Curriculum* (1987), to name a few. Public education has long been perceived to be in a state of crisis.

This sense of continuing crisis is not likely to abate, as changing demographics (see Chapter 1) raise new problems or intensify old ones. Increased poverty among schoolchildren, major changes in family structures, and an increasing number of minority students pose some significant questions: How well equipped are we to deal with the increasing racial and ethnic diversity that is altering the shape of our schools? What are the special implications of this diversity for English teachers? What is our stance on the "English only" movement (a movement represented by legislation in some states that mandates English as the only legal language)? How can we capitalize on student differences rather than attempting to ignore or eliminate them? How can we build more understanding relationships with the community? All of these questions suggest possible crisis situations.

The two ideographs with which the word "crisis" is written in Chinese combine the ideas of *danger* and *opportunity*. The Chinese also have a proverb that says that you can't get the tiger cub without entering the cave and facing the mother tiger. For us, entering the cave means facing conflicts in values and in the distribution of power. Two major areas of conflict over values and power are in the content of the curriculum and in the structuring of the environment in which students learn. Conflicts over the curriculum center on issues ranging from the number of required courses to the censorship of a particular book. Conflicts over the structuring of the environment center on the issues of tracking and school choice. Both of these areas of conflict suggest dangers, but both also contain opportunities for positive action.

Conflict over the Curriculum: Censorship

Conflicts over the curriculum may occur between teachers and students, colleagues, parents, the school board and school administrators, and the community, though the nature of the conflict may well be different in each case. Students may reject and hence neglect parts of any curriculum they find boring and pointless. Colleagues who will be teaching your students in succeeding years may feel that you ought to "cover" certain materials they think students should have as background for their courses or that you should stress things they—but perhaps not you—feel are important. Some school administrators may wish to avoid friction with the school board and the community and hence to avoid, in turn, anything controversial in the curriculum while others may take the lead in educating the community and changing attitudes. The school board, responding to pressures from parents and the community, may also wish to avoid controversy by approving only "safe" materials or may encourage innovation. Individual parents, religious groups, political organizations, or community members at large may object to materials on a variety of grounds. Swearing, vulgarity, and sexual content are some of the most frequent targets. Racist or sexist implications draw attacks from some groups, while others object to "liberal" views that challenge traditional notions of authority with regard to family, religion, or state. English teachers are especially vulnerable to challenges of this kind, since the books studied in English classes often treat complicated and controversial issues and may contain passages that must be seen in the total context of the book to be understood and justified.

A sensitive treatment of one such bitter conflict between the schools and the community is to be found in James Moffett's *Storm in the Mountains: A Case Study of Censorship, Conflict and Consciousness.* (See Suggested Reading at the end of this chapter.) Moffett recounts a 1974 censorship case in Kanawha County, West Virginia, where a textbook series he had designed was attacked by individuals and groups who felt that their traditional values were being threatened. The conflict spawned violence, including shootings, fire bombings of buses and schoolrooms, school boycotts by parents, and sympathy strikes by miners. Reverberations from the controversy included objections to the text series in other states as a result of the national publicity given to this case. In his book, Moffett asserts that the "content of textbooks has been very limited ever since 1974" because of a form of "censorship" imposed on authors by nervous publishers.

Moffett wrote his account more than ten years after the original incidents and after revisiting Kanawha County and talking with some of the people who had been involved in the controversy. From that vantage point he writes:

> I was dismayed, hurt, and angry when these book-banners knocked down the program on which I had spent over three years of full-time work and which I had expected to spiritualize some of public education. But I understood these people. Hearing them in the interviews was like listening to voices from the past, not just from my youth but from many visits to West Virginia with my wife and daughters.
>
> My heart is with them. They are right about many things or at least right in a sense, at some level of understanding. They should *not* have had my books crammed down their throats. . . . (But I grieve too for the suffering of those school administrators and teachers torn by the forces around them. I know how they feel too.) The curriculum should *not* be a

standardized thing forced on all alike (James Moffett, *Storm in the Mountains: A Case Study of Censorship, Conflict and Consciousness* [Carbondale: Southern Illinois University Press, 1988], 103-4).

In returning to the place where his textbook series was denounced, Moffett engaged in a dialogue with his opponents that provided an opportunity to increase the understanding of both parties.

This illustrates one of the two most important principles to follow in avoiding difficulties with censorship: Grant your opponents the respect for the sincerity of their views that you would expect for your own. The other important principle is to try to anticipate potential objections to the texts you choose to teach. In her essay, "How to Write a Rationale in Defense of a Book," Diane Shugart emphasizes the need to be prepared for possible challenges:

> The teachers who have rationales in hand are able to show immediately that they have thought about what they are doing. Evidence of thought alone is sometimes enough to stop a censorship incident before it gets going. In addition, preparing a written rationale really does help us to think more clearly about the books we use and to resist more strongly any attempts to remove the books from the curriculum. It may be worth a little more effort if the effort helps us to keep our jobs and our academic integrity (in James E. Davis, ed., *Dealing with Censorship* [Urbana, Ill.: NCTE, 1979], 187).

After this first step of thinking out your rationale, the next step might well be a letter to parents explaining that rationale. Often teachers ask parents to give their permission for their children to read a book that might be a problem, and teachers may provide alternatives for students who do not have permission. If parental or community objections are made after the book has been read or assigned, the problem is a somewhat different one. In this case, the objector might be asked to write out a rationale for the objection, along with an answer to the question of whether he or she has read the whole book and considered the place of the offending passage(s) in the book as a whole.

As was the case with Moffett's later interviews, dialogue can bring increased understanding. Frustrating as these conflicts in values may be, they do testify to the interest that parents have in their children's education. In this book we have encouraged a critical, reflective approach to the classroom, a questioning of classroom practices by students and teachers. This invitation to question, extended to parents, may lead to a clearer idea about English teachers' intentions and to improved dialogue between parents, students, and teachers about the nature of language and learning.

When communication fails and legal action ensues, English teachers need to know where to turn for help. While local and state organizations are usually the best resources for dealing with local problems, there are also national resources available to teachers facing censorship cases. Box 10.1 lists two of those resources.

Censorship issues can arise in connection with student writing as well as with reading. If teachers publish student writing, as we urge them to do, they must try to anticipate any problems so that they take *intelligent* risks in giving students freedom to write naturally and honestly. The recent Supreme Court decision in the Hazelwood case holds that if publications are paid for by the school, then school authorities have the right to censor them. Even if money for publication comes from other sources, there is the issue of sensitivity to the feelings of parents and members of the community to consider.

Problems stemming from publication of student writing are sometimes hard to predict. Consider two recent cases (which are *not* hypothetical): When a local radio station changed its format, a school publication printed two editorials about the new format, one pro and one con. The student who wrote the negative review was harrassed by disk jockeys of the station and was attacked on the air. When a student wrote a short story in which a woman was abused by a man, the advisor accepted it for publication in the school literary magazine, but the principal suppressed the magazine, apparently uncomfortable with the presentation of this real-life situation because it might be seen as derogatory to women. The principal's reaction may have derived in part from being caught off guard by a phone call complaining about the story; the advisor had not told the principal about the story, nor explained that its point of view was sympathetic rather than antipathetic to battered women.

Teachers should keep administrators apprised of possible problems in student publications; they should likewise help students to think of constructive, noninflammatory ways to write about sensitive issues like AIDS or art censorship. The teacher who wishes to publish student writing without tidying up the spelling or the punctuation—because it is more authentic and students then "own" their work in a way they otherwise don't—may want at least to explain the rationale for this to parents and other readers.

The potential conflict between authenticity and correctness in publication of student writing points to another area in which values may clash. "Back-to-basics" proponents assert that students should be trained through drill to do well on national tests and to write error-free prose. Their opponents assert that error-free prose is not as important a goal as thoughtful and honest prose and that the way to achieve this kind of writing is not through drill on so-called basic skills.

Back-to-basics proponents may also advocate emphasis on learning facts and presenting materials that uphold traditional social views. Their opponents, on the other hand, may stress the process of questioning and arriving at concepts through the use of investigating, reasoning, and

---

BOX 10.1
NATIONAL ORGANIZATIONS CONCERNED WITH
INTELLECTUAL FREEDOM

Freedom to Read Foundation
American Association of School Lib-
  rarians
50 East Huron Street
Chicago, IL 60611
(312) 944-6780

National Ad Hoc Committee Against
  Censorship
American Civil Liberties Union
22 East 40th Street
New York, NY 10016
(212) 925-1222

---

imagining; they believe that the function of education is to promote changes that will improve the society. Depending on the set of values that prevails in a school, English teachers may find themselves forced to assign grammar workbooks or free to present important concepts about language in other ways.

Conflict over the Environment: Tracking

The way the learning environment is structured also affects what teachers are expected to teach different groups of students. Tracking, or ability grouping, is as controversial an area as censorship, and it often begins when students are in elementary school, thus affecting their entire educational careers. Tracking can take place inside classrooms (separating the Robins from the Bluebirds in a second-grade reading class, for example, on the basis of their reading proficiency), in specific subject areas (assigning some students in sophomore English to remedial, others to college-preparatory sections), or through different overall curriculum placements (in college prep, general, business, or vocational programs).

Tracking mechanisms are varied and complex, and they are based on different rationales. Some tracking is done on the basis of an assessment of supposed innate ability, derived from IQ test scores and teacher reports. In other cases the basis is an assessment of present proficiency, derived from objective tests and previous grades. Where different programs are offered, students' professional goals may be the basis for tracking, though counselors often play a significant role in encouraging or discouraging certain career choices as "realistic" or "unrealistic" for a given student.

English presents special problems for tracking, since it's more difficult to break English down into sequences for learning than it is, for example, to determine sequences for mathematics or a foreign language. Thus it's harder to determine what should come first in an English curriculum and what constitutes "advanced" work. There is also disagreement among English teachers, school administrators, school boards, parents, and the public at large as to what's important in the study of English. These disagreements focus on certain questions: Should teachers and schools emphasize preparing students for national tests like the S.A.T. and the Advanced Placement Exams (which help students prepare for and enter colleges) and those that are based on national norms for accomplishment at certain levels? Should English classes develop the skills in oral and written communication demanded by employers for certain kinds of jobs? Should students have a firm foundation in English grammar? Given students' future lives, what is the proper place for writing in the English curriculum? For the study of literature? Is tracking educationally sound? If there is to be tracking, what kinds of materials are appropriate for each track?

Proponents of tracking feel that students of supposedly similar needs and abilities should be grouped together, and that such grouping will provide a more "efficient" approach to subject matter. They point out that certain kinds of material are more appropriate for certain kinds of students than others, and that the speed at which material can be learned varies from student to student. They cite the difficulty teachers may have in teaching to a range of student abilities, asserting that tracking makes classroom management easier. Some parents are also staunch supporters of tracking, often because they fear that students of apparently lower abilities may require teachers to slow the pace of classroom learning and thus not provide sufficient challenges for the abler students. Other parents may demand accelerated or honors or advanced-placement classes in order to give their childen better preparation for college, in some cases even provide college credit.

Parents and community members often judge a school on the basis of its students' performances on national or statewide tests; these people may claim that tracking gives students better preparation for such tests. (Declines in national test scores have often been cited in the descriptions of "crisis" in our schools.) School millages and even real estate values in a community may depend on public perception of the quality of a school as it is supposedly reflected in its students' performances on national or state tests. Community members may not recognize that these tests cannot give a very accurate or complete account of what may have been gained in an English classroom. The dangers of trying to meet the "crisis" of declining test scores through teaching to tests, especially objective tests, have already been indicated (see Chapter 9). Teaching to a test is likely to result in drill, teacher lectures, and emphasis more on test-taking strategies than on other kinds of learning. The opportunity that the crisis provides is that it can give teachers the chance to reflect on their goals and the outcomes they desire for their students. Teachers should have clear rationales for what they do and should be able to justify their practices, both to themselves and to others. This kind of accountability is more meaningful than a record of test scores.

Another danger of tracking is that it means more than just that different material will be studied or that the pace of learning will be different; it usually results in different expectations and attitudes on the part of the teacher and student alike, and these in turn determine what students learn. As Jeannie Oakes points out in her pioneering study, *Keeping Track: How Schools Structure Inequality* (see Suggested Reading at the end of this chapter), tracking reinforces and tends to reproduce already existing social inequities in the public schools. Students in upper tracks have a chance to learn how to approach intellectual problems and how to communicate with others; students in lower tracks learn mainly good manners, submission to authority, and the need to follow directions. (See Box 10.2.) Thus tracking hurts supposedly "slower" or less able kids (most of whom in many schools are minorities), since most of the academic course choices and current resources and materials are available only to the upper-track students (most of whom in many schools are middle-class whites). Higher-track classes are generally smaller and focus more on creative and analytical skills, whereas lower tracks tend to focus on surface skills, taught with worksheets and drills.

Most crucial of all, teachers are likely to have low expectations for lower-track students and thus fail to provide any challenges for them; students are led to adopt the self-fulfilling prophecy that they can't succeed. Listen to Lynn who, during her pre-student teaching observation in a high school, observed two teachers who taught both "advanced" and "basic" sophomore classes:

> Janet treated her two classes very differently. She'd begin the basic classes in a very stern manner, giving students a series of commands. During class she often gave them worksheets to complete, which asked them to underline parts of speech and fill in blanks about correct usage. She asked students to read aloud in class quite a lot, and she didn't seem to notice that several students put their heads down on their desks and slept while others were reading. She said that students in this class didn't have the skills they needed for writing, and as a result she didn't usually have them write more than a sentence. She also said these kids weren't responsible enough to work in small groups.
>
> Janet began her advanced class in a relaxed manner—she laughed and joked with students as they came into the room. She spent a lot of time discussing the literature students had read outside class. They really discussed some pretty complicated issues, and she had them write papers on topics related to the literature. They had to bring drafts of their papers to class and talk about them in writing groups.
>
> Anna, the other teacher I visited, treated all her classes in pretty much

BOX 10.2
KEEPING TRACK: SOME STUDENT RESPONSES

As reported by Jeannie Oakes in *Keeping Track,* when questioned about the most important thing they had learned in their classroom, students from high-track English classes gave the following responses:

I have learned to form my own opinions on situations. I have also learned to not be swayed so much by another person's opinion but to look at both opinions with an open mind. I know now to have a good solid opinion on a subject I must have facts to support my opinion. Decisions in later life will probably be easier because of this.

I've learned to study completely, and to know everything there is to know.

I have learned to speak in front of a group of people, and not be scared to death of everyone.

To know how to communicate with my teachers like friends and as teachers at the same time.

I have learned to be creative and free in doing things.

The most important thing I have learned in this class this quarter is how to express my feelings.

How to organize myself and present an argument.

I'm learning to communicate with large groups of people.

How to express myself through writing and being able to compose the different thoughts in a logical manner; this is also a class where I may express my creativity.

Learned to think things out. I've learned to look in depth at certain things and express my thoughts on paper.

I have learned to be more imaginative.

I have learned that in high school the English classes treat you more like an adult.

I've learned to analyze stories that we read. I like this class because the teacher doesn't put thoughts into your head.

It teaches you how to do research in a college library.

Learned to analyze famous writings by famous people, and we have learned to understand people's different viewpoints on general ideas.

Oakes goes on to report that the responses of students in low-track English classes who were asked to identify the most important thing they had learned in their classroom were very different from those of the high-track students:

Behave in class.

Self-control.

I have learned that I should do my questions for the book when he asks me to.

Manners.

How to shut up.

Write and get my homework done.

Working on my P's and Q's.

I have learned about many things like having good manners, respecting other people, not talking when the teacher is talking.

I learned about being quiet when the teacher is talking.

To learn how to listen and follow the directions of the teacher.

I think the most important is coming into class and getting our folders and going to work.

Learn to get along with the students and the teacher.

I've learned how to get a better job and how to act when at an interview filling out forms.

I learned that English is boring.

To spell words you don't know.

Job training.

—Adapted from Jeannie Oakes, *Keeping Track: How Schools Structure Inequality* (New Haven, Conn.: Yale University Press, 1985), pp. 67–72, 87–9. Copyright © 1985 Yale University Press.

the same way. At the beginning of the hour, she called kids by their names as they came in and often chatted with them about what was going on in their lives. She told me she thought it was important to get to know students as people and she sometimes visited them at home. She also took part in a weekend retreat sponsored by the school every year, where they talked about improving relationships among students from different ethnic groups. She also had students who were working independently or in small groups on what she called community based projects.

While I was observing in Anna's classroom, I got a chance to talk to some of the students and look at their work. I didn't see very great differences between the advanced and the basic students. Anna expected a lot of each of them. Actually, some of the students in the advanced class seemed to have weaker skills than many of those in the basic class. And I think several of those in the basic class could have gotten along o.k. in the advanced class. In both classes she gave the kids opportunities to teach each other.

Janet very clearly illustrates the dangers of tracking; Anna, in contrast, made the most of the tracking situation, and her students tended to live up to the higher expectations she had for them. Psychological experiments have shown that when teachers are told that an average class is a group with exceptional or above-average abilities, the students in the class perform better. What the teacher expects and how the teacher treats students seem to be more important factors in the students' success than the group the students are in. Summarizing sixty years of research on ability grouping in schools, Jeannie Oakes says, "*No* group of students has been found to benefit consistently from being in a homogeneous group" (Oakes, p. 7.)

Conflict over the Environment: School Choice

The struggle for control of schools and the values they represent sometimes takes the form of debates about how much choice parents should have in selecting the schools their children will attend. Since support for schools comes from tax dollars, with the amount of support determined by special millage elections, school boards and school administrators must be especially sensitive to public opinion and public wishes and demands. The increasing popularity of "choice" initiatives, voucher plans, and other related strategies—like the conflicts about tracking and censorship—are further indications of the desire of increasing numbers of parents to have some control over their children's education. John Chubb and Terry Moe, the authors of the controversial *Politics, Markets and America's Schools,* are among the proponents of organizing schools through "market control," as private schools do, rather than through "democratic control," as most public schools do. In several states there have been movements to encourage tax-supported alternative options for education (including home schooling). Minnesota allows open enrollment across public school district lines, and Milwaukee allows some low-income students to attend private schools with the support of public funds. In Oregon, an open-enrollment policy governs all public education.

While some people see school choice plans as a way to give parents more say about their children's education, others see them as potentially deepening the segregation that already exists in the public schools. In Milwaukee, a plan to create a school designed to target supposedly at-risk African-American males is causing considerable controversy in light of court decisions over the last thirty-odd years to desegregate schools.

Other educational planners suggest that in larger urban areas, like New York City and Chicago, a more democratic approach to changing the schools would be to give teachers or parents—or both—more local control over their schools. This approach to school improvement through decentralization—often coupled with a drive to make schools smaller—is an attempt to give individual schools more power and make them more responsive to community needs. If parents play a part in shaping the curriculum under such a plan, teachers may well find themselves assuming a more collaborative role with members of the community.

School/Community Interaction

In any event, teachers should recognize the fact that neither schools nor English classes can or should exist in isolation. Community and school interact in diverse and complicated ways. The kind of information published by the Chamber of Commerce in some communities—the socioeconomic status of the community, its crime rate, its racial and ethnic composition, and the amount and kind of education characteristic of its citizens—points to factors that frequently help shape what occurs in an individual English class. These factors can, for example, determine whether funds will be available for new texts; whether a controversial book is likely to be censored; whether a classroom will be clean and well maintained; and whether students will come to class well fed, well rested, and ready to learn.

Other, often less obvious characteristics of a community also contribute to the shape of the schools and their programs. The attitude of the local media toward education, the public standing of the school superintendent, the role played by community agencies ranging from parole offices to YMCA boards, the percentage of students who hold jobs, and the number of single-parent homes all help determine whether school newspapers and yearbooks can rely upon support from local businesses, whether taxes will be raised to support salary increases for teachers, whether counselors will be available to work with troubled students, and whether students will have the opportunity to participate in school plays and debate teams.

The most important, and most obvious, connection between school and community is that students move back and forth between the two, constantly bringing the community into the school. (See Box 10.3.)

Schools likewise contribute to the shape of the community. They send messages—in the form of test scores, dropout rates, college acceptances, programs for special populations, sports events and musical productions, teacher strikes, administrative appointments, and physical appearance of buildings—that influence real estate development and business and industry recruitment within the community. By filling, as they are increasingly asked to do, various social service functions, schools can make contributions to the community that are not strictly educational and that contribute to community spirit. An individual English teacher who encourages students to enter writing contests, publishes student work—whether by placing it in local store windows or by producing class books—

BOX 10.3
THE AURA OF AVENUE D

Seward Park [High School], at best, could tilt the pH of Richie's values toward the decent. But every afternoon he went home to Avenue D and every morning he arrived with the aura of Avenue D on him. He personified the true dilemma for Seward Park, which is not the infrequent violence within the building but the incessant violence beyond its walls, floating like a toxic cloud.

Somebody calls somebody a bitch. Somebody flirts with someone else's girlfriend. Somebody insults somebody's brother-in-law. Somebody gets burned in a drug deal. None of these incidents have the least to do with Seward Park, yet any one has the potential to convulse it, for Seward Park is the crossroads of neighborhoods, ethnic groups, and extended families.

—From Samuel G. Freedman, *Small Victories: The Real World of a Teacher, Her Students & Their High School* (New York: Harper & Row, 1990), p. 358.

and fosters schoolwide reading programs helps enhance both community pride and school status.

The interests of the school and the community, however, may not always coincide. The reasons for teaching English that we discussed in Chapter 1 may be viewed differently by school and community at any given time. Teachers, for example, may argue that English instruction should emphasize personal growth, while the community may set a high priority on preparing good workers. Members within the community may also be in conflict. Parents of college-bound children may argue for more advanced-placement courses, while other parents may want a better shop program. And often there isn't enough money for both. Even more fundamental disagreements may arise over the ultimate purpose of the school: Should the school devote its energies to upholding traditional values and helping students adjust to society, or should it help students to question the status quo and seek ways to improve society? Such questions call for wide-ranging dialogues between teachers, school authorities, and members of different segments of the community.

The role of the English teacher in such dialogues is to foster improved school/community relations by discussing rationales for what is emphasized in the English classroom frankly and openly with the members of the community. Teachers must also seek to explain the more complex or unfamiliar forms of student assessment, such as primary-trait scoring, portfolio evaluation, and performance assessment (see Chapter 9). Assessment often seems to be the most visible element in the interactions between school and community, and parents may be unaccustomed to evaluation of student writing selectively, or to taking organized account of oral presentations and student participation in discussion. English teachers can also help school/community relations by involving members of the community in their classrooms. There are many ways to do this. (See Box 10.4.)

The curriculum itself can also be designed in ways to narrow the gap between the English classroom and the "real world" of the community. The whole-language movement, which approaches language as social construct, provides one example of such a curriculum. (See Box 10.5 and also Chapter 7.) In the whole-language approach, students are considered "curricular informants"; their "life experiences" serve as the starting place for what happens in the classroom. Together, teacher and students explore topics, engaging in conversations in which all participate and using language (as adults do) to communicate different points of view and to negotiate answers to complex questions. Such a curriculum by its very nature tends to become interdisciplinary, since the world outside the school is not divided neatly into subjects like English, history, mathematics, and social studies.

Although the language-as-social-construct approach may make it easiest to narrow the gap between the English classroom and the world outside the school, teachers following other approaches can find ways to achieve some of the same results. They can work out interdisciplinary units, sometimes in cooperation with colleagues in other departments. They can also utilize events and issues of the day as subjects for discussion leading to writing. A hurricane can prompt a classroom study of the effects of the storm, where students gather oral histories of individuals whose homes were destroyed, write explanations of meteorological factors, discuss resulting economic problems. During the Vietnam war, many high school classrooms were transformed by debates about the nation's role in that conflict; similar conversations took place during the recent war in the Persian Gulf. Debates about student rights in the late sixties changed the faces of classrooms to make them more sensitive to student concerns. Debates about the environment and war are part of the emerging curriculum of the early nineties. Debates on educational issues have been ongoing—in the 1980s these often focused specifically on the issue of whether schools should strive mainly for equity or for excellence, or whether they could achieve both.

With the changing demographics, it will be increasingly important for teachers to take advantage of the growing diversity among the students in their classrooms. It will also be important for students to see mirrored in some of the things they read parts of their own lives, and at the same time to learn something of other cultures and other perspectives. Monolingual English-speaking students can benefit from exposure to peers who are fluent in another language or knowledgeable about another culture. Enlargement of the canon of what's taught (see Chapter 4) will likewise expose students to greater diversity in the literature they read and will provide literary reflections of the culture of students whose

---

BOX 10.4
WAYS TO INVOLVE THE COMMUNITY IN THE CLASSROOM

1. A community "boosters" organization can raise funds or tap community businesses to obtain items not provided by the school budget—copy machines, computers, sets of books, tape recorders, video equipment, audio- and videotapes.

2. Community members can volunteer to tutor students needing special help or to supervise sections of the library.

3. Community members can help with the mechanics (typing, sorting, folding) of producing a class book or other publication.

4. Community members can organize and participate in celebrations of writing, where all students in a given class or school read selections from their work aloud to small groups of adults and receive responses.

5. Community members can serve as interviewees for classes learning to conduct interviews.

6. Community members can give book talks about "the book that changed my life."

7. Community members can help teachers to arrange and conduct field trips to plays, libraries, museums, or other local points of interest.

8. Teachers can ask parents or community members for suggestions about ways they might like to be involved with English classes.

---

heritage may not have been heretofore a part of the curriculum. The inclusion of a broader range of multicultural literature in the English classroom and the implementation of interdisciplinary approaches both bring the English classroom and the community closer together.

Professional Development

Building bridges to connect the English classroom with the rest of the world is part of what it means to become a true professional. Seeking and maintaining contacts with others in the profession is another part. Teaching can be very lonely work, and closing the classroom door to spend hour after hour with adolescents leaves many teachers hungry for adult conversation, particularly conversation about teaching. Contacts with other teachers also help you to continue that process of reflection so essential to remaining alive as a teacher. Avenues of professional development include establishing and maintaining a network with your peers, joining professional organizations, participating in the National Writing Project,

BOX 10.5
WHOLE LANGUAGE: STARTING NEW CONVERSATIONS

McInerney: Did I ever tell you the one about the first time my wife met my relatives? There were about fifteen of us at my Aunt Stella's house in Brooklyn and my grandmother was making a typical meal for my family, something like leg of lamb and lasagna. No connection to each other, but they were lying around the kitchen so she cooked them. So, we've got fifteen Italians sitting down, shouting across the table at each other, and here sits Carol, my wife. Now, she comes from sort of a Germanic background, a bit more reserved. She's waiting for everybody to sit down before she eats. My cousin, Dom, takes a few bites but then has to leave for a hockey game. My other cousin takes up where he left off on his plate. My grandmother's standing in the corner worrying that there's not enough food, and Carol sits there waiting. And I lean over and say, "If you don't start eating, it'll all be gone!"

Harste: I really love that upbringing of yours.

M: Now, am I stretching it to suggest that this is something like whole language? Don't hold back until it all falls into place, you've just got to do it.

H: That's a great place to start.

M: I felt like Carol when I first started teaching seven years ago. I heard the lectures, I read the books, I knew what whole language was about. But come the first day of school, here I am saying to myself, "Well, this basal [reader] isn't so bad." I couldn't decide how or where to begin.

It was weeks before I settled on journals as a starting point. Which brought up a similar problem—there's about a million ways to do journals. So I thought, "To hell with this handwringing." We just jumped in and hashed out the parameters as we went. And, like in a lot of whole language classrooms, one thing led to another.

H: Well, you would cast yourself as a learner then.

M: Right, because I'm uneasy projecting myself as someone who's the whole language expert. I'm a bit apprehensive when people visit my room. I know where my classroom *could* be and I know where it is now—not even close. . . .

H: I like to think of the classroom as a readers' and writers' guild. I think the key question that teachers need to ask is, how can I organize my classroom so that each person is allowed to have a voice and join the conversation?

I think that means that instruction has to begin in life experiences. Students need to make connections between their own lives and what is going on in school. Instead of reducing the world to problems for them, we need to begin with their concerns. For me, this boils down to using the child as your curricular informant.

M: Right. What works for you as an adult can also be applied to your elementary or secondary classroom.

H: And when you hear all these different voices, *new* conversations begin. That's the foundation of strong communities— difference, not like-mindedness. If everybody thinks the same, then there's no basis for a conversation. Well, we don't want everybody to

be the same. We don't want all whole language classes to look the same. It's the differences that can transform our thinking. . . .

M: Then the theory *is* the practice and the practice *is* the theory.

H: Right, right. Ken Goodman is the perfect example of this. Whole language really started with him. What he did was look at what real readers did when they read whole stories and, from this, he culled some principles of language. . . . He saw that children simultaneously use their knowledge of the flow of language (syntax), their knowledge of the world (semantics), and their knowledge of letter-sound relationships (phonics). . . .

M: We're talking about the late 1960s, right? This was really a revolutionary way of looking at reading instruction.

H: Exactly. And Ken went on with other principles: that language varies by the context of use; that language is learned *through* use; that language, by its very nature, is social; that learning is theoretically based; and that the hallmarks of learning are community and connectedness.

I think it's important to point out, though, that in addition to being a theory of language and a theory of learning, whole language is a theory of professional self-renewal. By using the child as our curricular informant, we have a self-correcting device built into our model of curriculum and curriculum development. It's really a call for teachers to reclaim their classrooms and participate in the development of a practical theory of language learning. . . .

M: And as we learn more from the kids, whole language will change.

H: Yes, and that's what's wrong with seeing it as some sort of immutable orthodoxy. . . . To the extent that teachers buy a package and simply administer a new kit or instructional routine, whole language is lost.

M: It's more of a negotiation, right? When you lose that give-and-take, you lose the essence of whole language.

H: If you take a whole language approach, there is no set of materials. Whole language teachers see teaching and learning as a relationship. They assume that children are already readers and writers, that what we have to do is support and expand the reading and writing that already is in place. Other approaches assume that you have to teach kids to read and write. There's a world of difference there, and it's reflected in how you organize and conduct instruction in the classroom. . . .

Try this. If I asked you, "What are the principles of learning that have guided you?" what would you say?

M: I guess my real concern in the classroom is to treat the children as I would want to be treated. Is that too biblical for you? It's true, though. That's my major guiding principle. If I was a kid in my class, would I like it? If I was learning this subject for the first time, what would I want to do?

That's putting a lot of faith in yourself and a lot of faith in your kids, but it works.

—"Whole Language: Starting New Conversations" is reprinted with permission from John McInerny and Jerome C. Harste. From PORTRAITS OF WHOLE LANGUAGE CLASSROOMS: ed. Heidi Mills and Jean Anne Clyde (Heinemann Educational Books, Inc., Portsmouth NH, 1990).

working on writing-across-the-curriculum projects, and joining a teacher-researcher group.

Peer Networks

Fellow students in your methods class and those with whom you share your experience of student teaching can be an important resource as you become a teacher. Not only do they contribute to your thinking as you develop ideas about teaching and share frustrations, they can also become part of an ongoing support group for you. Methods students have established class newsletters, arranged reunions, and set up periodic meetings with one another. These various forms of communication enable them to explore common concerns and continue to share ideas as they become more experienced teachers.

Professional Organizations

Attending a convention and talking with English teachers from a variety of schools can be a revitalizing experience. Similarly, reading an article or a book written by another English teacher about ways to address a specific problem can send you back to the classroom ready to face new challenges. Joining a professional organization will provide you these and many other opportunities to continue your development as a teacher. Your methods professor may encourage you to join the National Council of Teachers of English as a student member, and we heartily endorse that idea. The address for this organization is

National Council of Teachers of English
1111 Kenyon Road
Urbana, IL 61801

When you join NCTE you will receive a subscription to the *English Journal* as part of your membership; you will find many useful articles in this journal. In addition, you will receive information about the national convention (held annually in November), a catalog of NCTE books, and information about a variety of other meetings and materials of interest to English teachers.

In addition to joining NCTE, plan to join your state affiliate of NCTE. You can request information about the address of the state affiliate from the Urbana office of NCTE. Many state affiliates sponsor annual conventions (which may be more accessible than the national convention) and publish their own journals and newsletters. All of them provide a way of meeting other English teachers interested in sharing ideas.

The benefits of professional affiliation extend beyond gathering new information. Taking part in professional organizations can enable you to develop perspectives on controversial issues and be ready to take proactive stances on them. This means that you will be in a better position to educate other teachers, administrators, parents, and community members about what you do in the classroom.

The National Writing Project

The National Writing Project, a teacher-development program begun in the mid 1970s, offers summer workshops for experienced teachers interested in improving their skills in writing instructions. Based on the assumption that teachers of writing should themselves write, and that experienced teachers can learn from one another, NWP summer programs require participants to write extensively and to work in writing groups. In addition, many of the summer programs expect teachers to make presentations based on their work in the classroom. You can request information about the NWP program in your state from

National Writing Project
School of Education
University of California
Berkeley, CA 94720

Participation in a summer institute of the National Writing Project is usually sponsored by the school district in which you teach, and you may be expected to offer presentations to colleagues after you have completed the institute. To learn more about the NWP, you can read its newsletter, *The Quarterly*, which can be requested from the above address.

Writing Across the Curriculum

During the past couple of decades a movement described as "writing across the curriculum" (WAC) has emerged in both colleges and high schools. Based on the theory that writing facilitates learning, it has encouraged teachers in all disciplines to incorporate more writing into their classes as a way of increasing their students' learning. This does not mean that teachers in these disciplines are encouraged to take on the responsibilities of English teachers. Instead, WAC encourages teachers of history, math, science, and other disciplines to employ frequent informal writing to foster learning in the given field. Informal writing can include journal entries, exit slips, unsent letters, and a variety of other forms. You'll find more about WAC in

Fulweiler, Toby, ed. *The Journal Book*, Portsmouth, N.H.: Heinemann, 1989.
Gere, Anne Ruggles, ed. *Roots in the Sawdust: Writing to Learn Across the Disciplines*. Urbana, Ill.: NCTE, 1985.
Mayher, John, Nancy Lester, and Gordon Pradl. *Learning to Write— Writing to Learn*. Portsmouth, N.H.: Heinemann, 1983.

You may also wish to join the WAC Network. Network members receive mailings and participate in meetings at the annual convention of NCTE. The address is

WAC Network
Professor Christopher Thaiss
Department of English
George Mason University
Fairfax, VA 22030

Not surprisingly, English teachers are frequently asked to take leadership positions in developing a WAC program within a school. While this means additional responsibilities, it also represents an opportunity for professional development and a chance to get to know teachers in other disciplines.

Teacher-Researcher Groups

Research is an integral part of teaching, and it contributes to professional development. Teachers engage in a kind of informal research whenever they test ideas or lessons in the classroom or reflect upon the results of a unit or a semester. They can also design somewhat more formal research projects to address questions about how to achieve maximum effectiveness in a writing project, for example, or how best to assess student achievement in a particular area.

In designing and carrying out their research projects, teachers should employ the three kinds of reflection first described by John Dewey: *technical reflection*, which involves thinking about how best to achieve one's

---

BOX 10.6
MAKING A DIFFERENCE

For all the educational jargon and technology, for all the research and standardized testing, in the final analysis teaching and learning come from a relationship between two people. We count our greatest successes in little things, in memories. Kathy sitting at the computer and literally bouncing on the chair from excitement. Victor reading his own ghost story. Rick illustrating a letter to a third grader at an elementary school in another town in red and blue 3-D colors, so when you looked at it through a pair of cardboard glasses, it really was 3-D! Diane always being the first to read. Milton writing about his grandfather, and Bobby about his mother. Valerie grinning after a film and saying, "It's OK." Jim sending his hunting story off to the writing contest after laboring through two writing conferences and four drafts and showing up at the door with his letter. Sammy and Lelond at the door before the class started.

So what? What difference does it make? Perhaps little in the school or the school system. We're still asking questions—about ability grouping, about how we teach, about kids who fail. And questions about poverty and teen pregnancy, about alcoholic stepparents and breaking parole, about dropping out and self-esteem, about accepting responsibility and pride. They get to be big questions after a while. What difference does it make? It makes some difference to us, to re-learn some things we knew about teaching kids in a caring way and how that hurts sometimes because caring about people can hurt, but how we don't win anything without risking ourselves. And we don't grow without questioning how it's done and seeing if it can be done better another way. What difference does it make? For twenty kids, or some of them, maybe quite a bit.

—From Becky Howard and Tom Liner, "Ninth Grade, Low Level, Fifth Period: A Kind of Case Study," in *English Journal,* October 1990, p. 52.

goals once those goals have been determined; *practical reflection,* which involves thinking about both the means and the purpose of those means; and *critical reflection,* which involves a consideration of ethical and moral issues. Educational philosopher Maxine Greene says that if teachers are to "initiate young people into an ethical existence, they themselves must . . . break with the mechanical life, to overcome their own submergence in the habitual, even in what they conceive to be virtuous, and to ask the 'why' with which all moral reasoning begins" (*Landscapes of Learning* [New York: Teachers College, 1978], 46). (See Suggested Reading at the end of this chapter.) Research, for the teacher, must include observation of oneself as well as of the people and things in the world around one.

Becky Howard and Tom Liner combined observation and reflection in their research with an experimental ninth-grade English curriculum that they designed for low-track students. They began with an assumption to test: "The emphasis of the class is on writing, an activity typically avoided by teachers of low-level students who assume 'they can't do it.' We know they can do it, if we can reach them" ("Ninth Grade, Low Level, Fifth Period: A Kind of Case Study," in *English Journal* [October 1990], 47). Their research became an ongoing attempt to find things that would "reach" these students, who had been tracked by the school into the lowest group. The results (reported in Box 10.6) confirmed their assumption about the abilities of their students, although there could be no final solutions for some of the social problems responsible for their students' previous failures. Most important, Howard and Liner found that teaching these kids was a rewarding experience because they came to care about them. "For all . . . the research and standardized testing," they say, "in the final analysis teaching and learning come from a relationship between two people."

And caring teachers can make a difference through their relationships with their students. The increasingly complex social forces we have been discussing here are important, and research and reflection may give you the satisfaction of understanding them better. But despite the undoubted importance of understanding these social factors, we hope that your greatest satisfactions as a teacher will come, as they do in good teaching, from that personal relationship of teacher on one end of the log and student on the other end.

Suggested Reading

COOPER, MARILYN M., and MICHAEL HOLZMAN. *Writing as Social Action.* Portsmouth, N.H.: Heinemann, 1989.

This book addresses the question of literacy from a social perspective; reading and writing are viewed as social activities.

DANIELS, HARVEY A., ed. *Not Only English: Affirming America's Multilingual Heritage.* Urbana, Ill.: NCTE, 1990.

This book asserts the need for celebrating diverse cultures and languages in schools and provides some means for implementing such a perspective.

DAVIS, JAMES. E., ed. *Dealing with Censorship.* Urbana, Ill.: NCTE, 1979.

A collection of essays by various teachers on a range of issues pertaining to censorship, this book includes a practical section on what resources are available.

DEWEY, JOHN. *The School and Society.* New York: Collier, 1899.

This inspirational book by a pioneering educational philosopher argues for a necessarily close relationship between social concerns and the process of schooling.

FREEDMAN, SAMUEL. *Small Victories: The Real World of a Teacher, Her Students & Their High School.* New York, Harper & Row, 1990.

This is an award-winning journalist's account of the joys and challenges in one inner-city teacher's classroom.

GARRISON, ROGER. "Graduation Before Graduation: Social Involvement and English." *English Journal* (October 1990): 60–3.

This article advocates having students do a community project through the English classroom and shares one successful way to do it.

GERE, ANNE RUGGLES, ed. *Roots in the Sawdust: Writing to Learn Across the Disciplines.* Urbana, Ill.: NCTE, 1985.

Gere has collected essays written by teachers in various areas about how they used writing to enhance the learning process in their classrooms.

GOODLAD, JOHN I. *A Place Called School: Promise for the Future.* New York: McGraw-Hill, 1984.

This is one of the best of several national studies on high schools in America; it includes suggestions for improving schools.

GREENE, MAXINE. *Landscapes of Learning.* New York: Teachers College Press, 1978.

A philosopher of education writes about the importance of the imagination and integrating the arts into literacy education.

HOWARD, BECKY, and TOM LINER. "Ninth Grade, Low Level, Fifth Period: A Kind of Case Study," *English Journal* (October, 1990): 47–52.

The story of one year in a "basic skills" writing class is written by the teachers who taught the class.

KIDDER, TRACY. *Among Schoolchildren.* New York: Harper & Row, 1989.

Like *Small Victories,* this account of one elementary teacher's classroom is written by an award-winning journalist.

MIRGA, THOMAS. "Today's Numbers, Tomorrow's Nation: Demography's Awesome Challenge for Schools." *Education Week* (May 14, 1986): 14–40.

This special issue of *Education Week* is devoted to short articles with statistics on changing demographics, with some concerns expressed about possible implications for education.

MOFFETT, JAMES. *Storm in the Mountains: A Case Study of Censorship, Conflict and Consciousness.* Carbondale: Southern Illinois University Press, 1988.

Moffett focuses on the Kanawha County, West Virginia, censorship case of 1974 involving his own innovative and controversial textbook series.

OAKES, JEANNIE. *Keeping Track: How Schools Structure Inequality.* New Haven, Conn.: Yale University Press, 1985.

This book shows how tracking reflects the class and racial inequalities of American society and in part helps to perpetuate them.

RIGG, PAT, and VIRGINIA G. ALLEN, ed. *When They Don't All Speak English: Integrating the ESL Student into the Regular Classroom.* Urbana, Ill.: NCTE, 1989.

A collection of essays by a variety of educators that detail successful classroom practices, this book is a positive approach to the multicultural, multilingual classroom.

SIZER, THEODORE. *Horace's Compromise: The Dilemma of the American High School.* Boston: Houghton Mifflin, 1985.

One of the best of a series of books that came out of several national commissions to study the state of American education, this one is supportive of teachers and suggests structural changes to empower them.

TYLER, RALPH. *Basic Principles of Curriculum and Instruction.* Chicago: University of Chicago Press, 1949.

This text develops a rationale for exploring the issue of the purpose of education as a basis for curriculum planning, and suggests procedures for formulating and implementing goals in terms of chosen purposes. The book deals with issues of evaluation, organization, and general principles of curriculum design.

ZEICHNER, KENNETH. "Alternative Paradigms of Teacher Education." *Journal of Teacher Education* 34 (1981): 7–24.

This teacher/educator's essay opposes the typical emphasis in teacher preparation on technical expertise and advocates an experience-based approach grounded in the reflective practice of the prospective teacher.

Index